Explorations in Applied

Explorations in Applied Linguistics 2

H. G. Widdowson

Oxford University Press
1984

Oxford University Press
Walton Street, Oxford OX2 6DP

Oxford London New York Toronto Melbourne Auckland
Kuala Lumpur Singapore Hong Kong Tokyo Delhi
Bombay Madras Calcutta Karachi Nairobi
Dar es Salaam Cape Town

and associated companies in
Beirut Berlin Ibadan Mexico City Nicosia

OXFORD is a trade mark of Oxford University Press

ISBN 0 19 437088 7

© H. G. Widdowson 1984

This book is sold subject to the condition that it shall not, by
way of trade or otherwise, be lent, re-sold, hired out, or
otherwise circulated without the publisher's prior consent in
any form of binding or cover other than that in which it is
published and without a similar condition including this
condition being imposed on the subsequent purchaser.

All rights reserved. No part of this publication may be
reproduced, stored in a retrieval system, or transmitted, in any
form or by any means, electronic, mechanical, photocopying,
recording or otherwise, without the prior permission of
Oxford University Press.

Phototypeset by Tradespools Ltd, Frome, Somerset

Printed in Hong Kong

To my sons: Marc-Alain and Arnold

Contents

Acknowledgements

Acknowledgements are made to the following from whose texts the papers below have been taken.

Professor R. B. Kaplan and Newbury House for 'Applied Linguistics: the pursuit of relevance', published in *On the Scope of Applied Linguistics*, edited by R. B. Kaplan 1980.

Longman, for 'New starts and different kinds of failure', published in *Learning to Write: First Language/Second Language*, edited by A. Freedman, I. Pringle, and J. Yalden, 1981.

The Council of Europe, for 'Procedures for discourse processing', published in the Addendum to Document CC-GP4 (81) 43, 'Towards a more comprehensive framework for the definition of language learning objectives'.

Gunter Narr Verlag, for 'Types of linguistic sign in texts', published in Texte in *Sprachwissenschaft, Sprachunterricht, Sprachtherapie*, edited by W. Kuhlwein, 1983.

Pergamon Press and the British Council, for 'The deviant language of poetry', published in *ELT Documents* 115.

The Finnish Association of Applied Linguistics, for 'Reference and representation as modes of meaning', *AFinLa Yearbook 1983*.

Teachers of English to Speakers of Other Languages, for 'The use of literature', published in *ON TESOL 81*, for 'ESP and the curse of Caliban', published in *ON TESOL 80*, for 'Course design and discourse process', published in *MEXTESOL 81*, and for 'Competence and capacity in language teaching', published in *ON TESOL 82*.

Newbury House, for 'Criteria for course design', published in *English for Academic and Technical Purposes. Studies in Honour of Louis Trimble* edited by L. Selinker, E. Tarone and V. Hanzeli, 1981.

SPEAQ Journal, for 'Teaching language as and for communication', published in the *SPEAQ Journal* Vol. 4, No. 2, 1980.

The author would like to express his thanks to Winifred Evans, for all her secretarial help.

Introduction

The papers in this book are further enquiries into issues raised in its predecessor of the same title, and in particular they seek to discharge the responsibility of applied linguistics, as stated in the earlier book (and restated in the first Section of this one), to devise a coherent model of linguistic description which will be relevant to language teaching.

As before, the papers here are in some respects a varied assortment. They were prepared at different times and so mark different stages in the conceptualization of the matters concerned. Some focus attention on descriptive issues, others attend more closely to pedagogic ones. Again, some papers were written within an academic framework and key their arguments in with the publications of other people, acknowledged by citation and reference in the approved scholarly fashion; other papers, more popular in intention and designed to be performed, dispense with these accoutrements of scholarship altogether.

But beneath the appearance of variety of presentation, there is a pattern of recurring ideas which are taken up from the previous book and bear upon the common applied linguistic purpose I have referred to. They are all concerned with the formulation of a relevant model of language which will serve as a source of reference for a principled approach to language teaching. And they all subscribe to the assumption that if language teaching is to develop the ability to use language as a resource for communication in the natural manner, then what is required is a model of language use rather than one based on linguistic analysis of the kind that has conventionally informed the practice of teaching.

The formulation of such a model has to be expressed in terms which allow it to be assessed as description, but it also has to be shown to be relevant to pedagogy. Hence the varying emphasis on descriptive and pedagogic issues in these papers. The variation in mode of presentation is a function of their applied linguistic purpose. There would be little point in proposing a model of description as relevant to teaching if the description and the discussion of its relevance were not made accessible to teachers. At the same time, of course, the model on offer has to make some claim to validity as description. There are obvious risks in thus attempting to reconcile the requirements of both validity and relevance. Often, of course, one finds oneself in no-man's land, a target for snipers in entrenched positions on both sides, one espousing the cause of practicality, the other the cause of theoretical rigour. But these risks are the occupational hazards of applied linguists and I do not see how they can be avoided.

As in the previous book the papers here have been sorted into sections. Some of them (as for example in Sections Five and Six) are concerned primarily with the working out of pedagogic implications and some (as in Section Three) with more technical matters of description. In other cases (as for example in Sections Two and Four) descriptive and pedagogic issues are given equal prominence. But in all sections and in all papers the dual perspective is presupposed.

Although all sections are meant to bear upon the general theme, each is also supposed to have its own independent coherence and to be comprehensible without reference to the others. Within each section, the papers are placed in approximate chronological order of first appearance, so it is possible to trace the development of a particular line of enquiry. This means that the sections do not follow on from each other in linear fashion but run, as it were, in parallel, so that the last paper in a particular section will often reflect the same stage of thinking as the last one in a different section (one might compare, for example, Papers 9, 15, and 18). The only exception to this chronological principle of ordering is in Section Four where it seemed to me to be preferable to show the development of descriptive ideas first before bringing in the question of teaching.

The way the papers have been arranged will, I hope, not only help to bring different areas of enquiry into focus but will also reveal the process of enquiry itself. For these papers, like those in the previous book, are intended to be illustrations of the *kind* of investigation that I believe is necessary if the different techniques of language teaching are to be given rational endorsement in principle, as they must be if methodology is to have any real meaning. Both modesty and scepticism prevent me from believing that anything in this book, or its predecessor, has any real permanence. Its value lies in the possibility that others might be provoked into pursuing explorations of a similar kind, but with greater skill and to better effect.

All the papers in this collection were written since I joined the Department of English for Speakers of Other Languages at the University of London Institute of Education six years ago, and owe a good deal to the support and stimulating influence of my colleagues and students there. They, together with all those people at conferences and seminars in various parts of the world who encouraged me with their approval must bear some responsibility for this book.

H. G. Widdowson
May 1983

SECTION ONE
Theory and practice

The papers in this first section provide the conceptual setting for those which follow. They are all concerned with the principles which relate theory to practice and which, in my view, define applied linguistics as an area of enquiry bearing on the techniques of language teaching.

Paper 1 is a variation of a paper published in the first volume of *Explorations in Applied Linguistics* under the title 'The partiality and relevance of linguistic descriptions'. Indeed, certain passages from the earlier paper are repeated here, placed now in a different pattern of argument but contributing to the same conclusion: that in applied linguistics our task is to look for models of language description which relate to the experience of the learner as user. This paper, then, indicates quite explicitly a continuity of thinking from the previous book, and sets the scene for this present one.

Paper 2 takes up the same theme but associates it with more general epistemological issues. It seeks to show the culturally relative nature of all systematic enquiry and the implications of this for the status of statements which claim to give a scientific account of human behaviour. This paper bears on the whole question of whether we can, or should, expect any such statements to provide *explanations* rather than partial representations of reality which can facilitate our *understanding* (cf. Ochsner 1979).

Both of these papers talk about the difference between analyst-oriented models of language system and participant-oriented models of language use, claiming primary relevance for the latter with regard to the practices of language teaching and learning. Both are somewhat circumspect about theory. The third paper in this section, on the other hand, proclaims its importance.

There is no contradiction here. Papers 1 and 2 argue against too ready a reliance on theory which has not been assessed for relevance; Paper 3 argues for the need to adopt a theoretical orientation to the teaching task itself, whereby techniques are tested in the operational conditions of the classroom as implementations of principles explicitly formulated in advance. All the papers in this section, then, subscribe to the basic belief that effective practice depends on theory, but that the theory has to be relevant to the purposes of practice and has to yield principles which can be interpreted and tested as practical teaching techniques.

1 Applied linguistics: the pursuit of relevance

The term *applied linguistics* suggests that its concern is with the use of findings from theoretical studies of language for the solution of problems of one sort or another arising in a different domain. The close association of applied linguistics with language teaching (to the extent, in some quarters, of virtual synonymy) is based on the belief that such findings must necessarily be relevant to the practical teaching of languages. It would seem to be self-evident that since linguists study language and teachers teach it, there must be a relevant connection if only one could find it. It seems perverse to question such a belief. Nevertheless, that is what I propose to do. The relevance of linguistics cannot, I think, be taken for granted because it is not obvious that the way linguists conceive of language is the most appropriate for teaching purposes. I want to suggest that the main business of applied linguistics should be the establishing of appropriate concepts or models of language in the pedagogic domain without prejudging the issue by supposing that a relevant model of language must inevitably derive from a formal model of linguistic description in a technical sense.

The following is a representative statement of the belief that I wish to question:

> This is the main contribution that the linguistic sciences can make to the teaching of languages: to provide good descriptions. ... The best suited linguistics is the body of accurate descriptive methods based on recent research into the form and substance of language. There is no conflict between application and theory; the methods most useful in application are to be found among those that are most valid and powerful in theory. (Halliday, McIntosh and Strevens 1964: 167)

In case it is objected that I am quoting from an out-of-date book, here is a more recent expression of the same view:

The relevance of the linguistic approach to language teaching is that it provides by far the most detailed and comprehensive descriptions of language. ... The linguistic approach is responsible for determining how we *describe* what we are to teach. (Corder 1973: 30-31)

It is interesting to compare these declarations of faith with the more cautious comments of Chomsky:

It is possible—even likely—that principles of psychology and linguistics, and research in these disciplines, may supply insights useful to the language teacher. But this must be demonstrated, and cannot be presumed. It is the language teacher himself who must validate or refute any specific proposal. There is very little in psychology or linguistics that he can accept on faith. (Quoted from Allen and Van Buren 1971: 155)

I think it is the responsibility of applied linguistics to demonstrate whether or not linguistics can provide insights of use to the language teacher and to investigate other sources of insight in the search for relevant models. This paper attempts a preliminary exploration of the issues. I shall argue that it is possible—even likely—that linguistics, as customarily conceived, may *not* be the most suitable source for a practical teaching model of language.

We can begin with an example given in Halliday *et al.* (1964) of what we must assume to be a 'good description' derived from 'accurate descriptive methods'. It is the formal distributional definition of the noun as a word class which is contrasted with the bad, old-fashioned conceptual definition. This, of course, is a standard demonstration of the merits of structural linguistics. Halliday *et al.* make the usual point that notional or conceptual definitions of a noun, as the name of a person, place, thing, etc., are vague and misleading:

Conceptually defined categories can be held precisely because they are incapable of exact applications; some of the definitions have survived to this day, protected by a cosy unreality. But it is doubtful if any English schoolboy, having to find out whether a certain word is a noun or not, asks: 'Is this the name of a person, place, or thing?' More probably he will test whether it has a plural in -*s*, or whether he can put the definite article in front of it. Since he is probably required to decide that 'departure' is a noun whereas 'somebody' is not, he is more likely to reach the right conclusion by this method. (Halliday *et al.* 1964: 145)

What needs to be noted here is that application is conceived of as an analytic procedure. The formal definition is preferred because it is more helpful when it comes to *finding* nouns. Although this might be an activity required of schoolboys, it is not an activity normally required of language users. Indeed, when a language user begins to identify nouns, one can be fairly sure that he is no longer attending to what is being said. It is only when we assume the role of analyst (as the schoolboy may well be directed to do) that we set about finding and testing word classes, and we only assume such a role when our normal procedures for *using* such classes for communicative purposes break down. Now one may readily concede that the old-fashioned notional definitions do not yield very satisfactory syntactic categories for the analyst, but it does not follow that they do not capture a certain conceptual reality for the user. The question then arises as to whether a relevant model for teaching language is to derive from that of the analyst or from that of the user. If they are incongruent, and if there are grounds for preferring the user's model, then there *is* a conflict between what is useful in application and what is valid in theory.

But are the two models incongruent? I believe that in certain important respects they are, in that they are related to two quite different ways of conceiving of language. The analyst represents language in terms of an abstract system by devising a model which must conform to principles of scientific enquiry. There can be no tolerance for vague notions, imprecision, and ambiguity. The emphasis must be on 'accurate descriptive methods'. Now it may be that such a model can be seen as representing in some sense the underlying knowledge that users have of their language, but it is knowledge that they are generally unaware of since they are never called upon, in normal circumstances, to manifest it but only to realize it as communicative behaviour. And communicative behaviour is vague, imprecise, and ambiguous. This is because it draws on resources for meaning in the language which cannot always be reduced to linguistic rules since they just have not been encoded as such in the language system, and because language behaviour *has* to be imprecise if it is to function effectively as communicative interaction. I shall return to these points presently.

What I am suggesting is that the very exactitude required of the analyst's model makes it essentially inadequate as an explanation of user behaviour. It also makes empirical validation very tricky, perhaps ultimately impossible. It is not a matter of performance being an imperfect reflection of competence, of the analyst's model being but poorly represented in behaviour because of a variety of rather tiresome incidental circumstances. The point is that they are two distinct modes of reality. Competence in the Chomskyan sense is a set of abstract rules which are manifested through analytic models of description made as explicit as possible in the interests of scientific enquiry. Performance is a realization of language resources for communicative purposes. Some of these resources will, of course, correspond to rules specified by the linguistic analyst, in which case the rules can be said to have 'psychological validity'. In other cases, however, the user will have concepts, will use communicative procedures which the analyst cannot capture, or the analyst will have rules which he has to apply but which the user will need to ignore. In brief, the analyst devises rules which represent an ideal knowledge system whereas the user draws on the whole range of communicative resources, in Halliday's terms the whole meaning potential, of his language and employs procedures for making sense. These are alternative models of language: the analytic representation of formal language on the one hand and communicative realization of natural language on the other. Obviously they must correspond in some way; otherwise linguistics would have no empirical content at all. But (to use Chomsky's own words) it is a relationship which 'must be demonstrated, and cannot be presumed'.[1]

I have claimed that there is a radical difference between the analyst's model of language and the user's. It is a claim that I must now try to substantiate. To do so I want first to return to the conceptual definition of the noun. For analytical purposes it is necessary, or so it would appear, to reject this definition in favour of a formal one. A noun, the analyst tells us, is not *really* the name of a person, place or thing, but a distributional class. Yet the language user does, it seems, associate this syntactic class with a semantic concept, so that *reflection, suffering, pride*, and so on are conceived as entities, capable of assuming roles as participants in propositions and also of shifting their meaning to person, place, or thing within the semantic range of noun-ness in metaphorical use.

The sense of noun-ness comes from an awareness of the potential resources available in the language for expressing meanings which happen not to be reduced to rule. But this potential can be realized in a particular message form even though it is not given formal recognition in the code. This is particularly striking in poetry, which very commonly achieves its effects by such realizations. Consider first the following rather extreme example (which I have chosen for reasons I will explain presently):

anyone lived in a pretty how town
with up so floating many bells down
spring summer autumn winter
he sang his didnt he danced his did
(e e cummings)

Here the syntactic environment requires that *did* be understood as a noun. In the code, however, it is not a noun but an auxiliary whose function is to carry tense for a lexical verb. As such one might say that *did* incorporates the semantic features of past tense and verb-ness and that is all. Now, it happens that in English these two semantic features are not encoded as a noun: there is no noun in English which expresses, let us say, past time and process and nothing else. The features are in some sense 'there' as potential meaning resources in the language but unrealized in the code. So Cummings creates a noun which has those features: *did*. We might paraphrase the expression *he danced his did* as something like 'he danced his way through all his activities in the past'. But this, of course, only gives a general indication of the meaning: the full semantic impact depends on our recognition that here we have a fusion of verb-ness, noun-ness, and past time. If we had no conceptual sense of the meaning potential inherent in word classes, there would be no way of understanding the poem.

Of course, there remains a good deal more to understand; and one may feel that the poem is too obscure to be worth bothering about. The reason I chose to comment on it is that it was at one time at the centre of a good deal of discussion among linguists, and this discussion illustrates very clearly the limitations of the analyst's representation of language and its remoteness from the experience of the user. What troubled the analysts was essentially this: if a grammar represents rules which will generate all the sentences of a language, what do we do when we come across actually attested sentences, like those in Cummings, which cannot be generated? If we tinker with the grammar so that it will generate such sentences, we have to accept that it will also generate all kinds of other peculiar sentences which have not been, and probably never would be, attested. One solution that was offered (Thorne 1965) involved writing different rules for the poem from those of standard English, treating the poem, in effect, as the sample of a different language. In this language *did* is a noun. No doubt from the analyst's point of view, this solves the problem and his grammar of English is preserved. What about the user, though? It does not solve the problem for him quite simply because there is no problem there in the first place. Whereas the analyst *has* to resolve whether *did* is a noun or not in order to write a rule, the user, who is not in the rule-writing business, does not need to do so and indeed does not want to do so: *did* is both noun and verb and its meaning depends on the ambiguity remaining unresolved.

In the case of Cummings, the analyst can solve his difficulty. In other cases, however, where the deviation from rules seems less extreme, the problem proves more intractable. Consider the following lines:

Move him into the sun—
Gently its touch awoke him once,
At home, whispering of fields unsown,
Always it woke him even in France,
Until this morning and this snow.
If anything might rouse him now
The kind old sun will know.
(Wilfred Owen)

Here the inanimate noun *sun* is associated with lexical items—*whisper, kind, old* which require us to reclassify it semantically as human. The difficulty is that we cannot write a rule for the language of this poem which carries out this reclassification for the simple reason that *syntactically* the noun remains inanimate, as the pronoun *it* makes clear. So what we have here is a new lexical item which is not and cannot be accounted for by any rule, but which is created from resources available in the language. The sun is both human and inanimate and, as I point out elsewhere (Widdowson 1974), it is crucial to an understanding of the poem that this ambiguity remains unresolved.

The language user, then, is able to understand even when the rules which purport to represent his competence are violated. How can this be? Here was another troublesome question. A grammar not only represented rules which would account for all the sentences of the language but which accounted also for the language user's ability to understand all the sentences. Yet there were sentences—semi-sentences—which violated the rules and still were comprehensible. After considering this problem, Katz comes to the conclusion:

The task a speaker performs when he understands a semi-sentence involves, in addition to his use of grammatical knowledge, the use of knowledge of another kind. (Katz 1964: 402)

This knowledge of another kind is what I have been referring to as an awareness of the potential meaning resources of the language and of the ways in which they can be realized. This realization occurs in contexts of actual communication. It makes no sense to ask how a language user manages to understand a deviant sentence because a sentence is not a unit of use but of analysis. It is a device for manifesting rules, not for realizing resources. This is why it is such a frustrating business trying to get subjects in experiments to make judgements on sentences: there will always be a natural tendency to shift from analysis to use and to try to process the sentences as communicative expressions. This is the problem of empirical validation which I mentioned earlier: how do you get your subjects to assume the required analytic role, and if you do, what is the point of your experiment, since you have lost them as normal language users? I think it is likely that the sentence is, in the words of T. S. Eliot:

> ... an abstraction
> Remaining a perpetual possibility
> Only in the world of speculation.
> (from *Burnt Norton*)

A fair amount of poetry seems to be getting into this paper, and it might be thought that the points I have made about user interpretation and analyst description only apply to such rather outlandish uses of language which trade in curiosities like metaphor and ambiguity. But metaphor and ambiguity are not aberrant features of language use, although they are commonly represented as such in language analysis. It is a normal and essential quality of natural language that it should allow for metaphor for a creative use of its total resources: otherwise it would not have the flexibility it has to have to adapt to changing communicative purposes. But metaphors cannot be reduced to rule because once they are, they cease to be metaphors and become incorporated into the semantic system. The point about metaphors is that they depend on a disparity between the established rules of the code and the extempore exploitation on a particular occasion of potential resources for meaning which are not reduced to rule.

The essence of metaphor is that it represents ambiguity which can be reconciled with effective communication but which cannot be resolved by analysis. There are other aspects of ambiguity in natural language use which cannot easily be accounted for by 'accurate descriptive methods'. Consider the famous example:

1   Flying planes can be dangerous.

If we adopt an analytic role and consider this as a sentence then we must recognize that there is an ambiguity here. We can resolve it in the familiar way by postulating two deep structures which by transformational accident assume the same surface form. One of them is roughly equivalent in meaning to:

2   It can be dangerous to fly planes.

The other is roughly equivalent to:

3   Planes which fly can be dangerous.

Or is it? One notes that the information contained in the relative clause here is pretty vacuous. It is surely of the nature of planes to fly. It seems nonsensical to use a defining relative clause to express a defining feature of the noun itself. Perhaps, then, there is another ambiguity here as between a defining and a non-defining relative clause interpretation, the latter being paraphrasable as:

4   Planes, which fly, are dangerous.

This, if not actually semantically ill-formed, is again oddly redundant, to say the least, but these do not exhaust the possibilities. If we are thinking of paraphrases which might count as equivalent to the original sentence, the following is surely also a candidate.

5   Planes can be dangerous when they fly.

It seems reasonable to trace a transformational process with possible surface outputs as follows:

6   Planes can be dangerous when they fly.
    Planes can be dangerous when flying.
    Planes can be dangerous flying.
    Flying planes can be dangerous.

Now the difficulty about all this is that the relative likelihood of any of these being considered the 'deep structure' seems to depend on how the structure is lexicalized and how far the lexicalization can be understood as representing a reasonable statement. In the present case we might wish to reject 3 and 4 as semantically deviant and in consequence opt for 5. But in cases where the structures are lexicalized differently, the order of likelihood may alter quite radically. Consider, for example:

7   Old men forget.

The paraphrase:

8 Men, who are old, forget.

is nonsense. So here we must reject a deep structure equivalent to **4**. A deep structure equivalent to **3**, on the other hand, makes perfect sense:

9 Men who are old forget.

So does one roughly paraphraseable as:

10 Men forget when they are old.

If we alter the lexis, however, we get a different state of affairs. Consider:

11 Brave men tremble.

Here we would be inclined to reject

12 Men tremble when they are brave.

because it seems to make no sense or rather because it is difficult to make sense of it as a possible statement.

There are two problems for analyst-user relations emerging from this discussion. The first is that the analyst is required to specify precisely the range of possible underlying structures associated with a particular surface form and in so doing he creates ambiguities in the model which would never actually be realized as ambiguities by the user because the forms which resolve them would not count as satisfactory statements. In other words, the ambiguity in the sentence does not correspond with ambiguity in language use: it is a function of the analysis. It arises from a requirement to be precise which extends beyond the needs of the user. Confronted with any of the foregoing examples of language in the context of a discourse, the user will draw on procedures for making sense (described in Grice 1975 under the general heading of the 'co-operative principle'). Whereas the analyst has to disambiguate by reference to syntactically equivalent structures in the code, the user disambiguates by reference to pragmatically relevant information in the context. The two modes of operation are quite distinct.

Another way in which user and analyst operations differ takes us back to the previous discussion on metaphor. The point was made then that the effect of metaphor depends on avoiding the resolution of ambiguity: the user keeps two meanings in his mind at the same time. The same observation can be made about the different meanings incorporated into one form that we have just been considering. Thus in the case of 7, the user is not obliged to select one alternative in preference to another: he may accept both simultaneously. The two alternatives need only to be understood as consistent one with the other in the context in which they occur. Sometimes, of course, the discovery of consistency comes as a surprise as in puns and other kinds of joke, but the ability to appreciate comic effects is part of a more general ability to hold different meanings in the mind concurrently. Like metaphors, jokes are simply particularly striking examples of the normal operation of natural language use. But the analyst cannot cope with concurrent meanings: he has to work disjunctively. His role is rather like that of somebody having to explain a joke: the explanation will spell out the linguistic detail, but it cannot recreate the communicative effect.

What I have been trying to show is that the analyst's description and the user's experience of language are necessarily quite different.[2] Analysis must, of its nature, be exact. Communication, on the other hand, cannot be. This is not a matter for regret. If meanings could be precisely specified then there would be no need for the kind of negotiation which lies at the heart of communicative behaviour, whereby what is meant is worked out by interactive endeavour. There would be no room for the practical reasoning, the ongoing accomplishment of making sense that the ethnomethodologists talk about (see, for example, Turner 1974, Cicourel 1973, Gumperz and Hymes 1972).

Here, perhaps, we are at the heart of the matter. For analysis to be valid it must be precise: for communication to be effective it must be imprecise. Precision in analysis is achieved by the observer taking up a detached position, by disassociating himself from participation. I just do not know how the model that results from such detachment is to be validated. There are times when one feels intuitively that it captures something vital about linguistic knowledge, that it touches on the truth of the working of the mind. There are times when one feels that the model simply generates its own complexity according to the principles of a kind of intellectual Parkinson's Law. Whether and to what extent it can be made to correspond with the user's model, is, it seems to me, a major theoretical question of central concern to applied linguistics (see Note 1). It may be that the user's view can be taken into account by the analyst, and there are signs (see Widdowson 1978a) that the attempt is being made, with the increasing concern in recent research with the communicative properties of language.

Meanwhile, however, the applied linguist is faced with the problem of appropriateness. In the past, the assumption has been that it is the analyst's model rather than the user's which represents the 'real' nature of language. The changes in pedagogic approach—grammar translation, direct method, oral-situational, structural, functional, and what have you—have not altered the basic allegiance. Only in approaches which seem to bypass linguistics and applied linguistics altogether, like Suggestopedia, do we see a real concern with the user of the language rather than with the language he uses (see Stevick 1976, 1980). This belief in the necessary relevance of linguistic analysis has led us into all manner of strange error. Thus, when linguists proclaimed that language was really structure and language was really speech, we created a monstrous hybrid: the oral structural approach. Learners had to produce sentence patterns in repetitive drills to learn the underlying structures of a language and had to do this orally on the grounds that speech is the natural form that language takes. Nowadays we have notions instead of structures because we think that linguists are now indicating that language is really made up of case categories, semantic concepts, and speech acts. If applied linguists want to be taken seriously they really must examine the question of relevance with more critical perception.

Throughout this paper I have talked about analytic models without differentiation. That is perhaps an excusable simplification since by virtue of being analytic they all do, it seems to me, have common characteristics which set them apart from the user's experience of language. If, however, we are to give more attention to the user's model as having at least equal claim on our concern in our search for relevance (and I have been proposing that we should), then we do need to differentiate. Users come in different shapes and sizes. They are of different ages, different levels of cognitive development, different cultures. We have to take account of these (and no doubt other) differences.

In a paper with a particularly apt title with regard to our present discussion (*The relevant models of language*), Halliday suggests ways in which the child's concept of the nature of language differs from that of the adult. He claims that the adult user's concept or model is essentially a representational one, one which concentrates on the function of conveying information. But this, he says, is only one element, and perhaps not a particularly salient element, in the child's multifunctional model of language.

Halliday, then, points to a lack of congruence between the model of adult and child users of language. The same theme is taken up in

Olson (1972). Here an interesting distinction is made between 'sentences as descriptions' on the one hand and 'sentences as propositions' on the other. By the former, Olson seems to mean language items understood in terms of contextual relations and, by the latter, language items understood in terms of code relations. With reference to my own view of the matter, therefore, the analyst naturally inclines to take sentences as propositions while the tendency of the user is to take them as descriptions. Of course, the user can, as I have already indicated, shift to the analytic key and treat language propositionally (in Olson's terms) when he needs to do so, that is to say, on those relatively rare occasions when the lack of contextual information forces him back to a consideration of the code. The observation that Olson makes which is of interest to us here is that it appears that the child lacks the ability to shift to an analytic view and to recognize that one sentence implies another (i.e. the ability to manipulate the code to arrive at paraphrase equivalents). He makes the comment:

> While these implicational relationships (i.e. between sentences as propositions) are implicit in ordinary language, they appear not to be noticed or exploited in either the language of children or in the ordinary language usage of adults. This may be the case because such implicational relations derive from a different point of focus than that involved in ordinary conversational use of language. In the first use of language (i.e. descriptions), the language is completely transparent to the reality that lies behind it; one focuses on the world through the language. In the second use, the focus is on the propositions themselves and their relation to other propositions rather than to the reality specified by the sentences; this latter requires a divorce of language from reality. (Olson 1972: 163)

What Halliday and Olson indicate, in different ways and from different points of view, is that the child user's model of language may be very different from that of the adult user. But models may also differ between adults and children from different cultures. The whole area of enquiry which goes under the general heading of 'the ethnography of communication' is relevant here (see Bauman and Sherzer 1974, Gumperz and Hymes 1972). Also of relevance, of course, is the work of Labov and others on the varying prominence given to different functions of language by different social and ethnic groups within a speech community (see, for example, Bernstein 1971, Labov 1972). Then there are the broad distinctions that can be made in personality type between convergers and divergers (see Hudson 1966): or, for that matter, between the hedgehog and the fox (Berlin 1957). These are all sources of insight for applied linguistics in its quest for an appropriate way of representing language to the learner.

I began the argument of this paper by objecting to a concept of applied linguistics proposed by Halliday (or, at least, proposed, one must assume, with his approval). I find to my satisfaction that I can end by quoting comments of his from a later source which support my view (and so contradict his own). They run as follows:

> If the teacher's image of language is narrower and less rich than that which is already present in the minds of those he is teaching (or which needs to be present, if they are to succeed), it will be irrelevant to him as a teacher. A minimum requirement for an educationally relevant approach to language is that it takes account of the child's own linguistic experience. ... (Halliday 1973: 19)

I think that it is the responsibility of applied linguists to consider the criteria for 'an educationally relevant approach to language' and to avoid the uncritical assumption that applied linguistics must necessarily be the application of linguistics. This (analytic) paraphrase is too restrictive and has proved in the past to be seriously misleading. It has allowed applied linguistics to avoid what I have claimed here is its central task: the pursuit of pedagogic relevance, the search for a model which will draw on and appeal to the learner's experience as a language user.

Notes

First published in Kaplan 1980.

1   For a brief, but particularly lucid discussion of the principles of formal analysis and the relationship between formal and natural languages, see Lyons 1977, Appendix 1. The discussion ends with the following comment:

> The goal of theoretical linguistics can be described as that of constructing a class of formal languages, all of whose members share certain general properties and each of whose members can be put into correspondence with some actual or potential natural language. It is as yet unclear whether this goal can be achieved. (Lyons 1977a: 169)

The point I make in this paper is that applied linguistics has tended to assume that the correspondence is self-evident. We need to work out ways of establishing the correspondence in relation to language teaching pedagogy just as psychologists have sought to establish it in relation to underlying cognitive processes (for a review, see Greene 1972).

2   This difference relates to the more general problem in the social sciences of observer-oriented, as opposed to participant-oriented, approaches to the description of human behaviour. In the pedagogic domain this corresponds to teacher-centred, as opposed to learner-centred, approaches to teaching. An applied linguistics model which took the user into account would, of course, be participant-oriented and would therefore provide the basis for a learner-centred methodology. One of the consequences of accepting the analyst's model is that it logically leads to a teacher-centred pedagogy of imposition rather than a learner-centred pedagogy of participation.

2   Models and fictions

How are we to name the activity we are engaged in when we attempt to work out a principled approach to the solution of practical problems in the acquisition and use of language? This is not a trivial question. One does not have to embrace extreme Whorfian doctrine to recognize that how a thing is called can have a critical effect on how it is conceived. And this can have important consequences on how we conduct our enquiries and how they appear to potential sources of research funds. Our activity has commonly been called *applied linguistics*. A metathetic alternative has been suggested: *linguistics applied*. What do we understand by these two terms and which of them provides the most appropriate designation for what we do?

I assume that, semantically, the difference between the two expressions is that in the case of *applied linguistics* we have a type classification, what Bolinger refers to as a 'characterization' (Bolinger 1952) whereas with *linguistics applied* we do not. We might compare *Lost paradise* with *Paradise lost*. On the one hand a type of paradise, a palm-fringed beach perhaps, thronged with lotus eaters; on the other hand, the fall of man, the unique loss of Eden. Thus applied linguistics can be understood as a kind of linguistics, like historical linguistics or folk linguistics. This presumably allows its practitioners to define an independent perspective on the general phenomena of language and to establish principles of enquiry without necessary reference to those which inform linguistics *tout court*—and *tel quel*. With linguistics applied we do not have this option. Whatever we do with linguistics, however we apply it, the informing principles which define this area of enquiry, already pre-established, must remain intact. Any other principles we invoke must be auxiliary operating principles and have to do not with theory as such but with the technology of application.

It seems to me, then, that with linguistics applied the theory of language and the models of description deriving from it must be those of linguistics. As an activity, therefore, it is essentially conformist. Applied linguistics, on the other hand, can develop its own non-conformist theory, its own relevant models of description. Both lines of approach have their dangers. The tendency of linguistics applied will be to dance attendance to whatever tune is currently in theoretical fashion. The tendency of applied linguistics will be to dance around in circles with no tune at all. For linguistics applied, therefore, the question of central concern is: how far can existing models of description in linguistics be used to resolve the practical problems of language use we are concerned with? For applied linguistics, the central question is: how can *relevant* models of language description be devised, and what are the factors which will determine their effectiveness?

This first question takes us at once to the theoretical status of linguistic models. Linguistics claims to be a science, like physics. It must, therefore, conform to general principles of scientific enquiry, and in particular it must avoid intuitive contamination in the interpretation of its findings. And it is here that we come against a major problem. Linguists have a way of claiming validity for solutions which seem peculiar and make no appeal whatever to ordinary intuition on the grounds that language, like God, moves in a mysterious way and outside the range of the common man's awareness. On the other hand, this does not inhibit them from commending solutions because they seem 'intuitively correct' and disapproving of those which seem to be 'counter-intuitive'—these expressions are of high frequency in the literature. So it is that the linguist finds a way of both having his cake and eating it too. For although intuition may serve as a source of hypotheses, it cannot scientifically be used to test them or to provide them with a mark of approval. Geoffrey Sampson, for one, is very insistent on this point. In his discussion of the evidence for linguistic theories he says:

> We do not need to use intuition in justifying our grammars, and, as scientists, we must not use intuition in this way. (Sampson 1975: 70)

Sampson argues that linguistics, like any other science, is, and must be, empirical. But it seems that in order to meet this requirement, linguistics has to restrict its attention to a fairly narrow strip of language phenomenon: most of what is of human interest about language behaviour is left out of account. This, of course, is Hockett's objection to Chomskyan grammar: it leaves out of account, he says 'just those properties of real language that are most important' (Hockett 1968: 10). This is reminiscent of E. M. Forster's remark about Henry James: 'Most of human life has to disappear before he can do us a novel' (Forster 1927: 147). This reference to literature is not gratuitous and I shall have more to say about fiction presently.

Sampson argues that linguistics is a science, like physics. Other people are not so sure. Here is Peter Matthews:

> Is there a true analogy. ... between a 'science' *like* linguistics and a 'science' *like* physics? The problem is not that linguistics is at this stage 'less advanced': will the descriptive linguist ever be able to propose an ordinary mathematical theory for a language, will he ever be able to falsify a 'theory' by one observation, will he ever be able to construct an absolute test of his predictions? Surely we delude ourselves if we imagine that linguistics will be 'like physics' sometime in the future. ... (The problem) is rather that the extent of our data is in principle not precise. Languages change, and language interacts continuously with other forms of social behaviour. ... We cannot even be expected to account for 'all of the data', simply because we do not know what 'all of the data' means! (Matthews 1972: 77 quoted in Bolinger 1975: 551)

We must surely accept the possibility that human knowledge and behaviour are just not the same kind of phenomena as those which are independent of human agency, that they are intrinsically participant, first and second person phenomena which cannot be detached to be third person data of an objective kind and are not therefore susceptible to scientific enquiry. But if this is so, what then is the status of statements in linguistics?

This is not the place, and I am not the person, to enter into the complexities of epistemology. But I would like to make an informal observation or two which might have a bearing on the question. Central to the issue is the matter of the privileged position of the enquirer. In the physical sciences, the enquirer is trained in detached analysis, in putting the phenomena he wishes to investigate at a remove from the immediacy of perception and intuition. In this way he aims at correcting the distortions of the human factor. What this involves, in effect, is the acquisition of a secondary culture of a non-participant kind defined by the philosophy of science and apart from the popular beliefs and values of participant primary culture. From the vantage point of this secondary culture, the scientist can reveal a different, third person reality, which will often run counter to that which is popularly accepted. He can, furthermore, demonstrate its truth, though until the respectability of such a secondary culture was established and its practical consequences made clear this truth was commonly condemned as heresy.

But now how does all this apply to the linguist as scientist? Can he detach himself and take up a privileged observer's position in the same way? I do not think so. The linguist is of necessity a participant: like other social scientists he enacts the data he analyses so that there are no separable facts out there, as it were, open to objective validation. We get a model of behaviour (that of the linguist) used to analyse another model of behaviour (that of the common man), one set of cultural assumptions, which are secondary and superposed, used to interpret another set of cultural assumptions, which are primary and acquired through ordinary socialization.

So it is that the linguist is not a representative speaker/listener. He comes from a different culture and so is able to analyse in detachment. The data he produces are devised to demonstrate the general underlying rules of language he has inferred. The sentences that linguists present have the same sort of status as the components of kinship analysis presented by anthropologists: devices for the design of ideal systems. But what cognitive reality do they have for people who use language and enact kinship relations in the ordinary business of social life? What is their empirical status?

As soon as a language user is presented with a sentence he quite naturally converts it into an utterance. His culture prevents him doing otherwise: he will associate the isolated linguistic expression with a likely context of occurrence and interpret it accordingly. If you train him to do otherwise, he loses his innocence and at the same time his usefulness as an informant. He becomes tainted by foreign influence.

The linguistic analyst, in conformity with the secondary cultural principles he embraces, represents language as a system in a steady state, with each term in its place in peaceful co-existence with others—a picture of classical harmony and well-formed order. An artefact, a cultural construct. For really there is conflict, an intrinsic instability—with rules moving into dominance or decline. And every use of language is a resolution of this conflict, the ex tempore exploitation of the meaning resources available for expressing the variety and contradictions of human experience; in short, as T. S. Eliot puts it:

> a raid on the inarticulate
> with shabby equipment always deteriorating.
> (from *East Coker*)

The linguist presents his view of the world, his model of reality. Shift the perspective and you get a different view, and a different reality. The linguist's model has no privileged patent on the truth, it is open to investigation by another, that model by yet another, and so on. Now, of course, it can be very interesting and enlightening to see how one set of cultural values interprets another and the exercise can yield all kinds of insights, but there is no way, as far as I can see, of establishing which is true and which is not.

What I am saying is that the linguist, in common with other social scientists, simply fashions his data to fit a particular set of cultural assumptions. Further, he will be inclined to interpret behaviour according to his own predispositions. Liam Hudson has this to say about psychologists and his remarks apply, *mutatis mutandis*, to linguists as well:

> The truth is that, to a remarkable extent, psychologists do research in their own image. One notices this daily. Psychologists with high I.Q.s do research that reflects well on those with high I.Q.s. Neurotic introverts show that neurotic introverts do well at school and university. Convergers do research that bodes well for convergers; divergers, for divergers. ... Just as novelists draw on their experience, so too do psychologists. We would both be cut off, otherwise, from the springs of our intellectual vitality. (Hudson 1972: 129)

We return to fiction. It seems to me that models of human behaviour in the social sciences are comparable in status and function to the representations of human behaviour in novels or plays or any other art form. Both depend upon idealization procedures which in effect yield prototypes of a kind which we can set into correspondence with actual and non-idealized reality. There is not, and cannot be, any direct empirical link between either of them and the external world. Descriptive models and fictional representations create idealized norms of human behaviour which we cannot accept as a plausible pattern against which actuality can be compared. Their function is not to be correct but convincing, to serve as a means towards a more perceptive awareness of what we do and who we are. Hamlet and Heathcliff do not carry conviction as characters because they have empirical counterparts among our acquaintances. If they did, they would diminish into insignificance. So it is with models of linguistic description. Their value, as a kind of art form, depends on idealization and a detachment from empirical validation.

Linguistic theories, I suggest then, are fictions. This is a perfectly respectable thing to be. As Harré points out, the fictionalist view of theories has a long history. He describes it like this:

> As an aid to thinking a plausible theory may be a very powerful tool, and by using known laws of nature in describing the behaviour and nature of the entities with which it deals it gains plausibility. But the entities themselves have no more reality than the characters of fiction, and the terms which are used to describe and particularly to refer to them are like the names and addresses of characters in novels. (Harré 1972: 81)

I find the notion of a theory as an aid to thinking an appealing one. You do not *apply* a theory which is a fiction, any more than you apply a novel. What you do is to use it to develop your awareness of what a useful model of behaviour might be for your particular purposes. In this view, a linguistic model is of value only to the extent that it can help us towards a definition of what an applied linguistic model should be.

So we come to the second question I posed at the beginning. What would a relevant model of language in applied linguistics look like: what assumptions, beliefs, values would it need to satisfy? What would be its cultural character, if you like? It would, I think, have to be congruent with the knowledge and attitudes of language users, and be developed, therefore, in accordance with membership categories of the kind that ethnomethodologists have made familiar. It would attempt to record the language user's intuitive, imaginative as well as rational awareness of the nature of language and would accord as much respect to the operations of the right as to those of the left cerebral hemisphere.

It naturally follows that applied linguistic models of language would vary according to the kind of language user concerned. They would be consumer based. Halliday (1964) (severely savaged in certain purist quarters) with its argument in favour of relating adequacy to specific relevance indicates an appropriate rationale for the applied linguist. Again, Halliday (1969), concerned as it is with relevant models of language points us, I think, in the direction we might go. Thus the relevant model of language for teachers of literature will take into account the cultural perspectives of literary criticism and aesthetics. The relevant model for students of physics doing a course in ESP will take into account the philosophy and methodology of science. The relevant model for learners in a particular cultural context will take into account the traditions, values, beliefs, and customary practices of that culture and the way language is used to express them. In all such cases, the starting point is the need and purpose that the model of language must provide for. You do not start with a model as given and then cast about for ways in which it might come in handy. You start instead with a characterization of the learner and his circumstances: his behaviour and beliefs, his habitual patterns of thinking, his conventional attitudes to language, the extent and influence of literacy and other social patterns of cultural transmission and control, and so on. All these, and more, are factors which might affect the model of languages to be presented. The relevance of the learner's first language has long been recognized and interesting work has been done recently on the matter of language distance (see Corder 1979, Kellerman 1979). But questions of social and psychological distance, as discussed, for example, by Schumann (1978), are of equal importance in the design of effective applied linguistic models. We are concerned with language as the rightful property of language users, not as the special preserve of the linguist.

The issue of directionality is critical here, as it is for sociolinguistic studies (see Cooper 1980). Linguistics applied works in one direction and yields descriptions which are projections of linguistic theory which exploit the data of actual language as illustration. Applied linguistics, as I have characterized it here, works in the opposite way and yields descriptions which are projections of actual language which exploit linguistic theory as illumination. My own belief is that it is only by preferring applied linguistics to linguistics applied that we shall achieve something which is relevant and accountable in terms of usefulness and avoid the kind of ethnocentrism and cultural imposition that has marked so much of language study and teaching in the past. There are signs of this preference emerging in recent work. But we have a long way to go and there will be many an alluring linguistic Will-o'-the-wisp to lead us astray from the path of our intentions.

Note

Paper presented at the BAAL Annual Meeting, Manchester Polytechnic, September 1979, and revised for publication in *Applied Linguistics* Vol. 1, No. 2, Summer 1981.

3   The role of theory in practice

One of the lesser known of Gulliver's travels takes him to the Island of Balnibarbi, somewhere in the Pacific. What strikes Gulliver about this place is its poverty and inefficiency:

> I never knew a soil so unhappily cultivated, houses so ill contrived and so ruinous, or a people whose countenances and habit expressed so much misery and want.

It is not long before he discovers the reason for this sorry state of affairs. The island is full of academic institutions, dedicated to the pursuit of abstract speculation and engaged on research whose effects are disastrous to the well-being of the people. Gulliver visits the most prestigious of these, The Grand Academy of Lagado, and there meets some of the academics. One of them has been working for eight years on a project for extracting sunbeams out of cucumbers. Another has devoted a lifetime's fruitless toil in trying to convert human excrement back to its original food. Another is working on an extensive scheme to grow crops not from seed but from chaff. It is not surprising that such research has only succeeded in laying the land to waste, blighted by an excess of scholarship.

The situation in Balnibarbi might seem familiar to cultivators in the field of English language teaching. And to bring the point nearer home, I should mention that there is in this Grand Academy of Lagado a school of languages engaged in researches of a similarly abstruse and fanciful kind. One example is a scheme for dispensing with language entirely:

> ... and this was urged as a great advantage in point of health as well as brevity. For it is plain that every word we speak is in some degree a diminution of our lungs by corrosion, and consequently contributes to the shortening of our lives. An expedient was therefore offered, that since words are only names for *things*, it would be more convenient for all men to carry about them such

things as were necessary to express the particular business they are to discourse on ...

There is, however, a practical difficulty in applying this theory:

> ... if a man's business be very great, and of various kinds, he must be obliged in proportion to carry a greater bundle of things upon his back, unless he can afford one or two strong servants to attend him.

Again, this will perhaps strike chords of recognition: academics dreaming up theories of language of suspect validity and no practical value, and infecting practitioners with a misplaced belief in their applicability, with language these days replaced not by a bundle of things but a bundle of notions, functions, categories, speech acts, structures deep and surface. Dean Swift, thou shouldst be living at this hour!

There is, I think, a deep distrust of theory among many people concerned with the practical business of language teaching. They see it, at best, as an academic indulgence of no real relevance, at worst as an insidiously disruptive influence on sound practices based on experience. On the one hand the theorist is represented as a harmless enough figure, though loaded with undeserved prestige; on the other hand, he is represented as a dangerous mountebank, peddling nostrums that do more harm than good. What I should like to do on this occasion is to argue for the significance of theory in even the most practical of language teaching activities and to indicate how it can be seen as a means of bringing the efforts of academic departments and language schools into a complementary relationship.

Let me begin with the concept of training as applied to teachers of language. The term 'training' is generally understood, I think, as a process whereby a person (or any other animal for that matter) is provided with certain techniques in order to achieve certain objectives. These objectives are clear, specified in advance. So training can appropriately be associated with apprentice plumbers, motor mechanics, long distance runners. To be sure, the techniques may be complex and intellectually demanding, but the idea of training presupposes that the objectives themselves pose no problem. You train *for* something, to achieve some predetermined goal. The focus of attention is not on the definition of what is to be achieved but on the most effective means of achieving it.

Now how far is training, defined in this way, a satisfactory process for the development of effective teachers? Some people of the brass tacks nitty gritty school do talk as if training as I have defined it were all that is necessary by way of professional qualification: the acquiring of routines and techniques for manipulating classes in the presentation and practice of language. But this, as I have suggested, implies that the purposes are unproblematic, that the objective of the exercise is established in advance. And this, as we all know, is just not the case. It is not enough for teachers to know *what* to do to organize situational demonstrations, structural drills, pair work, group work, role play and what have you, they must also know *why* they are doing these things, how these activities contribute to the development of language learning. And the question *why* leads them to a consideration of the nature of language, how it is acquired and used as a means of conceptual thinking and social action, how language abilities interrelate, the nature of learning and how it is achieved, and so on. In short, the question *why* leads them into theory.

Of course, one might argue that theirs is not to reason why but simply to get on with the job. The problem here, though, is that you can't get on with the job unless you are clear in your mind about what the job is. And in language teaching this problem is well in evidence: the question of what it is we are trying to achieve is controversial, a matter of continuing enquiry, and an issue that has to be confronted in the very act of teaching. Otherwise the techniques that are used, no matter how ingenious, are directed into a void. Language teaching, in order to be effective in practice, must have a theoretical dimension because without it there is no objective, and no eventual purpose. All that is left is technique dressed up with nowhere to go, the dreary humdrummery of routine for its own sake.

Now when I say that practical teaching must have a theoretical dimension, I do not mean that it must be based on proven theory. I mean, rather, that the teaching practitioner must have a theoretical orientation to his task. Let me elaborate on this point because I think it is an important one and the source of much misunderstanding. One could argue that effective teaching is a matter of applying in the classroom the findings of theoretical research. So if research indicates that learning is a matter of shaping behaviour by habit formation, then the teacher devises a methodology based on drill. If research indicates that learning is a matter of taking cognitive initiative, then the teacher directs his methodology towards problem solving. If research yields a model of language which focuses on the formal properties of linguistic systems on the surface, then the teacher represents language in terms of overtly different sentence patterns; if, on the other hand, a model of description deals with underlying and covert relations in deep structure, then the teacher, too, takes a deep breath and plunges into the depths.

The dangers of this kind of dependent application are obvious. Every time there is a shift of theoretical fashion, a reversal of previous findings, the teacher is presented with a dilemma: either he gives up following the hunt and settles for what he has got, thereby running the risk of becoming old fashioned, fixed in his ways, a fuddy duddy; or he scampers off in hot pursuit, changing his ways to conform to current thinking, thereby running the risk of becoming unreliable, impractical, a fly-by-night. Both the fuddy duddy and the fly-by-night are familiar figures on the English Language Teaching scene: the former stolidly for structural syllabuses and closely controlled methodology, believing that recent thinking either introduces familiar ideas in fancy dress or unfamiliar ideas that are too fanciful to be of use; the latter, the fly-by-night, prattling on about notions and functions and role play, authentic language and autonomous learning, believing that past practices must be abandoned in favour of the new enlightenment.

Both fuddy duddies and fly-by-nights, which, we will agree, reflect no credit on our profession, emerge in our midst because of a mistaken view that the theoretical element of language teaching lies in the direct application of theory to pedagogic technique. In this view the researcher works on theory, passes his findings out to teachers, who then adjust their practice accordingly. In Pit Corder's words, teachers are in this way consumers of theories. As I have already indicated, I think this view is mistaken. It invests the researcher with too much authority and the teacher with too little. Here on the one hand is the researcher abrim with scholarship, expert in abstract thinking, precise in his experimentation, a purveyor of theoretical insight. Here, on the other hand, is the humble practitioner waiting to be shown the way, agape for guidance, his expertise, such as it is, derived only from experience, a consumer of theoretical insight. But the researcher is, on closer inspection, not such an impressive figure after all. In his thinking he casts about for ways of making conceptually coherent schemes out of a mass of complex phenomena and to do this he has to idealize, restrict, and so in some degree to diminish the data he deals with in the interests of clarity. And since one man's idealization is another man's misrepresentation, the conceptual schemes based upon it will always be vulnerable to attack by people who feel that too much of what is essential has been left out of account. So it is that Chomsky's formulation of the scope of linguistic description is now rejected by many in favour of one which embraces communicative competence. I have no doubt that this formulation too will be challenged before long. 'And thus the whirligig of time brings in his revenges.' Theorists live very unstable lives in a state of perpetual insecurity. It is wise not to place too much reliance on what they say.

But this, it might be objected, applies only to the speculative side of the researcher's activities. What about experimentation? Surely this is meant to convert abstract theorizing into hard fact, definite conclusions that we can depend upon. Now the point about experiments is that they are controlled and control means, again, a measure of idealization. The experimenter seeks to establish a relationship between two things by altering one thing, the independent variable so called, and seeing what effect this alteration has on the other thing, the dependent variable. Now the validity of his operation obviously requires that all other factors that might have an effect on the dependent variable should be eliminated, so that the experimental conditions represent an idealized version of conditions in the real world. But this of course means that the findings can only be interpreted with reference to the experimental conditions, and so express a *relative* truth. It cannot be assumed that they hold good in the non-idealized world where variables are free to act and interact and counteract. So even if a certain experiment were to give convincing substantiation to a particular hypothesis about learning language, it does not follow that such a finding should directly determine teaching procedures, since the classroom which provides the context for teaching abounds with variables which are neither controlled nor accounted for.

If theorizing and experimentation cannot be depended upon to give us findings that we can apply in the practical domain, then what purpose do they serve? There is a temptation here to draw the wrong conclusion, to read all this as a confirmation of one's distrust in theory and to dismiss these academic activities as airy fairy irrelevancies, games people play in the Grand Academy of Lagado. But I would argue that the real relevance of these activities lies not so much in the findings they yield, as *products* for consumption, but in the *process* of enquiry itself. The theoretical dimension of teaching comes in not as an application of the findings of somebody else's research but as an application of procedures for conducting research of one's own, suggested by these findings no doubt but related to classroom activities, and part of the pedagogic process. From this point of view, the controlled experiments of the researcher do not produce *facts* for instant assimilation and use, but identify *factors* that call for further enquiry in the context of the classroom.

This is what I mean by a theoretical orientation. The teacher, I have argued, needs to ask why he follows certain routines, or otherwise these routines are simply empty ritual, gestures in the void. He must be able to formulate problems based on an analysis of short term and long term objectives and then be able to test out solutions through teaching activities. Every teaching experience can be considered as an experiment whereby the teacher first undertakes a conceptual analysis of the problem he wishes to solve, then designs activities in the classroom by way of trial solutions, controlling the variables as best he can. What this amounts to is pedagogy made more systematic and exploratory, more critically self-aware and accountable, a pedagogy which has assessment built into the experimental process of teaching itself and which sets up no great divide between teaching and research.

To achieve this theoretical orientation to the teaching task one needs to go beyond training as I defined it earlier and into education. That is to say, one needs to develop an intellectual independence, an ability and inclination to explore by conceptual analysis and experiment. We need to encourage enquiring minds, which do not submit to the drudgery of humdrum routine without question and which are not easily persuaded to join the mindless march behind the latest banner. In short, we need educated teachers rather than teachers that are just trained. But, as I have tried to show, this does not mean that the importance of practice is diminished. On the contrary its importance is enhanced by being provided with a perspective which gives it an essential purpose as teaching techniques become exercises in experimental method. In this view, training is an element in what we might call applied education and not an end in itself.

We are all, I think, aware of the consequences of educational deficiency in our field. People talk disparagingly about swings of the pendulum, bandwagons, new fads, and are inclined to put the blame on the theorists. But an idea only develops into a fad when the conditions are favourable to its growth and when it is uncritically accepted; and if there are fads in our profession at the moment it is because they meet a need for novelty and teachers lack the will or the ability to assess the validity and relevance of the ideas put forward. Fads in other words are the consequence of educational failure. You do not, in an open society at any rate, avoid them by a censorship of innovatory thinking because to do that would be to stop up all springs of enquiry and all hope of progress. This presumably is one reason why education is so crucial in a democratic system and perhaps why totalitarian states can replace it in part with training.

Of course, a theory which happens to suit the needs of the time or fit neatly into prevailing prejudice is particularly difficult to resist and it is here that education is given its severest test. An interesting example of this, in a domain not usually associated with language teaching, is discussed by Galbraith, in his book *The Age of Uncertainty* (1977). It concerns the case of the Reverend Henry Ward Beecher who, in the late nineteenth century, put forward a theory to solve the tricky problem that Darwin had posed about the origin of species. The devout parishioners of Beecher's church in Brooklyn understandably could not easily reconcile the idea that man was created in God's image in a matter of moments in the Garden of Eden and the idea that man was descended from the monkey at the end of a long evolutionary process. Fortunately, the Reverend Beecher was at hand with a theory that effected the necessary reconciliation. This is how Galbraith describes it:

> His reconciliation involved a distinction between theology and religion. Theology, like the animal kingdom, was evolutionary. Such change did not contradict the Holy Writ. Religion was enduring. Its truths did not change. Darwin and Spencer belonged to theology; the Bible was religion. So there was no conflict between natural selection and the Holy Scripture.

and Galbraith adds the comment:

> I do not understand this distinction, and it is fairly certain that neither Beecher nor his congregation did either. But it sounded exceptionally good. (Galbraith 1977: 57)

To move now from theology to pedagogy, and into the ELT field: the notional-functional syllabus, like the structural syllabus before it, must have sounded, and must still sound, exceptionally good to some teachers, and the temptation to accept it as a creed and to suspend a critical investigation of the theory in favour of immediate application, as in the case of the Reverend Beecher's flock, must have been and must still be very difficult to resist. But it is just this kind of temptation that has to be resisted, and it is the responsibility of teacher education to create conditions that will encourage resistance. But who is responsible for teacher education? I come now to the question of co-operation, the bringing together of our efforts in complementary relationship that I referred to earlier.

It is the business of University departments like my own to educate teachers and this we aim to do by encouraging the conceptual analysis of current practices in ELT and relating this, to an extent not always recognized, to the actual classroom context through sessions of supervised teaching practice. So what we seek to do is to provide a theoretical orientation to practical work. But this orientation needs to be extended and sustained beyond the actual period of formal study leading to certificate or diploma or degree. It needs to be sustained as a part of continuing teacher education whereby the classroom is seen as the setting for ongoing experimental research, a place where ideas can be put to empirical test. This does not mean, as I have pointed out, that the classroom is converted into a laboratory decontaminated of intervening variables. The classroom retains its identity as a place of complex interaction. The controls that are applied are those which are called for in the interests of effective pedagogy. The research is part of the teaching activity itself.

It is in the provision of facilities for ongoing education of this kind that the language schools can complement the efforts of the academic sector and can make their most telling contribution to developments in ELT. The language schools, quite properly, emphasize the practical side of language teaching, just as university departments quite properly emphasize its theoretical side. The danger is that this emphasis might drift into exclusive concern. The universities need to recognize that theory must be accountable in practice; the language schools need to recognize that practice is made more effective by theory. This recognition is not always easy to achieve, even less easy to act upon. Academics will always be tempted into intellectual enquiry for its own sake, and in the intricate mazes of scholarship can easily lose the thread that leads them out of the labyrinth and back to the outside world: like denizens of The Grand Academy of Lagado groping for the truth. The stereotype of people in language schools, on the other hand, represents them not so much as groping as grasping. Their temptation, I suppose, is to seek the achievement of short term practical results by the most direct and economical route and to shy away from a long term investment in research. The criterion for assessing a teaching technique tends then to be reduced to the simple question: Does it work?

I have heard the expression 'It works' used as the highest commendation of a teaching technique. But the fact that something works is not in itself a cause of commendation. All sorts of things 'work'. A candle 'works' as a source of light: long distance runners carrying messages in cleft sticks 'work' as a means of communication, but neither of these, I assume, would be commended in favour of electricity or radio. The fact that something works should lead us to enquire into the principles of its working so that we can look for something that works better. The expression 'It works' should not mark the end of investigation but the beginning. Similar remarks might be made about another familiar expression of commendation: eclectic. Too often it seems to mean a random lucky dip, a rummage around for techniques. But eclecticism is no good unless one enquires into the principles of selection, unless, in other words, it is informed by theory.

The effectiveness of practice depends on relevant theory: the relevance of theory depends on effective practice. The two are in complementary relationship, each sustaining the other, and ensuring that the field of ELT is an area of both valid academic enquiry and viable commercial enterprise. There should be no conflict here, no divergence of interests, with gropers on the one side, graspers on the other. We have a common objective, a joint responsibility for the development of English language teaching. In these times of economic stringency when we are forced to look at the most effective way of using reduced resources, it is of particular importance that we should recognize this responsibility and seek collaborative ways of discharging it. It may not only be our credibility that is at stake but our very survival.

Note

Originally presented as the Gretta Smith Memorial Lecture at the Annual Meeting of the Association of Recognized English Language Schools (ARELS), November 1981.

SECTION TWO
Discourse: the use of written language

All four of the papers in this Section characterize written language use as a form of non-reciprocal interaction and indicate what roles the writer and reader must assume as discourse participants.

Paper 4 makes its way to such a characterization through a general consideration of the nature of language use. It takes up the point previously made in Paper 1 that the language user does not communicate by simply conforming to linguistic rules but by realizing the meanings which are available as a resource in his language and which are only partially accounted for by systemic description. This realization is achieved when the language items in the actual utterance are appropriately related to contextual factors. This being so, meaning must be a matter of negotiated settlement between interactants. The question then naturally arises as to how such a settlement can be brought about when the interactants are not actively participating in the negotiation itself, when there is a physical dissociation of participant roles, as in writing and reading.

The differentiation between the manifestation of rules in sentences and their realization in utterances has, no doubt, a somewhat familiar, not to say hackneyed air to it by now, but in this paper I seek to show how it logically leads to a particular way of conceiving of the writing and reading processes. It also makes further appearances later in the book, notably where it is reformulated as a distinction between different types of linguistic sign (in the papers of Section Three) and where it provides the basis for distinguishing between competence and capacity (in Paper 18).

Paper 5 in this Section concentrates particularly on the implications that the interactive nature of written discourse has for the role of writer. A number of issues arise here, corollaries to the main argument, which are taken up in subsequent papers. One of them concerns correctness. This, it is suggested, may be a matter of conformity beyond communicative requirement and so relate to what I refer to as the indicative or identifying function of language. This topic is taken up again in Paper 18. Another issue relates to the matter of skill automation, whereby operations on phonology and syntax are carried out below the level of conscious awareness, leaving the mind free to interpret the larger units of discourse structure. The need for such automation as a necessary condition for effective communication is discussed further in Paper 16. What these larger structural units might be is a central question dealt with in the papers of Section Three.

Paper 6 develops points raised in Paper 4 about focal and enabling acts in discourse. It begins by emphasizing the need to recognize the importance of language as a means of conceptualizing, of fulfilling, in Halliday's phrase, an ideational function, as well as a means of conveying what has been conceptualized. These two operations, the formulation of propositions and their effective conveyance to another person, need to be co-ordinated on every occasion of communication by means of discourse negotiation. The question again arises as to how this is to be effected when the interactants act independently of each other, as they do in writing and reading. The suggestion made in the paper is that the writer creates discourse by the process of expansion whereby he prepares his conceptual content so as to make it accessible to the putative reader, whereas the reader derives this content from the textual record of the discourse by the process of reduction whereby the facilitating elements, their duty discharged, are filtered out. What this means with reference to the observations made in Paper 4 is that the reader has to distinguish between the focal acts, which express the essential substance of the writer's intent, and the enabling acts, which simply serve as a means of conveyance.

The last paper of this Section (Paper 7) restates the main points of the previous ones and then moves the argument forward by noting that the receptivity of the addressee to an intended message depends on two factors: the extent to which it is actually understood, its accessibility, and the extent to which s/he is willing to acknowledge it as justified, its acceptability. Acceptability is then related to general questions of social motivation concerning territorial and co-operative imperatives, dominance, dependency, and degrees of affiliation. It is here that the nature of the writing and reading processes as types of social interaction is made most explicit. Accessibility is related to the notion of schematic structure, and this is a major topic of the papers in the Section which follows.

4   The realization of rules in written discourse

Reading is most commonly characterized as an exercise in linguistic analysis, an activity whereby information is extracted from a written text which signals it. The information is thought to be *there*, statically residing in the text and in principle recoverable in its entirety. If, in practice, the reader cannot recover the information it is assumed that he is defective in linguistic competence. Such a view represents written language as the manifestation of syntactic and semantic rules and the reader's task as a matter of recognition. I want to propose an alternative view: one which represents written text as a set of directions for conducting an interaction. From such an interaction, which in effect creates discourse from text, the reader derives what information he needs, or what information his current state of knowledge enables him to take in. Meanings, in this view, are not contained in a text but are derived from the discourse that is created from it, and since this will be determined by such factors as limitation of knowledge and purpose in reading, these meanings can never be complete or precise. They are approximations. What I want to propose, then, is an approach to reading which focuses on the procedures which the language user employs in making sense of written communication.

These procedures must, of course, draw on a knowledge of linguistic rules but are not to be equated with them. The application of linguistic rules in dissociation from a context of use yields sentences. These are simply devices used by analysts for the purpose of exemplification. To me, therefore, Chomsky's definition of competence as the speaker/hearer's knowledge of the sentences of his language makes no sense. What the speaker/hearer knows are the linguistic rules of his language which the grammarian exemplifies by inventing sentences and which the speaker/hearer can also exemplify if ever called upon to play the role of analyst. Asked to say a sentence in English, one might produce:

Poor John ran away.
The farmer killed the duckling.
Seymour cut the salami with a knife.

and so on.

But the language user is not normally called upon to say a sentence, to manifest rules in this way; what he does is to realize rules to fulfil some communicative purpose. So if one were to cite sentences like this, one could legitimately be asked the question: 'What do *they* mean?' because this appeals to a knowledge of the linguistic rules they exemplify. But the question 'What do *you* mean?' is unanswerable, because it is addressed not to the meaning of sentences but to the meaning of utterances.

The farmer killed the duckling.

Which farmer? What duckling? What do you mean? What on earth are you talking about? The sentence has signification because it exemplifies rules of syntax and semantics, but it has no communicative value because it has no context as an utterance which would provide it with one.

All this is no doubt obvious enough. But the distinction between sentence and utterance is so crucial to an understanding of how language is used in reading, or any other communicative activity for that matter, that it is worthwhile dwelling upon it at some length. The sentence and the utterance are alternative expressions of linguistic rules. The sentence manifests the rules for the purpose of demonstration or display, whereas the utterance realizes the rules for the purpose of communication. The sentence is a unit of analysis whose meaning or signification is established by paradigmatic association with other sentences. Thus the signification of, for example:

They travelled there by train.

can be established by reference to other sentences like:

He travelled there by train.
He is travelling there by train.
He is travelling there by bus.

and so on.

The utterance is a unit of use whose meaning, or value, is established by its syntagmatic combination with other utterances in context. Thus the value of:

They travelled there by train

will depend on what information is available in the circumstances of utterance. For example:

The Smiths decided to go to Broadstairs for their holiday. They travelled there by train.
The Browns decided to go to Paris for Christmas. They travelled there by train.

One might make the same sort of observation (as Chomsky himself points out) about an expression like:

John's picture

If we treat this as a sentence constituent, we can only assign it a very general signification associated with the possessive. Only when such an expression is used can we understand what particular value it realizes: whether it refers to the picture *of* John or a picture he has bought (or is buying or intends to buy or has failed to buy) or a picture he has painted (or intends to paint or is always talking about painting) and so on. The possibilities are endless and beyond the scope of analytic specification.

Linguists commonly talk about language use in terms of a sequence of sentences, and of extending the scope of grammar 'beyond the sentence' as if texts were the same kind of unit as sentences but bigger. This, in my view of the matter, is a fundamental misconception. Sentences do not occur in language use although, of course, the linguistic rules which sentences exemplify realized in language use as utterances.

Nor does it make much sense to say that sentences *underlie* utterances. Utterances and sentences are independent and alternative modes of expressing rules and neither underlies the other. One can, of course, set a sentence in correspondence with an utterance and there may be occasions when this occurs, when normal communication is interrupted and the language user adopts an analytic role. But in general the communicative realization of linguistic rules as utterances and the analytic manifestation of linguistic rules as sentences are distinct modes of operation. The sentence, I suggest, is irrevelant to the study of text in its relation to discourse. It is irrelevant, too, therefore, to the process of reading.

Since the sentence is an exemplificatory device it cannot, obviously, express any deviation or modification of linguistic rules. Sentences must in all senses be exemplary instances and the linguist takes care to compile them in such a way as to represent the language system as a stable and self-consistent construct. But the system is, in fact, highly volatile with its elements in potential conflict. It has to be to serve its social function (see Slobin 1975). The linguist, by the judicious composition of sentences, keeps the factions apart and maintains the illusion of peaceful co-existence. But when the rules are realized in use one element may frequently dominate and neutralize others, a certain signification may be reduced to insignificance. Consider an example. The signification of the progressive aspect has recently been described by Leech and Svartvik as follows:

> The progressive aspect refers to activity *in progress*, and there-fore suggests not only that the activity is *temporary* (i.e. of limited duration), but that it *need not be complete*. (Leech and Svartvik 1975: 69)

Then they compose convenient sentences as follows:

> He wrote a novel several years ago (i.e. he finished it).
> He was writing a novel several years ago (but I don't know whether he finished it).

Such examples preserve the signification of the progressive as stated because the elements which accompany it—the lexical items and the adverbial phrase—are congruent with it. But what if we alter the examples as follows:

> He read the newspaper all morning.
> He was reading the newspaper all morning.

Now, because the adverbial itself indicates activity in progress in a way in which 'several years ago' does not, there is a lack of congruence in the first example between the non-progressive signification of the aspectual form of the verb and the progressive signification of the adverbial phrase. What happens is that the expression 'all morning' neutralizes the aspectual distinction be-tween simple and progressive so that we understand that in both cases what is referred to is activity in progress. Furthermore, in both cases the activity need not be complete, as is clear from the following sequences:

> He read the newspaper all morning. And now he's going to read it all afternoon.
> He was reading the newspaper all morning. And now he's going to read it all afternoon.

The point then is that although for the purposes of exemplification we can devise sentences which preserve the signification of linguistic rules by representing them as consistent and complementary, in the reality of language use there are conflicts to be resolved. The meaning value of utterances is a function of this resolution. The realization of rules involves the use of procedures of interpretation which will make sense of linguistic elements and their relationship. The examples I have given suggest that one such procedure is to allow lexis to take precedence over syntax. That is to say, if the lexical items in an utterance suggest one interpretation and the syntax another, then it appears to be the case that the lexical items will modify the meaning of the syntax and not the reverse.

This suggests another basic difference between sentence and utterance, between the linguistic analyst's model of language and that of the user. In the sentence the syntax is primary and the lexical items serve a secondary and facilitating function: so long as they do not create conflicts of the kind I have illustrated they can be selected at random. Hence the banality of such examples as:

The man hit the ball.
John loves Mary.

and the self-conscious curiosity of such examples as:

The aardvarks will devour the pterodactyls today.
The draftsman may have bought an elephant.
(Thomas and Kintgen 1974)

The words do not matter. They are only there to give substance to the structure. But in language use it is the lexical items which are primary, and the syntax which serves a secondary and facilitating function.

It is for this reason that so much work in psycholinguistics has revealed so little about language use. Its central concern has been the investigation, by experiment and speculation, of how syntactic structure is processed in the act of interpretation. Fascinating though much of this is as an intellectual exercise, it tells us very little, I think, about how linguistic rules are realized in communication. Presenting people with a set of carefully contrived sentences in paradigmatic association will oblige them to adopt an analytic attitude. In such circumstances (as Labov and Krashen in their different ways make clear) they will focus on form and set about solving the syntactic problems presented to them. But language users are not experimental subjects finding their way through structural complexity any more than they are rats finding their way through mazes. If a piece of language like the following occurs as an utterance:

The pie baked by Aunt Gertie was eaten with custard.

people do not scratch their heads in puzzlement over passives and embeddings and deletions to disentangle the syntax before deciding that it was Aunt Gertie who baked the pie and not the reverse and that it was probably not her, after all, who was eaten with custard. Some psychologists have discovered, apparently to their surprise, that so called non-reversible passive expressions like:

The flowers are being watered by the girl.

are more easily and more quickly understood than reversible expressions like:

The dog is chasing the cat. (Slobin 1966)

It seems to me quite simply what subjects do in these cases is to abandon their analytic role and understand these expressions as possible utterances. The lexis, therefore, distracts them from the syntax as it tends naturally to do in language use. Again, Fillenbaum (1974) finds that if subjects are presented with pieces of language like:

Don't print that or I won't sue you.

they will understand, and remember it, as:

If you print that, I'll sue you.

Again, what happens here, I suggest, is that subjects in effect convert the sentence into a plausible utterance, one which is in accord with what they know about the world.

The point that I have been trying to make, somewhat laboriously perhaps, is that we must escape from the idea that understanding discourse is a question of interpreting sentences, whether on their own or in combination. Discourse occurs as a realization of linguistic rules in the act of making sense and this inevitably involves an engagement with the language user's cognitive and experiential reality. Sentences are artificial constructs which are detached from such reality by definition and so have nothing to do with discourse. So it is that we can have utterances which do not correspond with sentences, which can only be understood in defiance of linguistic rules as codified by grammarians. Poetry offers the most obvious instances and there is a considerable body of rather unedifying literature which deals with the question of how the deviant sentences in poems are to be accounted for in grammatical terms. The answer is that they cannot be so accounted for because they are not sentences. If you give experimental subjects sentences like the following:

> The child is father of the man. (Wordsworth)
> In my beginning is my end. (T. S. Eliot)

> When will you ever, Peace, wild wooddove, shy wings shut,
> Your round me roaming end, and under be my boughs?
> (Hopkins)

let alone more curious instances like:

> Me up at does
> out of the floor
> quietly Stare
> a poisoned mouse
> (e e cummings[1])

you may well elicit the analytic judgement that they are not well-formed. But as utterances in contexts of use they can be understood. Now one can, of course, claim that deviations of this kind are peculiar to poetry and can therefore be dismissed as peripheral. But precisely the same principles of interpretation apply to non-poetic discourse. Consider the following:

> Was there a holiday tomorrow?

Here we have an ungrammatical sentence, which is to say that this string of words does not manifest the linguistic rules of English. But I can attest its occurrence as an utterance in the following circumstances. My neighbours had been arguing about whether or not there was to be a school holiday on the following day and when I arrived the wife had gone off to find out. When she returned her husband greeted her with this question. It makes sense. Or, rather, everybody made sense of it. It realized linguistic rules in appropriate fashion. Nobody but me noticed any oddity.

Whereas the manifestation of rules, therefore, is restricted to what can be conveniently codified, the realization of rules involves the exploitation of the total resources for meaning inherent in the language. Thus the language user can create meaningful paradox out of semantic anomalies as in expressions like:

> Boys will be boys.
> Business is business.

He can transcend the limits of conventional reality as sanctioned by the common code by devising metaphor, or by manipulating the sound system to meaningful effect, or by the deliberate contrivance of ambiguity as, for example, in:

Say hullo to the good buys.

which one sees at Heathrow Airport, or the following, which appeared recently on posters advertising the *Times* newspaper:

Pioneers in sound recording.
What comes up must go down.

There is a powerful potential in language existing, as it were, between the lines of rewrite rules and dictionary entries which provides for nuance and subtlety, for fresh perception and the exploration of experience. It enables me, as a user of English, to recognize, for example, that there is more to tense than grammarians specify. And this other dimension is realized when I read these lines from *The Ancient Mariner*:

The sun's rim dips, the stars rush out,
At one stride comes the dark.

where the present tense makes a sudden appearance in the middle of a narrative in the past tense. It is realized, too, on more everyday occasions when I read headlines like:

Bomb explodes in Bond Street
Begin agrees to Israeli withdrawal

and know that this means that the bomb *has exploded* and Begin *has agreed* and that there is no question of these being present events or habits. (See again Leech and Svartvik 1975.)

I have talked about the realization of rules as distinct from their manifestation. The question to consider now is how this realization is brought about. It is brought about (as I have already implied), by the employment of certain procedures which provide linguistic elements with appropriate interactive value. The context itself does not determine the meaning of utterances, any more than does the code itself. Jakobson (Jakobson and Halle 1956) talks about the two as 'interactants', but code and context do not just interact on their own. As Firth pointed out:

Logicians (and grammarians, we would add) are apt to think of words and propositions as having 'meaning' somehow in themselves, apart from participants in contexts of situation. Speakers and listeners do not seem to be necessary. (Firth 1957: 226)

A human agent is required to apply the necessary procedures to relate code to context. You cannot account for any kind of behaviour by simply stipulating rules. Rules belong in the domain of knowledge and you have to know how and when to apply them if they are to be effective in the domain of actual behaviour. What sort of procedures, then, does the language user have at his disposal for realizing linguistic rules to achieve appropriate communicative behaviour?

First, there are certain procedures, I think, which are based on assumptions of normality, and which language users will apply unless there are other factors which deter them. These procedures derive from what Halliday calls the 'good reason' principle. For example Bever (1970) talks about the tendency to interpret noun-verb-noun sequences as referring to actor-action-object. Clark and Clark (1977) suggest a whole list of similar processing strategies. What such strategies indicate is that the language user has certain definite ideas about how one usually talks about things so that he is conscious of a set of basic utterance types constituting a reference for the normal realization of rules. This is what Chomsky's 'kernel sentences' are, I think, and accounts for the 'psychological reality' that he claims for them. But they are not, in my terms, sentences: they are ways of organizing propositional content which have a high utterance potential. As such they represent a set of initial expectations. This does not mean, of course, that for the *analyst* these sequences are any more basic or any deeper than others, which is why Chomsky abandons his kernel sentences after 1957. What it does mean is that the subject will tend to process sentences of this kind more readily than others because he will identify them with normal utterance types expressive of a kind of unmarked and standard view of reality.

In language use, however, other procedures are brought into play which provide good reason for modifying these assumptions of normality. For what is said in the course of a conversation or in producing a continuous passage of prose does not simply make independent reference to a single state of affairs. It serves to relate information to what the interlocutors already know. Thus the propositional content of an utterance is organized so that it sustains an ongoing interaction whereby the knowledge of the addresser is adjusted to the knowledge of the addressee to their mutual satisfaction. The procedures whereby this is brought about have been described by Grice (1975) as deriving from what he calls the 'co-operative principle', which finds expression in a set of maxims relating to: quantity (make your contribution as informative as is required and no more), quality (do not say what you believe to be false), relation (be relevant), and manner (avoid ambiguity and obscurity, be brief and orderly).

The application of procedures of this kind enables the language user to realize linguistic rules for propositional development as is demonstrated, for example, in Sacks (1972). Such procedures also enable him to identify conditions to be met in the performance of different illocutionary acts, even when these conditions are given muted expression in the interests of social acceptability—also, of course, an important aspect of co-operation. This has to do with what Labov (1972) calls 'modes of mitigation and politeness' and with what Searle has discussed under the heading of 'indirect speech acts'. (Searle 1975). These procedures are also brought into play of course in the realization of rules of discourse as described in Labov and Fanshel (1977).

Gricean maxims constitute general directions for conducting an interaction and Grice makes particular reference to conversation. The work referred to in the preceding paragraph, too, is centrally concerned with spoken language. I want now to consider how they are used in written discourse. Let us look first at the producing end of the operation. The writer has something he wishes to convey to an absent addressee. This addressee, he assumes, will have certain kinds of knowledge in common with himself: knowledge, for example, of linguistic rules, of the conditions that have to be met for the performance of illocutionary acts, and knowledge too of the universe of reality to which he intends to refer. The writer will also assume that his addressee will be sufficiently curious to learn what he has to say to co-operate in its conveyance. But the writer must put the co-operative principle into operation first: he has to decide what information he can count on the addressee already having and what information he needs to provide, and how he must provide it, in order to get his message across. Taking these decisions involves him in the conduct of an interaction in which he attempts to anticipate the reactions of the addressee. The act of writing is the enactment of an exchange, with the writer taking on the roles of both interlocutors.

It is this playing of a dual role, I think, that makes writing so difficult. It is often suggested that the main problem in learning to cope with written language lies in the change of medium from sounds to spellings. I do not think this is so. Although there may, of course, be some difficulties in establishing correspondence across media, the principal problem has to do with a change in the *manner* in which communication is carried out, from a reciprocal exchange in which meanings can be openly negotiated to a form of interaction which is non-reciprocal and which requires therefore that negotiation be carried out covertly through the process of internal enactment that I have referred to. Literacy introduces a new mode of social behaviour and raises all kinds of complex cultural issues which are perhaps not always fully appreciated by those involved in its promotion. It is a mistake to suppose, as linguists and language teachers have tended to do, that speech and writing are simply alternative media for the manifestation of language (see Widdowson 1978b, Chapter 3).

The writer, then, has certain communicative intentions: he wants to report certain events, describe certain states of affairs, conduct an argument, and so on. To do these things, he has to enact an exchange whereby he anticipates the reactions of the addressee to what he says. It follows from this, I think, that we should be able to distinguish between two principal types of act that the writer performs. The first type, which I will call *focal* acts, have as their purpose the expression of the facts, ideas, views, and so on which the writer wishes to convey and which represent his initial purpose in writing. The second type, which I will call *enabling* acts, serve to facilitate this conveyance. The focal acts relate to the writer's role as addresser: their function is to express his message. The enabling acts relate to his role as addressee: their function is to anticipate reactions from the prospective reader which might interfere with the transmission of the message. They are, if you will, *counteracts*. Let us look at an example. A writer (in this case J. K Galbraith) wishes to make the following point:

> In 1859 India was one of the best governed countries in the world.

This constitutes a focal act. But the addressee, of course, may not agree with what is said and, knowing this, Galbraith goes on to anticipate the possible objection by a series of statements which support his point and facilitate its acceptance:

> Persons and property were safe. Thought and speech were more secure than in recent times. There was effective action to arrest famine and improve communications.[2]

This kind of enabling act anticipates the reaction: 'I don't agree.' There is another kind of enabling act which anticipates the reaction: 'I don't understand.' Whereas the first kind of counteract, let us call it a *justification*, anticipates a reaction to the illocution that is being performed, the second, let us call it a *clarification*, anticipates a reaction to the proposition that is being expressed. Consider another example (this time from John Lyons):

> As commonly applied, the distinction between languages and dialects is based very largely upon cultural or political consideration.

Since the reader may not immediately understand what is meant by this, the writer provides a gloss in the form of an example:

> Many of the so-called 'dialects' of Chinese, for example, are more distinct from one another than say, Danish and Norwegian, or even more strikingly, Dutch and Flemish, which are frequently described as different 'languages'.[3]

This, of course, is a very general and incomplete account of what goes on but it will serve to suggest the kind of interaction the writer must be involved in.

The physical result is a text, a collection of linguistic clues which the reader must interpret in order to reconstitute the interaction. This reconstitution can never be complete because this would entail an exact correspondence between the writer's intention and the reader's interpretation and this in turn would entail a coincidence of individual realities. Communication can of its nature only be approximate even when it is conducted through reciprocal exchange. It will be particularly imprecise when there is no possibility of checking its effectiveness by open negotiation. Consider for a moment some of the things that could go wrong. The writer might over-estimate the reader's knowledge of the reality he is referring to and leave too much to be inferred. In this case an absence of enabling acts will make him obscure. Conversely, he may underestimate the extent to which the reader shares the same reality and in this case he will produce a prolixity of enabling acts which will distract the reader from the focal information. In both cases there will be communicative dysfunction which is traceable to the writer's misjudgement, to his mismanagement of the interaction. He will not have put the co-operative principle into effective operation. For we must note that Grice's maxims cannot simply be automatically applied: some of them, for example, are in potential opposition. Thus in respect to the maxim of manner at a particular point in developing an interaction, the writer may have to decide whether to be brief at the risk of obscurity or ambiguity, or whether to ignore the injunction to be brief in the interests of greater clarity.

The reader, too, has his problems. He may quite simply not have the linguistic competence necessary to recognize the clues to meaning that the writer provides. This difficulty has always been acknowledged by language teachers and sometimes it has been represented as the *only* difficulty. But there are others. The reader may allow his own reality, his own attitudes and ideas, to override his ability to perceive the clues. His purpose in reading may be such as to lead him to focus on information that is not intended to be focal. Or he may have no purpose in reading at all and no interest in what the writer has to say, in which case he will, of course, be reluctant to co-operate. This difficulty is all too familiar in language teaching.

If reading and writing activities involve the realization of linguistic rules to create discourse, in the way I have suggested, then certain consequences follow which are of direct relevance to the teaching of these abilities. To begin with, meaning is not contained in texts: it is a function of the discourse that is created from the text by interactive procedures. The text is the *product* of the writer's efforts, actual and perceptible on the page, but it has to be re-converted into the interactive *process* of discourse before meanings can be realized. The text may be genuine in that it represents the record of the writer's interaction but it has to be authenticated as discourse by the reader. Genuineness is a property of the text as a product. Authenticity is a property of the discourse as a process. To touch on a pedagogic point here, in passing, it would seem to follow that so called 'comprehension' questions should not be directed at an analysis of the text product, as is commonly the case, but at developing the discourse process (see Widdowson 1977).

The meaning that is thus derived from a text can never be total or complete because it is conditional on the extent to which different kinds of knowledge of writer and reader correspond, and the extent to which the reader is prepared to engage in the interaction on the writer's terms. What a reader gets out of a text will depend on his interest and purpose in reading, as well as his ability to relate what is said to his own knowledge of the world. A corollary to this is that the effectiveness of communication in written language corresponds to the degree of congruence between writer intention and reader interpretation: it is a measure, therefore, of the reader's success in reconstituting the writer's original interactive discourse from the textual clues provided. This reconstitution will crucially depend on the writer and reader sharing knowledge of different kinds: knowledge of linguistic rules and how they are realized by general procedures in accordance with the co-operative principle, knowledge of the subject matter referred to, knowledge of particular conventions of communication, like the rhetorics (or registers, if you will) of certain specific universes of discourse. It follows from this that reading cannot be dissociated from norms of social behaviour and cultural values. It is contingently and not essentially a linguistic affair. What also follows from this is a paradox which those who talk of promoting international goodwill through a common language must find difficult to accept: that those with whom we communicate best are the people with whom we already have a common understanding and with whom, therefore, we have least need to communicate. Conversely, we can communicate least with those we need to communicate with most.

Notes

This paper was presented at a seminar on the teaching of reading skills organized by the British Council and the Goethe Institut, Paris, October 1978, and published in the proceedings (von Faber 1980) and in *Recherches et Echanges*, Tome 4 No. 2 Juin 1979.

1 These lines are quoted by Chomsky. He comments as follows:

> This poses not the slightest difficulty or ambiguity of interpretation, and it would surely be quite beside the point to try to assign it a degree of deviation in terms of the number or kind of rules of the grammar that are violated in generating it.
> (Chomsky 1965: 228)

Elsewhere in this book he observes:

> ... it is clear ... that the notion 'grammaticalness' cannot be related to 'interpretability' (ease, uniqueness, or uniformity of interpretation) in any simple way, at least. (Chomsky 1965: 151)

These remarks would seem to support the position I argue in this paper and elsewhere that the linguistic analyst's model of language, which accounts for grammaticalness, is essentially different from that of the language user, which must crucially account for interpretation. It follows (or so it seems to me) that language use cannot be a matter of sentence interpretation at all.

2 Extracts taken from Galbraith 1977.
3 Extracts taken from Lyons 1970, chapter 1.

5   New starts and different kinds of failure

In my experience writing is usually an irksome activity and an ordeal to be avoided whenever possible. It seems to require an expense of effort disproportionate to the actual result. Fortunately for my self-esteem, this experience is a common one. Most of us seem to have difficulty in getting our thoughts down on paper. Certainly T. S. Eliot did, whose poem *East Coker* provides me with my title:

> ..... every attempt
> Is a wholly new start and a different kind of failure.
> Because one has only learnt to get the better of words
> For the thing one no longer has to say, or the way in which
> One is no longer disposed to say it.

Of course, Eliot was referring to the writing of poetry. But one does not have to be a poet biting the truant pen to suffer the agonies of written composition. To be sure, if one is simply dropping a line to relatives or writing a letter in conformity with established routines there is much less of a problem. This affords us a clue to the difficulty, which I will return to a little later. For the moment let us note that getting the better of words in writing is commonly a very hard struggle. And I am thinking now of words which are in one's own language. The struggle is all the greater when they are not.

Why should writing present such difficulties? And what exactly *are* these difficulties? They are clearly not linguistic in any straightforward sense since they are not solved by the acquisition of linguistic competence. What I want to do in this paper is to consider possible answers to these questions and so to define the objectives that the teaching of writing should aim to achieve.

I will begin by stating the obvious. Writing is a communicative activity and so is carried out in accordance with certain general principles which underlie the use of language in communication. We may move towards a specification of what these might be by considering what happens when language is put to communicative use in spoken interaction.

(A) is conversing with (B). The conversation involves the engagement of two kinds of knowledge: knowledge of linguistic rules and knowledge of the world of fact and social convention. To the extent that such knowledge is shared, the interaction will proceed satisfactorily. If there is a lack of shared *linguistic* knowledge there will be an increasing reliance placed on shared *world* knowledge, and the reverse. If (A) does not know (B)'s language, communication is clearly going to be a difficult business. Not impossible though. It is surprising what can be achieved if the interlocutors share a knowledge and view of the world and are motivated by common or congruent interests and intentions.

Thus pidgin languages arise to facilitate and extend contacts and collaboration already established without a common language. They do not spring immediately into being. And as lovers know, there can be communion without overt communication and then no words are needed. So it is that John Donne and his mistress achieve understanding by silence:

> Our soules, (which to advance their state,
> Were gone out,) hung 'twixt her, and mee,
> And whil'st our soules negotiate there,
> Wee like sepulchrall statues lay;
> All day, the same our postures were,
> And wee said nothing, all the day.
> ('The Exstasie')

Unfortunately, we cannot entirely rely on the congruence of world view and the negotiation of souls (although, as we shall see, negotiation of a different kind does have a central role to play). We must grant that a lack of a shared language is normally a serious impediment to communication, while noting, nevertheless, that a shared language is not a necessary condition on interaction. A common language by no means guarantees mutual understanding. It provides the means whereby a context of shared world knowledge and social convention can be created. But such a creation of context is not always easy to accomplish. If (A) and (B) share the same knowledge of linguistic rules, they have the possibility of establishing a common frame of reference, but they will need to work at it and failure is frequent.

The point I am trying to make (and in the attempt illustrating the difficulty I am trying to explain) is that communication is a matter of transferring information of various kinds from the context of (A)'s world knowledge to that of (B) and that linguistic rules *facilitate* the transference. They are a means to an end not an end in themselves. It is not enough to have a knowledge of linguistic rules: one also needs a knowledge of how to use them. Consider a simple example of what Schegloff (1972a) refers to as 'formulating place'. Suppose that in the course of a conversation, (A) asks (B):

Where do *you* live?

What is (B) likely to reply? We cannot say, of course, because we have no information about the frame of reference that has been set up between them. We know what the sentence means, but we do not know what the speaker means. The utterance may occur in the context of a discussion on the relative advantages of urban and rural life, for example, and in this case (B) will interpret it as referring to a type of locality and perhaps reply:

I live in the country.

A different reply, like:

I live in Townsend Road

would relate to a different frame of reference (see van Dijk 1977 Chapter 5). It would be informative but not relevant. On the other hand, if (A) and (B) have established that they live in the same town and (B) is making reference to where *his* house is, then a reply like:

I live in Townsend Road

would be relevant. It might not, however, be sufficiently informative. In that case, (A) and (B) might have to build up a frame of reference which makes it so. For example:

A Where do *you* live?
B Townsend Road.
A Where's that?
B Off Charles's Street.
A Near the cemetery?
B That's it.
A I know.

Alternatively, (B) might himself take the initiative in frame making:

A Where do *you* live?
B Townsend Road.
A Where's that?

B Do you know where the cemetery is?
A Yes.
B Do you know Charles's Street?
A Yes.
B Well Townsend Road is just off that.
A Right.

What (A) and (B) are doing here is using linguistic rules to negotiate an effective transfer of information, to achieve a convergence of knowledge. Notice that the negotiation ends not when the meaning of the expression is precisely specified but when the interlocutors are satisfied that they know enough to serve their purposes. This is a crucial point. In communication we are not concerned with what an expression means but what the producer of the expression means by using it and the receiver will only negotiate that meaning to the extent that he needs to: once he feels satisfied that for the purposes of the interaction there is sufficient convergence of knowledge then he will close the negotiation. This means that communication is always relative to purpose. It is never precise but is always only approximate.

An attempt to achieve precision beyond communicative requirements will in fact tend to disrupt the interaction. In Garfinkel (1972) there is a demonstration of this. Garfinkel instructed students to 'engage an acquaintance or a friend in an ordinary conversation and, without indicating that what the experimenter was asking was in any way unusual, to insist that the person clarify the sense of his commonplace remarks'. The following is one of the results:

> On Friday night my husband and I were watching television. My husband remarked that he was tired. I asked, 'How are you tired? Physically, mentally, or just bored?'
> **Subject** I don't know, I guess physically, mainly.
> **Experimenter** You mean your muscles ache or your bones?
> **S** I guess so. Don't be so technical.
> (After more watching)
> **S** All these old movies have the same kind of old iron bedstead in them.
> **E** What do you mean? Do you mean all old movies, or some of them, or just the ones you have seen?
> **S** What's the matter with you? You know what I mean.
> **E** I wish you would be more specific.
> **S** You know what I mean! Drop dead!
> (Garfinkel 1972: 7)

But this, you may say, is an example of ordinary casual conversation, commonplace talk, where there is of course no premium on precision. What about kinds of communication like that of scientific exposition which requires a more exact conveyance of information? Even in these cases, exactitude is only relative to particular communicative requirements and much must be left unspecified. And here I can cite the philosopher Karl Popper in my support:

> ...the idea of a precise language, or of precision in language, seems to be altogether misconceived... *The quest for precision is analogous to the quest for certainty*, and both should be abandoned.
>
> I do not suggest, of course, that an increase in the precision of, say, a prediction, or even a formulation, may not sometimes be highly desirable. What I do suggest is that *it is always undesirable to make an effort to increase precision for its own sake— especially linguistic precision—since this usually leads to loss of clarity*, and to be a waste of time and effort on preliminaries which often turn out to be useless, because they are bypassed by the real advance of the subject: *one should never try to be more precise than the problem situation demands*. (Popper 1976: 24 emphasis as in the original)

It is, in fact, self-defeating to strive for precision in language use beyond the requirements of the communicative occasion: a point which, as language teachers, we do not always bear in mind.

I am suggesting then that communication by means of language involves the use of linguistic rules to negotiate the transfer of information and so to extend an already existing area of shared knowledge of fact and convention. The success of the transfer is to be measured by reference to the extent that it satisfies the recipient's requirements for the information. Meaning, in this view, is a function of the interaction between participants which is mediated through the language. I will refer to this process as *discourse*. The language used to mediate the process can be recorded or transcribed and studied in detachment. This I will refer to as *text*: the overt trace of an interaction, which can be used as a set of clues for reconstituting the discourse. It is our only source of evidence about the linguistic rules used in the mediation of meaning.

But the text will not reveal how these rules are actually realized in the discourse process. It will indicate *what* rules were used but not how they were used, it will reveal what linguistic knowledge the participants have but not how this knowledge is actualized as communicative behaviour. Thus if we record an interaction we can subsequently note how the resultant text manifests certain syntactic features, how it illustrates the use of cohesive devices as discussed in Halliday and Hasan (1976) and the resources available in the language for organizing information so as to ensure propositional development across linguistic units. But text will not itself reveal the plans (Miller, Galanter, and Pribram 1960) which have to be implemented to achieve the complex communicative task, and which of these plans have been automated as routines in long term memory. Clearly the native speaker is not making conscious choices when he operates the basic rules of syntax: if he did his working short term memory would be too overburdened to make conceptual connections with his existing knowledge and so would be unable to service the discourse process (see Levelt 1975). It has to be borne in mind that a focusing on linguistic forms as such will tend to inhibit the natural use of these forms for communicative purposes. The language learner has somehow to learn them so that they make no claims on his attention when he is using them. This, I think, has always been a central problem of language teaching pedagogy. We might agree that what the learner needs to acquire is fluency in a foreign language rather than accuracy in its manipulation (see Brumfit 1979a). But if fluency is to be an ability within competence and not simply a facility of performance, it has to be sustained by linguistic knowledge which can be assessed by measures of accuracy and which can be held in reserve as a back-up resource for occasions when repair is needed in communicative activity. Fluency and accuracy are complementary and interdependent phenomena: the problem is to know how the dependency works in natural language use and how it can best be developed in the process of language learning.

So far I have been making reference to spoken communication. I want now to turn to writing. And I want to suggest that written discourse too represents an interactive process of negotiation. But whereas in spoken discourse this process is typically overt and reciprocal, in written discourse it is covert and non-reciprocal. Thus in a spoken exchange the participants alternate in open negotiation of meanings, as we have seen, each taking turns to contribute to the interaction. The writer, however, is solitary; the person to whom he wishes to transfer information is absent and often, to some degree, unknown. This means that the writer has to conduct his interaction by enacting the roles of both participants. Since there is no possibility of immediate reaction he has to anticipate what it is *likely* to be and provide for any possible misunderstanding and unclarity arising from a lack of shared knowledge. The writer, then, has a basic conveyancing problem: he has certain information to impart for some illocutionary or perlocutionary purpose—to inform, to impress, to direct action, and so on, but he has to prepare the ground and set up conditions favourable to the reception of such information. He does this by continually shifting his function from initiator to recipient, from 'speaker', as it were, to 'hearer', enacting the interaction by playing the role of each participant. Consider an example: here is a text from Gombrich's *Art and Illusion.*

> The Greek revolution deserves its fame. It is unique in the annals of mankind. What makes it unique is precisely the directed efforts, the continued and systematic modifications of the schematic of conceptual art, till making was replaced by the matching of reality through the new skill of mimesis.[1]

This can be derived from the following discourse:

> *The Greek revolution deserves its fame.*
> Why?
> *It is unique in the annals of mankind.*
> In what way unique?
> *What makes it unique is precisely the directed efforts, the continued and systematic modifications of the schematic of conceptual art, till making was replaced by the matching of reality through the new skill of mimesis.*

Or again: this time a text from Gregory's *Eye and Brain*:

> Almost every living thing is sensitive to light. Plants accept the energy of light, some moving to follow the sun almost as though flowers were eyes to see it. Animals make use of light, shadows, and images to avoid danger and to seek their prey.[2]

This can be derived from the following discourse:

> *Almost every living thing is sensitive to light.*
> Give me an example.
> *Plants accept the energy of light, some moving to follow the sun almost as though flowers were eyes to see it.*
> You said almost every living thing. What about other examples?
> *Animals make use of light, shadows, and images to avoid danger and to seek their prey.*

And so the discourse is enacted by the writer shifting roles and so anticipating reactions like 'What do you mean?' 'So what?' 'Can you be more explicit?' 'Can you give an example?' and so on.

I have said that this conducting of covert interaction fulfils the essential conveyancing function of the discourse process. But it can also change the character of the information the writer wishes to convey. For although he may start out with some fairly clear idea of what he wishes to say, the very interactive process he enacts continually provides him with a different point of view which may yield insights and cognitive connections which he would not otherwise have perceived. The interaction not only *facilitates* the conveyance of information but also *generates* the thinking process. So it is that in writing one so frequently arrives at a destination not originally envisaged, by a route not planned for in the original itinerary. It is worth noting that when we instruct students to draw up a plan of an essay before writing and then to conform to it closely as they write we may be inhibiting the interactive process that generates written discourse.

The result of this discourse, this covert non-reciprocal interaction, is a text: words on a page. But written text differs from spoken text in a number of ways. For one thing, spoken text is of its nature transient and can only be recorded by outside intervention. When it is made permanent by tape or transcription some idealization interferes so that it is only a partial record of the discourse. In the case of written text, it represents a record not made by an outside third person observer but by the active first person participant. In this respect it is a true record. As far as it goes. For, of course, it usually represents only part of the discourse: it does not as a rule reveal the second person reactions which the writer anticipates by enacting the other participant's role, as it were, by proxy. There are, of course, exceptions. In some kinds of discourse, significantly those whose purpose is simple exposition, we find some textual record of the second person side of the interaction. The following, for example, comes from a popular account of the laws of physics:

> The law of conservation of energy says simply that in any isolated system the total amount of energy remains unchanged.
> *Is this true in the examples we have so far?* Take the case of the two balls recoiling elastically from a collision... We saw that the balls' total kinetic energy was the same after the collision as before. *But what about the situation at the instant of collision?* At that instant both balls are stopped dead. In other words they have no kinetic energy. *Where has that gone?*[3]

One way, indeed, of characterizing the difference between types of writing would be by reference to the degree to which the discourse is textualized. The textual record is never, however, complete: the vicarious second person contribution is always left to some extent presupposed.

Written text, then, does not generally record the interaction itself but only the result of it. When the reader comes along, therefore, he has to create an interaction from the partial record provided: he has to convert the text into a discourse. The extent to which the reader's discourse corresponds to that of the writer will depend on a number of factors, some of which I will mention presently. For the moment let us note that written text is of its nature an accurate record of the writer's first person activity in the discourse he enacts although this does not therefore determine the reader's second person activity in discourse he derives from such text.

There is another difference between spoken and written text that it is important to mention. Spoken text is a direct and immediate linguistic reflection of the actual interactive process and is simply contingent on the discourse. Once a particular discourse is enacted in spoken exchange, its traces in text disappear unless recorded for some particular reason—for later analysis for example. So in spoken exchange the text as such does not matter to the participants: it is simply the consequence of the discourse. We do not usually concern ourselves unduly with fashioning spoken text because we recognize its temporary and non-recurrent character and we concentrate on the discourse process rather than the textual product. Hence spoken text tends to be untidy, to exhibit syntactic irregularities, incomplete and overlapping expressions, false starts, and so on. With written text, however, the case is different. This is of its nature a record made by an actual participant to be used for the recreation of discourse. The text is not contingent but essential and must have existence beyond the discourse which it records. It is therefore an artefact, deliberately fashioned for the use of others. As such it has to meet certain standards of social acceptability. This means that it has to be tidy, correct, well formed. It must keep up appearances. The writer not only has to design his text so that it effectively records his participation in discourse and provides for the interaction of the reader, but also that it conforms to correct linguistic etiquette. Accuracy, in this way, becomes a necessary condition for fluency.

Of course, as with any other kind of social behaviour, constraints of correctness will vary in their force depending on the public one is exposing oneself to. The writer will be aware of them to a greater or lesser extent, according to who he judges his prospective readers will be. To return to a point I made at the beginning, one is not likely to agonize over correct textual composition when dropping a line to relatives. Writing a letter to *The Times* is a very different matter and might well involve reference to a manual of English usage, the Oxford English Dictionary, and Roget's Thesaurus. The more public and permanent character of print commands respect for what is socially acceptable.

It follows, I think, from the textual and discoursal character of writing that I have been describing that the writer is confronted with two kinds of task, and (to refer to my title) runs the risk of two different kinds of failure. Firstly, he has to conduct a covert interaction with a presumed interlocutor and record his first person participation in such a way that the reader will be able to derive a coherent discourse from it. He has to produce a text which has appropriate discourse potential. This means that he must follow the co-operative principle, as described in Grice (1975), even though there is no actual person to co-operate with. Thus, if he *over*-textualizes, he will fail by being verbose: if he *under*-textualizes, he will fail by being obscure. At the same time, he has to produce a text which conforms to standards of social acceptability, which is correct and cohesive as a linguistic artefact. So it is that the writer's rendering of discourse as text is so much more difficult than the reader's interpretation of the text as discourse. For the reader can afford to be cavalier in his treatment of text: he will derive from it whatever information will serve his purpose in reading and so he will frequently ignore the directions for following the discourse which the writer originally enacted on his behalf. Some of these directions will be irrelevant, since they are based on assumptions about the knowledge and purpose of the reader which turn out not to be applicable in particular cases. Typically the reader will focus on lexical items inferring and predicting meanings by reference to what he already knows and what he needs to know. And he can do this, of course, at considerable speed. Effective reading as a normal social activity is not a matter of completeness or correctness but of convenience and adequacy. But the writer must plod on, making allowances for all kinds of possible reactions, designing well formed textual patterns which the reader may well ignore. The reader can afford to focus on lexis, only turning his conscious attention to syntax when this strategy fails to yield the information he needs. For the writer, on the other hand, engaged as he is in correct text composition, syntax must always be there to reckon with.

Let me now try to relate this discussion to pedagogic matters. Learning to write involves learning how to cope with the two tasks I have described. In the first place the student has to learn how to conduct a non-reciprocal interaction by adopting a dual participant role, anticipating the reactions of a presumed interlocutor. He must be aware of the function of language as a device for negotiating the transfer of information by reference to shared knowledge. This means that the student should always have some idea of who he is meant to be interacting with, of what shared knowledge he can assume, including a knowledge of conventions of rhetorical organization which characterize different types of discourse. He should have some idea, too, of the purpose of the interaction. This involves relating the act of writing to some preceding situation. For in normal circumstances we do not just sit down to write when the spirit takes us. We are impelled to do so by some previous event or state of affairs: a political outrage that calls for a letter to the editor, a lack of funds that requires a request to rich Aunt Maud. Writing is a provoked activity, it is located in ongoing social life. The act of writing is not a wholly new start (to refer again to my title): it is a continuation. So the student should know who he is meant to be addressing and why. These are, after all, normal conditions for writing, and without them there can be no basis for interaction. You cannot negotiate anything unless you know who you are negotiating with and for what purpose and unless you know the conventions of the particular kind of negotiation you are engaged in. If these necessary conditions are not provided, then the business of putting words on a page becomes not a social activity but a language exercise: a manifestation of linguistic rules for display and not a realization of linguistic rules for communication. If the student does not recognize writing as a fundamentally interactive enterprise, then he will be forced to produce text which has no derivation from discourse: a piece of language existing in isolation for its own sake. Production of text for its own sake is not writing as a communicative activity but simply an exercise in linguistic composition.

This interactive aspect of writing is likely, I think, to represent a different sort of difficulty for first language learners than for second or foreign language learners. Learning to write one's own language involves a shift in mode of discourse, from one which is reciprocal interaction through spoken exchange to one which is non-reciprocal and covert. It has often been suggested that the principal difficulty in learning to read and write has to do with the recognition of sound–spelling correspondences: hence, for example, Pitman's initial teaching alphabet, ita. My own feeling is that this transfer of textual medium is much less of a problem than the transfer of discourse mode that I have referred to. To put it another way, I think the main difficulty has to do not with how language is manifested but with how it is realized in communication. With foreign learners, however, it may be that often the central problem *is* textual rather than discoursal. If the foreign learners have already learnt how to write in their own language, then they will have acquired the essential interactive ability underlying discourse enactment and the ability to record it in text. Their problem is how to textualize discourse in a different language. The teacher's task here is to get the learners to exploit their knowledge of the discourse process, acquired through their mother tongue, by realizing it through the linguistic rules of English. It is important to note that foreign learners of English come to the classroom with a great deal of experience of how language in general is used in communication. If we deny them access to that experience by presenting them with a model of language which is not congruent with it, then we impose learning problems upon them of our own devising. We must accept the possibility that many learning difficulties derive from the very pedagogy that is designed to solve them.

The first task in the learning of writing, then, relates to the production of text as a reflection of the discourse process. The second relates to the production of text as an acceptable well-formed artefact. Here again, I think, we have a difference between mother tongue and other tongue situations. The social pressure to conform by producing correct text in one's own language is familiar to anyone who has been subjected to formal schooling. We are made to feel the stigma of incorrect spelling and grammar from our earliest years. In the first language situation, correctness of text has the character of correct social comportment. If you get it wrong, you are likely to suffer some loss of status and what you have to say may not be taken seriously. There can be severe consequences for not conforming. But in the foreign language situation these social constraints may have little or no force since they do not belong to the learner's own society. The language is not his own and is not enmeshed in social values. It therefore becomes extremely difficult to eradicate those errors in a written text which do not reduce its effectiveness as a discourse record. If the foreign learner has no sense of the social propriety of correctness in the foreign language, as is typically the case, then he will obviously find it difficult to achieve. The teacher may cajole, the examination threaten, but the essential social pressure is absent. The second language situation is perhaps a different matter since here the language to be learnt does, by definition, have a role to play in social life so there is the possibility of the learner feeling obliged to adjust his linguistic behaviour to the accepted norms.

Perhaps this is an appropriate moment to make an observation about creative writing as a learning activity in relation to the points I have been making. Exercises in creative writing can no doubt be justified in a number of ways but it should be noted that they can lead to an avoidance of the central problem of interactivity as I have described it because they encourage communion with self rather than communication with others, and represent writing as a personal rather than a social activity. Furthermore, they cannot of their nature come to terms with the issues of acceptability since originality is, by definition, not constrained by conformity. There is no formal way of distinguishing between the deviation of unintended error and deliberate violation of rules for literary effect.

The two kinds of task I have tried to describe can be related to two aspects of language as social behaviour. On the one hand, language use is communicative: it involves the conveying of information by interactive negotiation. On the other hand, it is indicative: it involves the presentation of self as a social person, and so reveals the extent to which one's behaviour is socially acceptable. In producing written text the communicative aspect presents a difficulty because of the non-reciprocal character of the interaction; and the indicative aspect presents a difficulty because one has to be particularly careful of one's linguistic comportment.

But now another problem arises. I spoke earlier of how a knowledge of linguistic rules is automated so as to leave the mind free for higher order communicative operations. Effective communication commonly requires the unconscious manipulation of linguistic rules. The mind can then engage with conceptual organization and negotiation because the lower level syntactic plans have been automated, pushed down into long term memory, below the threshold of immediate awareness. What this automation appears in part to involve is a kind of idiomization process, whereby linguistic patterns are stored in the memory as whole units with potential communicative function so that they do not need to be composed on each occasion of use. The mind acquires a set of adaptable clichés. But if writing requires particular attention to correctness, as I have suggested, then there is the problem that unless syntactic rules have been thoroughly automated, then mental resources will be so preoccupied with achieving linguistic correctness that there will be little spare capacity for communication. In this case, very common in the second and foreign language situation, there will be a focus on the text for its own sake, and its discourse function will be neglected.

I have tried to indicate certain difficulties about writing and the different kinds of failure that can arise in consequence. How we might cope with them in teaching English as a foreign or second language is another question. We need, I think, to devise a methodology which focuses on the interactive character of writing and develops in the learner an ability to produce text which derives from discourse and provides for discourse recreation on the part of the reader. (See Widdowson 1979: Paper 13.) At the same time, text producing activities of this kind should provide incidental linguistic practice so as to ensure the automation of syntax. Only when a measure of automation has been achieved can one turn to the tricky question of how one can set up conditions of social pressure which will persuade the learner of the importance of appearances and of the need to behave linguistically in accordance with accepted etiquette.

Dr. Johnson tells us that:

A man may write at any time, if he will set himself doggedly to it.

Perhaps; but it will help a man (and a woman, too, we should add) to know what kind of task he must set himself to, so that his doggedness can be directed in some way. In this paper I have tried to define this task in the hope that such a definition might help in the development of an effective methodology for the teaching of writing.

Notes

Paper presented at the Conference of the Canadian Council for Teachers of English (CCTE), Ottawa, May 1979. Published in Freedman, Pringle, and Yalden, 1983.

1 Extract from Gombrich (1960).
2 Extract from Gregory (1966).
3 Extract from Rottman (1962).

6 Conceptual and communicative functions in written discourse

All movements which attempt to set up a new scheme of values, whether these be political or pedagogic or whatever, are subject to distortion and excess. Practical action requires the consolidation of ideas into simple versions which can be widely understood and applied. This is a necessary process if the movement is to have any kind of stability and substantial effect in the practical domain. We cannot all the time be tinkering with theory 'besely seking with a continuell chaunge', as Sir Thomas Wyatt puts it. The problem of application is: how can we consolidate without misrepresentation? How can we prevent our simple versions from being misleadingly simplistic?

The movement I am concerned with here is that which proclaims the primacy of communication in language. Its manifesto (to pursue the metaphor), which can be collated from a range of writings by different hands, contains expressions like 'notions', 'functions', 'speech acts', and assertions like 'There are rules of use without which the rules of grammar would be useless' (Hymes), 'The object of linguistics must ultimately be the instrument of communication used by the speech community' (Labov), 'Languages are learnt for the purposes of communication' (Wilkins), etc. I am a member of this movement myself, and have indeed contributed to its general manifesto. But I am beginning to get a little worried about how it is being interpreted and implemented. There are signs, I think, of distortion and excess in the understanding of ideas and their application to practical pedagogy. What I aim to do in this paper is to reconsider certain issues relating to a communicative approach to language teaching, with particular reference to written discourse, and so to rewrite part of the general manifesto in my own terms. I intend this to be not another example of continual change but a consolidation.

The first problem to tackle is a terminological one. The term 'communication' is commonly interpreted in a narrow sense to refer to what language users do with their language when engaged in social activity. That is to say, there is a tendency to equate it with 'categories of communicative function', illocutionary acts: promises, requests, orders, descriptions, definitions, and so on. But as Chomsky points out, the ability to communicate in this sense presupposes the ability to use language in the formulation of thoughts:

> ... communication is one of the functions of language. In communicating we express our thoughts in the hope that the listener understands what we are saying. We may be hoping to persuade him, to inform him that we believe such-and-such, and so on. The function of language for the expression of thought is not 'opposed' to its communicative function; rather it is presupposed by the use of language for the special purposes of communication. (Parret 1974: 52)

The dependence of communication, in a wider sense, on this conceptual function of language has not always been fully recognized. Thus although Wilkins talks about semantico-grammatical categories, which are conceptual, as well as categories of communicative function, it is the latter which have attracted most attention and their relationship with the conceptual categories has been largely left unexplored and unexplained. Again, in Searle's work, it is the illocutionary element in the speech act that has been seized upon, even to the extent in some quarters of assuming an equation between speech acts and illocutionary acts. The proposition, the conceptual element, in the speech act, has not been very much considered. This neglect is to some extent sanctioned by Searle himself since he represents the proposition as essentially only a condition on the effective performance of the illocution: it serves, as it were, a facilitating function. But one could shift the emphasis, as Chomsky appears to do, and say that it is rather the illocution which facilitates the expressing of the proposition. There seems to be no obvious way of deciding, in principle, whether it is preferable to think of the illocution as primary, with the proposition serving as the means for performing it, or of the proposition as primary, with the illocution serving as the means for conveying it.

I want to argue that neither proposition nor illocution is primary and that we shall continue to run the risk of distortion and excess if either is given emphasis at the expense of the other. Language is naturally used both for the framing of thoughts and for their conveyance for some purpose in social interaction. The central issue is how these two basic functions operate in communicative use, or to put it another way, how the language user reconciles the operation of these functions in discourse. My agenda is as follows. First a discussion of these functions, then a consideration of how they are realized in written discourse, followed by a suggestion of how they relate to the procedures of reduction and expansion in reading and writing. My general purpose is to reinstate conceptual activity in the context of communication as a whole.

There have, of course, been a number of proposals for defining the functions of language—Buhler, Malinowski, Jakobson, Hymes, Halliday have all had a turn at it. I, in my turn, want to suggest that there are (or at least, it is helpful to postulate that there are) two principal functions: the conceptual and the communicative.

The first of these functions provides the individual with a means of establishing a relationship with his environment, of conceptualizing and so, in some degree, controlling reality. This is language used for thinking, formulating concepts, fashioning propositions. It is essentially, to use Halliday's term, 'ideational', and it provides for the private security of the individual by enabling him to define his experience. Halliday puts it this way:

> Language serves for the expression of 'content': that is, of the speaker's experience of the real world, including the inner world of his own consciousness. ... In serving this function, language also gives structure to experience, and helps to determine our way of looking at things, so that it requires some intellectual effort to see them in any other way than that which our language suggests to us. (Halliday 1970: 143)

The second function serves a social purpose. The individual is necessarily involved with his fellow men so that he needs language not only to formulate his ideas but to convey them to others in the process of performing social activity of different kinds. So language has also to have a communicative function so that the individual can *do* as well as think, can engage in social interaction as well as in private cognitive activity. This function of language is essentially (to use Halliday's term again) 'interpersonal':

> Language serves to establish and maintain social relations: for the expression of social roles, which include the communication roles created by language itself—for example, the roles of questioner or respondent, which we take on by asking or answering a question; and also for getting things done, by means of the interaction between one person and another. ... (Halliday 1970: 143)

I have mentioned Halliday's ideational and interpersonal functions. He postulates a third function: the textual. Where does this come in? According to Halliday it provides the means whereby language makes links with itself so that individual sentences are fused into texts. This oddly anthropomorphic notion seems to be at variance with the descriptions of the other functions, which are based on human agency. Indeed, Halliday sets up his functional grammar in direct opposition to the idea that language structure develops in detachment from its use in servicing human needs. The textual function is surely more consistently considered as the means whereby the language user organizes propositional content so that it is effectively conveyed. The textual function, in other words, serves a communicative purpose: its business is to provide alternative versions of propositions so that they are appropriate to the state of shared knowledge and the dynamism of sharing knowledge at a particular point in an interaction.

Here, then, is the simple scheme I want to draw up. Language serves the individual as a means of conceptualizing reality, of establishing some control over his environment. In this role it formalizes knowledge and facilitates thinking. This is the conceptual function. Language also provides the means for conveying basic conceptual propositions, for setting them in correspondence with those in the minds of other people, and for using concepts to get things done in the business of social interaction. The adjustment of propositions so that they fit into the changing situation of shared knowledge is the 'textual' aspect of the matter. The use of such propositions to conduct social business, to perform illocutions of different kinds, is the 'interpersonal' aspect of the matter. Both are features of the communicative function of language.

Linguistic theory has, of course, tended to focus on one or other of these two basic functions, with language teaching often following suit. Thus Firth objects to de Saussure because he neglects the communicative in favour of the conceptual (Firth 1957) and Lyons objects to Firth because he neglects the conceptual in favour of the communicative (Lyons 1966). The basic difference between Wittgenstein of the *Tractatus* and Wittgenstein of *Philosophical Investigations* can be referred to a shift of focus from the conceptual to the communicative. It is interesting, I think, to review transformational-generative grammar with reference to this distinction. In Chomsky (1957) for example, we can regard the kernel sentence as the formulation of a basic proposition, a conceptual unit (which is why it has the 'psychological reality' that Chomsky claimed for it). Transformational rules can be seen as devices for preparing this proposition for communicative use as an element in text (they are, in this sense, rules of performance, as Labov has pointed out; see Labov 1972: 226). The illocutionary, as opposed to the propositional, aspect of the communicative function came late into the field. It is this aspect which Ross (1970) and Sadock (1974) attempt to account for in their proposals for the performative analysis of sentences. So transformational generative grammar, like the systemic grammar of Halliday, can be seen to have a functional basis, even though it may not be explicitly acknowledged.

The conceptual/communicative distinction I have been making is also quite useful, it seems to me, in a consideration of early work in psycholinguistics which attempted to test the derivational theory of complexity. Experimenters were anxious to get subjects to treat sets of sentences as conceptual units, but the natural inclination of the subjects, of course, was to treat them as communicative units. And researchers came to realize that communicative factors such as difference of attention focus (Olson and Filby 1972) and contexts of plausible denial (Wason 1965) had an effect on interpretation time (see Greene 1972 and McRae 1978 for a useful survey of this research). Greene refers to these factors as 'semantic'. They are not, they are pragmatic: they have to do not with the conceptual formulation of base propositions but with conditions on their conveyance for some communicative purpose. They have to do, therefore, not with semantic meaning, the conceptual signification of sentences, but with pragmatic meaning, the communicative value of utterances. Transformational rules, in the view I am proposing, are communicative and not conceptual in function and they are naturally only used when some base proposition needs to be fashioned to fit a particular context. If there is no context and subjects are asked to interpret linguistic expressions in parallel by internal reference, then they are forced to treat them conceptually. The extent to which they are able to actually do this will be a measure of their ability to solve a certain kind of cognitive problem which may have little or no relationship to the processing of natural language.

I said that both transformational-generative grammar and systemic grammar have a functional base in that their different components can be associated with the two primary functions I have talked about. But this association is historical and indicates how the internal structure of language reflects the functions it has evolved to serve. Once evolved, this structure provides a resource for both conceptual and communicative functions, so that in use one cannot identify parts of a linguistic unit as having an exclusive connection with one function or another. Thus, Halliday shows how the following expression 'John was throwing the ball' can be analysed as a convergence of choices from systemic options which derive from different functions. Ideationally we have actor/process/affected (John/was throwing/the ball), interpersonally we have modal/residual (John was/throwing the ball) and textually we have theme/rheme (John/was throwing the ball) and given/new (John was throwing/the ball) (Halliday 1968: 211). But this does not mean that the ideational structure is only relevant to the formulation of a conceptual proposition. Once a language has developed as an instrument for social interaction, its total resources are available for private purposes as well.

But of course languages continue to evolve and their evolution is the consequence, I think, of recurrent reconciliations of these private and social functions. Halliday, in common with most linguists, represents grammatical rules as inhabiting stable systems in peaceful harmony. But the very fact that they have to serve different purposes creates conditions of internal strife. In describing the language system one can represent different options as converging neatly into a unified product, but in using the system there are conflicts to be resolved in the process. And these resolutions, these reconciliations of private and social requirements (a feature of human life in general of course and not confined only to the use of language) are the source of language change and of language development in acquisition. Slobin has relevant remarks to make on this matter. He refers to 'four basic ground rules which a communicative system must adhere to'. These are: (a) be clear, (b) be humanly processible in ongoing time, (c) be quick and easy, and (d) be expressive. He goes on to say:

> Language is always under competing pressures to conform to all four of these charges. Because the pressures are inherently competitory, languages are constantly changing ... (Slobin 1975: 4)

> A gain in compactness or expressiveness of communication is often purchased at the expense of ease of processing or semantic transparency of message. (Slobin 1975: 5)

Now I want to suggest that the first two of Slobin's charges are essentially conceptual and the second two essentially communicative. That is to say, the requirements of clarity and processibility are basic to the formulation of propositions and relate to cognitive processing and storage, whereas the other two requirements relate to the conveying of propositions on communicative occasions. These latter charges can, I think, be associated with the Gricean maxims of the co-operative principle (Grice 1975).

As I see it, then, language works in two ways. On the one hand it provides for conceptual activity whereby clear and processible propositions are formulated in the mind. On the other hand it provides the means whereby such propositions can be conveyed in the most effective manner for particular communicative purposes. These two functions, potentially in conflict, have to be reconciled by negotiation on every occasion of social use. This negotiation is realized in discourse. We come to the second item on the agenda.

To engage in discourse is to try to find ways of expressing propositions so that they will be understood and, where relevant, acted upon. As Chomsky says, there are all kinds of reasons why one would wish to express propositions: to direct future action, to transfer information, to display knowledge, and so on. So the proposition can take on a range of illocutionary values. There is now a good deal of literature about the conditions that have to be met for illocutionary acts to be achieved and on the interpretative procedures which are engaged in the actual achievement. I am not now concerned with that 'interpersonal' aspect of the communicative function, but with the other, the 'textual' aspect, again leaving considerations of their interrelationship aside for the present. What I want to consider is how, in written discourse, the writer gets his propositional meaning across, and how the reader takes it in.

The problem for the writer is that he has to convey his propositions without the benefit of overt interaction which enables conversationalists to negotiate meanings by direct confrontation. This means that he has to anticipate possible reactions by in effect enacting the roles of both first and second person participants. He is engaged in a covert interaction, shifting roles in Socratic fashion to pose and respond to questions like 'What do you mean by that?' 'So what?' 'Can you give an example?' and so on. All the time he must provide for the possible lack of convergence of shared knowledge: of the world, of social conventions, of the language itself. So the propositional content he wants to transmit is elaborated to service what the writer judges to be an effective communicative interaction. Of course, this interactive endeavour does not only serve to facilitate the conveyance of propositions planned, as it were, in advance. The very interactive process involves a continual shift of perspective which will frequently yield new propositions, new conceptual connections not originally thought of. The writer's covert and non-reciprocal interaction not only provides for the conveyance of ideas but also helps to generate them.

The writer of course typically only records the first person participant's contribution to this interaction. This partial record of the discourse is written text. Turning now to the reader, his task is to derive a discourse from the text. The extent to which this derivation will reconstitute the writer's discourse will depend on how far it corresponds in actuality to the interlocutor the writer has presupposed. He may not need, or may not want, to follow the course of interaction so painstakingly plotted by the writer on his behalf. He can take short cuts according to the state of his knowledge, or according to his purpose in reading.

The writer's recording of discourse as text and the reader's derivation of discourse from text can, I think, be related to the process of *expansion*, as discussed in Labov and Fanshel, on the one hand, and to the process of *reduction*, as discussed by van Dijk on the other. And these processes can, in their turn, be referred to the two principal language functions I have been talking about: the conceptual and the communicative.

For Labov and Fanshel, expansion is a device for analysing spoken discourse. It consists of the following procedures:

1 We expand the meaning conveyed by the cues into the nearest equivalent in text terms, according to our best understanding of it.
2 We expand and make explicit the referent of pronouns to other utterances and events in other time frames.
3 We introduce factual material that is presented before and after this utterance, sometimes from widely separated parts of the interview.
4 We make explicit some of the shared knowledge between participants.

(Labov and Fanshel 1977: 49)

Such procedures are especially necessary for the analyst, concerned as he is with a third person rendering, when the discourse under consideration is very close to its conceptual source. This would be so when the shared knowledge and assumptions of the participants were such as to make conveyancing a relatively straightforward business, when there would be little need to make calculations and provisions for the establishment of common ground. In general, it will follow that the closer the correspondence of conceptual worlds, the smaller will be the communicative effort called for, and the greater the task of the analyst in textualizing the discourse to make it interpretable.

Procedures for expansion are not, however, the prerogative of the analyst. They must be available to participants too as a communicative resource in conversation. Again, there will be occasions when they have, as such, a particularly important role to play. This will be the case when one participant in an interaction does not, for one reason or another, have the inclination or capacity for communicative elaboration. In these circumstances, the other participant becomes the custodian of the co-operative principle and has to provide expansion to sustain the interaction. One example of such uneven distribution of communicative effort might be the discourse of psychotherapist and patient; another that of parent and child.

The familiar question now arises as to the relationship between the analyst's procedures for expansion and those of the participant. With respect to the first example, Labov and Fanshel point to the danger of disparity:

> ... the expansion itself is often a help to our understanding and plays a crucial role in the analysis of *interaction*. But the expansion can also be somewhat deceptive, since there is an interactive component of over-explicitness, which throws many of the actions into a wrong light ... Expansions magnify the strains and tensions in the social fabric and will produce distorted interpretation unless we remember that the expansion loses the important dimensions of backgrounding, which subordinates one form of social interaction to another ... Psychotherapists at the agency being studied expressed their appreciation for the insights gained, but remarked that this kind of analysis makes the therapeutic session seem like a type of 'warfare', and makes the relationships with patients seem much more abrasive than they actually are. (Labov and Fanshel 1977: 51)

On the other hand, with respect to the second example, parent and child discourse, Brown seems to imply an equivalence between participant and analyst expansion procedures:

> It is not necessary to rely on parents to provide glosses; the researcher can do it himself. Indeed, researchers cannot help doing it. The adult mind receiving a telegraphic utterance in a

given context quite automatically expands it into an appropriate sentence. (Brown 1976: 133)

It seems clear that expansion as a participant 'member' strategy will take on different functions in different kinds of spoken discourse and will accordingly vary in its approximation to the analyst's use of it as a methodological device.

I want to suggest that in written discourse the writer relies very heavily on expansion procedures to provide his conceptual meanings with the necessary communicative conveyance, since he is operating under conditions at the zero end of the co-operation scale. These conditions of non-reciprocal interaction lead to a convergence of participant and analyst perspectives. The writer is a participant in that he is enacting a discourse with an assumed and absent interlocutor but he is at the same time detached from immediate involvement and so he can, in third person analyst fashion, put himself at a remove from the interaction.

Expansion requires close attention to surface structure so that it is fashioned in such a way as to ensure the effective conveyance of information. Reduction, on the other hand, is a device for directing attention to the salient features of information, for stripping the discourse of its communicative integuments to get to the conceptual gist. The demonstration of such a procedure applied to written discourse appears in van Dijk (1977), where it is represented as the recovery of semantic 'macro-structures' by the techniques of deletion, combination, and generalization. The assumption seems to be that the analyst's reduction matches that of the participant. If the reader is regarded as taking a non-reciprocal role in interaction corresponding to that of the writer, such an assumption might seem reasonable. There is an important reservation to be made, however, which I will come to presently. Meanwhile, it is worth noting that reduction, like expansion, is a common resource in spoken interaction. Indeed both activities are described by Garfinkel and Sacks under the general heading of 'formulations':

A member may treat some part of the conversation as an occasion to describe that conversation, to explain it, or characterize it, or explicate, or translate, or summarize, or furnish the gist of it, or take note of its accordance with the rules, or remark on its departure from rules. That is to say, a member may use some part of the conversation as an occasion to *formulate* the conversation ... We shall speak of conversationalists' practices of saying-in-so-many-words-what-we-are-doing as formulating. (Garfinkel and Sacks 1970: 350, 351)

This quotation appears in Heritage and Watson (1979). They are concerned with reductive formulations and they, too, specify three operations: in their case, preservation, deletion, transformation. They give the following example of a solicitor, S, being interviewed on a radio programme:

S The inescapable facts are these, er in nineteen thirty-two when he was er aged twenty-three mister Harvey was er committed to Rampton hospital under something called the mental deficiency act nineteen thirteen which of course is a statute that was swept away years ago and er he was committed as far as I can er find out on an order by a single magistrate er sitting I think in private.

I How long did he spend in Rampton?

S Well he was in er Rampton and Mosside hospital er alternatively er until nineteen sixty-one.

I That's the best part of *thirty years.* (*formulation*)

S That's right.

Heritage and Watson comment as follows:

In this example, the interviewer's formulating utterance: 'That's the best part of *thirty* years' exhibits these three properties. Specifically, it *preserves* the length of time Mr. Harvey was in hospital whilst simultaneously *deleting* such information as: the names of the hospitals involved, the Act of Parliament under which Mr. Harvey was committed, what subsequently happened to the Act, the circumstances of his commital, and so on. At the same time, the interviewer's utterance *transforms* some of the information furnished to him (i.e., that Mr. Harvey entered hospital in 1932 and left in 1961) and re-presents this information as the outcome of an arithmetical operation: 'That's the best part of thirty years.' In furnishing the formulation, the interviewer re-describes or re-references parts of the information already delivered to him, thus preserving them in other words. (Heritage and Watson 1979: 130)

Although the properties of formulation, as presented here, and those of reduction as presented in van Dijk, can be seen to have some correspondence (deletion is common to both), it is not clear how the interviewer's formulating utterance can be understood as the semantic macro-structure of this conversation. And here we return to the question of the equivalence of analyst and participant reductions. The critical point about the interviewer's formulation is that it is made to further some conversational purpose. He selects the information he wishes to present as of particular relevance; he does not abstract the whole. And the same is true of reader reductions of written discourse. The communicative conditions provide the reader with the opportunity to recover the conceptual macro-structures of the writer's intention, but he may not wish to take advantage of it.

My argument then (to reduce or formulate it to its essential conceptual content) is this. Written discourse operates by means of the same basic interactive procedures as characterize spoken conversation but the absence of reciprocity calls for a different mode of exploitation. The writer is involved in a process of discourse enactment whereby conceptual content is expanded for conveyance, and in the absence of an active interlocutor to negotiate the course of the interaction, his expansions will tend to match those recoverable by analysis. This discourse process is partially recorded as a textual product. The reader reconverts this product into a process and so derives a discourse from text. This discourse, however, is reduced and this reduction yields not the underlying macro-structure of the writer's original formulation (so far as this is recoverable by analysis) but whatever conceptual content corresponds with the reader's state of knowledge and his purpose in reading. One might say, in general terms, that in writing expansion provides the means whereby the conceptual function can come to terms with the communicative, and in reading reduction provides the means whereby the communicative function can come to terms with the conceptual.

Let me, finally, return to the general theme with which I began. The teaching of languages should, I would agree (and have often enough asserted) be concerned with communication. But we must take care not to define this too narrowly. Our aim must be to develop in learners a capacity for using language for both thinking and acting so that they can exploit its meaning potential in discourse. This is not a simple matter of learning how to express a selection of notions or perform a selection of illocutionary acts. It is, more fundamentally, a matter of learning strategies (like expansion and reduction as I have presented them here) for reconciling conceptual and communicative functions in the discourse process.

I mentioned at the beginning the dangers of misrepresentation in simplifying ideas for practical application, and some might say that the present paper is itself a good illustration of this. Perhaps it might appear so. But my intention has been to try to correct distortion and discourage excess by presenting a more balanced model of language communication than is commonly promoted at present. Whether I have succeeded in my intentions is another matter. At all events (if I may end on a note of exhortation) the responsibility of applied linguists in this matter is clear: to mediate between the theory of language communication and the practice of teaching it without misrepresenting the former or misleading the latter. A difficult task, but if we do not achieve it we shall be discredited. And then another line from Sir Thomas Wyatt will become apposite: it is the opening line of the poem from which my first quotation was taken. It runs:

They fle from me that sometyme did me seke.

Note

Paper presented at the second Berne Colloquium on Applied Linguistics, June 1979, and published in *Applied Linguistics*, Vol. 1, No. 3, Autumn 1980.

7 Reading and communication

It is common these days to refer to reading as a communicative activity. But communication is a more problematic concept than its current popularity might suggest. The paradigm case is usually represented as a situation involving two people in face to face interaction: (A) and (B) in conversation, with the speaking role shifting backwards and forwards between them like a shuttlecock. But linguistic communication is not always of this reciprocal kind. When listening to a lecture or a speech, for example, communication takes place but there is no overt interaction, no turn-taking shuttlecock exchange. Although the listeners may be actively *engaged* in what is going on, they are not actually *participating* in the activity and so have no say in its organization. One may, of course, choose to challenge convention and seek to convert the monologue into an exchange by interrupting the speaker by questions or expressions of dissent. There are other communicative occasions, however, when it is not possible to intervene, even if one felt disposed to do so; when the only recourse is to disengage completely by switching off the radio, closing the book.

Reading is clearly an activity of this non-reciprocal kind. The question then arises as to how it is related to the paradigm case of conversation. Is it a derivative version in some sense? If so, in what sense? What is the nature of the derivation? These are the kinds of questions that I shall be concerned with in this paper: my purpose is to try to define the communicative character of reading.

We may begin with a consideration of the paradigm case: (A) and (B) talking to each other. The one taking the speaker role has some information to impart for some purpose. In general this purpose is to change the state of affairs that obtains in the mind of the addressee at the moment of speaking. (A) has reason to suppose that he knows something that (B) does not know and which he believes it is desirable for (B) to know. So he alters this state of affairs by passing this knowledge on and the situation then shifts into a new state, itself then subject to further change, and so on.

This goes on until one participant resists the change and breaks off the engagement or both participants arrive at a mutual agreement that the situation has reached a satisfactory state of stability, and bring the engagement to a close.

The general purpose of people talking, then, is to bring about some change or other by the transmission of information. The particular purposes associated with particular interactions will, of course, vary greatly. (A) might wish to convey information about his desires so that (B) can satisfy them, he may wish to instruct, to advise, to threaten, or command; he may wish to offer a service, or practise a deception, or impose an obligation. He may simply want to impress or escape from individual isolation. The reasons why people need to communicate with each other are varied and manifold and relate to the whole range of the individual's involvement in social life. Let us then consider what (A) has to *do* in order to successfully convey what he has in mind.

It might seem as if this is a simple enough matter of (A) encoding what he wants to say in the language he shares with (B). But the assumption here is that a commonly shared code automatically guarantees the common understanding of messages encoded in it, and this clearly is not the case. Suppose, for example, that (A) were to say:

The man is coming on Monday.

He (or she) is relying on (B) already knowing who this man is and why it should be a relevant bit of news that he is coming on Monday. So (A)'s utterance does not itself express the information. What it does is to act as a mediator between what (A) knows and what (B) knows. The utterance serves to bring two networks of knowledge together and the meaning of what is said is a function of this connection. To adapt McLuhan's well-known slogan: the mediation is the message. But very often the production of a single utterance will not be enough to connect up the two networks in this way, in which case the interlocutors have work to do to fix up a circuit. For example, (B) may not know, or may have forgotten, which man is being referred to and so may not understand what *proposition* is being expressed. We will give our example some human identity. (A) and (B), wife and husband, Mildred and George. A domestic scene.

Mildred The man is coming on Monday.
George Man? Which man? (*No connection. The message does not mediate.*)

Mildred You know, the builder. (*Circuit repair.*)
George The builder? (*Still no connection.*)
Mildred Yes, the builder. Don't you remember? He is coming to mend the leak in the boxroom ceiling. (*Still repairing.*)
George Oh, yes, that's right. Good. (*Message received and understood. Connection made, meaning achieved.*)

This is a case of propositional repair. But even if George *does* know who the man is, he may not know why Mildred thinks that his coming on Monday is worth mentioning. That is to say, even if he understands what *proposition* is being expressed by the utterance, he may still not grasp its illocutionary force. In this case, one can imagine an exchange of the following sort:

Mildred The man is coming on Monday.
George So what?
Mildred I thought you would want to know.
George I do know. You have told me twice already.
Mildred Well, I thought you might want to clear out the boxroom before he comes.
George Oh, I see. OK.

Gradually it emerges that what Mildred wants George to know is not only that the man is coming but that she wants him to do something about it. The message is not conveyed until George is led to realize that the utterance 'The man is coming on Monday' is meant to carry the illocutionary force of a request for action.

In both of these cases, the interlocutors are involved in negotiation in order to achieve the propositional and illocutionary value of the message. The last utterance in each exchange marks the successful connection. 'Oh yes, that's right. Good.' (I understand what you are talking about.) 'Oh, I see. OK.' (I understand what you are getting at.) The two worlds come together and the situation shifts into a new state.

Of course, if the two worlds, the two networks of knowledge, are already in close convergence, the need for negotiation is correspondingly diminished. So it is that, given the George and Mildred situation, the following exchange might occur:

Mildred The man is coming on Monday.
George I am going out tonight.

This can be understood as a perfectly coherent exchange if we suppose that George knows already that the man is to come to mend the ceiling and that this involves work in the boxroom beforehand. His utterance can then be taken to carry the message: 'I can't work in the boxroom tonight because I am going out.' So negotiation is not always necessary. When networks are interwoven by close acquaintance, messages are easy to achieve, sometimes without language at all.

But most communication calls for negotiation. It is necessary to establish the meaning of the message, to make it *accessible*. It is also necessary to make it *acceptable*. Why, after all, does Mildred not get to the point straightaway and say bluntly:

The man is coming on Monday, so clear out the boxroom.

Presumably because she might thereby provoke the response:

Who do you think you are ordering about?

or

Do it yourself.

If you intend to impose an obligation on somebody it is prudent to prepare the ground beforehand, to make him or her receptive to your purpose and the message acceptable. But even when there is no such imposition, the problem of acceptability arises because every occasion of interaction will tend to be an impingement on privacy. It is worth dwelling a moment on why this should be so.

People have need of social contact. It provides them with the means of collaborating in practical action. As Banton puts it:

Men must organize. In order to obtain food and shelter, to guard against period of shortage or misfortune, and to propagate their own kind, men are obliged to co-operate with their fellows. (Banton 1965: 1)

But contact is also necessary as a means of receiving 'strokes' of recognition and approval which sustain the internal organization of the individual self. Berne comments on this aspect of co-operation as follows:

The advantages of social contact revolve around somatic and psychic equilibrium. They are related to the following factors: (1) the relief of tension; (2) the avoidance of noxious situations; (3) the procurement of stroking; and (4) the maintenance of an established equilibrium. (Berne 1967: 18)

We may say, then, that people are acted upon by what we might refer to as the co-operative imperative. In language use this is expressed through what Grice calls the co-operative principle: a set of maxims which represent the ground rules we abide by when engaged in communicative behaviour. Thus when a conversation takes place, both interlocutors enter into a socially sanctioned agreement that they will not say more than necessary, that what they say will be relevant to the matter in hand, that they have some warrant in fact for what they say, and so on (Grice 1975). To put the matter briskly, social contact calls for a social contract. The management of human affairs depends on the assumption that people will co-operate to achieve understanding. Unless they do so, no negotiation is possible and communication is arrested. But there are risks involved.

Co-operation can only occur if those co-operating allow entry into each other's individual world, and this calls for caution. Human beings, in common with other animals, have a strong sense of private territory, their own circumscribed life space of ideas, values, beliefs within which they find their essential security. In communication, the socially sanctioned co-operative imperative requires the barriers which define this space to be lowered to allow entry. Not surprisingly, therefore, the entry is wary and circumspect. Interlocutors are anxious to avoid offence by seeming to intrude too abruptly, always aware that they are vulnerable to counter attack. So it is that it is in the interests of both parties concerned to be polite, to protect face, and self-esteem, to avoid an abuse of privacy (see Brown and Levinson 1978). Thus on every occasion of language use the co-operative imperative acting in the interests of social contact has to be reconciled with the territorial imperative acting in the interests of individual security. Of course there are occasions when the status or role of the interlocutors is such that customary circumspection can to some degree be dispensed with. One such case is when territory is shared, as it is in families. Familiarity may not always breed contempt, but it will always tend to breed complacency. Another case is when one interlocutor is so privileged in role or so powerful in status that he can invade the other's territory without any fear of reprisal. So it is that officers do not need to be polite to the rank and file. And teachers seldom bother to be polite to pupils. On most occasions of social contact, however, we have to be careful not to infringe rights and offend susceptibilities; we have to be aware of, and wary of, territorial claims.

The points I have made about the territorial and co-operative imperatives can be related to the drives which social psychologists identify as elements in social motivation. Argyle indicates that these drives can be ranged along two dimensions, which he represents diagrammatically as follows:

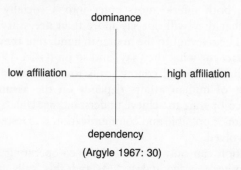

(Argyle 1967: 30)

The horizontal dimension here relates to the degree to which people feel they share a life space with those they are in contact with. In the case of low affiliation there will be little or no convergence of individual territory, whereas with high affiliation there will be a good deal. This dimension clearly corresponds to what Brown and Gilman (1960) refer to as solidarity. We may say, then, that a sense of high affiliation and solidarity derives from a recognition of shared experiential territory which reduces the risks of co-operation. Argyle's vertical dimension corresponds to Brown and Gilman's 'power semantic'. This has to do with the extent to which the individual asserts his own territorial claim in co-operative activity. If he is sufficiently confident of his own defences, then he will be assertive and seek to extend his space into that of his interlocutor, thereby exercising dominance. If he lacks confidence, he will invite incursions into his space, and be submissive and dependent. If assertion is frustrated, the result is aggression. If submission is frustrated, the result is anomie, a loss of the sense of social identity.

Linguistic communication has to be understood in relation to these factors affecting social behaviour in general. It can be characterized, I suggest, as a means of bringing individual worlds into convergence by negotiation. These worlds consist of constructs of knowledge and experience, frames of reference for interpreting events (cf. van Dijk 1977). Communication is achieved when the speaker formulates particular propositional content and illocutionary intent in such a way as to make them accessible on the one hand and acceptable on the other. Accessibility is achieved by an alignment of different states of knowledge so that a common frame of reference is created. Acceptability is achieved when the interlocutors locate their interaction on the power and solidarity dimensions and reconcile the conflicting forces of the territorial and co-operative imperatives. So it is that in conversation one is often chary of providing direct access to one's meaning in case it is not acceptable:

Look, you are not going to believe this but ...
I don't quite know how to tell you this, and forgive me if I seem to be critical but ...
I know that you have been through a hard time recently, but ...
and so on.

The greater the threat of disturbance to the ordered scheme of things which represents the internal security of the individual, the more necessary do protective utterances of this kind become. And of course, too much concern for acceptability may lead to obfuscation and a decrease in accessibility. The speaker may be so preoccupied in making sure that what he has to say is not too disturbing an intrusion into the hearer's privacy that the point of his utterance may be lost. The whole business of conversational interaction calls for considerable skill in negotiation.

I shall refer to this process of negotiation as *discourse*. The overt expression of the process takes the form of linguistic signals which can be recorded and studied in detachment after the event. These constitute the *text* of the interaction. A recorded text can be analysed as a product, simply as the manifestation of the linguistic code without regard to its character as the realization of discourse; and this, traditionally, is how it has been analysed in descriptive linguistics. The language user, however, does not deal with text as linguistic data in this way but as indications of communicative intent which have to be interpreted in flight, as it were, during the discourse process.

So much, then, for the nature of linguistic communication in general, as represented by the paradigm case of face to face interaction involving the overt negotiation of meaning through reciprocal exchange. But now what of written discourse? What of reading and writing? On the face of it these activities are very different from those of spoken interaction. There is typically no shifting of the initiative from one interlocutor to the other, so there can be no monitoring of effect, no adjustment to reaction, no open co-operation in the negotiation of meaning. The reader may give vent to snorts of disagreement, may scribble comments in the margin ('Rubbish!' 'Surely not!') but he cannot alter the development of the discourse as recorded in the text. It is the writer, it would seem, who is entirely in control of events. Indeed one might question whether, in the absence of such interaction, one can legitimately talk about written discourse at all. Is it not rather all text? To answer this question, we have to consider the relationship between text and discourse in spoken and written language use.

Written text differs from spoken text in two fundamental ways. First, it is fashioned by the producer for prospective use and cannot be realized as discourse until it is performed, as it were, as a separate and subsequent activity. Spoken text is the immediate reflex of discourse which disappears without trace unless recorded by third person intervention. The act of writing is the act of recording and if there is no record, no written communication has occurred. The act of speaking requires no record but only an immediate textual realization. Second, the written record is one-sided. Unlike spoken text it does not usually provide a representation of the entire interaction, but only the first person's contribution to it. Written text, then, is a partial record designed to have a delayed action effect, and as such is detached from discourse activity in a way that only analysis can achieve in the case of spoken language use. This detachment has important implications for reading, as I shall suggest presently.

But meanwhile the question remains as to how the writer, being the sole begetter of text, sending his signals out into the void for later reception, can be said to be producing discourse at all. He does so by means of a covert interaction whereby he anticipates the likely reactions of an imagined reader and negotiates with him as it were by proxy, by the vicarious assumption of the second person role. In this way he creates his own conditions for communication. He has something to convey and must calculate what additional information he needs to provide to facilitate the conveyance. In the course of his presentation, he shifts perspective to assume and so to assess the second person response and adjusts the development of his discourse accordingly. For example. Here is the beginning of a discussion on the relevance of the concept of role in the understanding of social behaviour:

A The basic psychological function of roles is to provide the individual with a fairly specific model for interaction.
B Why do you say it's a model?
A It is a model in the sense that any role is defined in terms of its relation to other roles.
B I'm still not quite clear. Give me an example.

A The role of parent is defined in relation to that of children.
B OK, I'm with you. Now go on to tell me about roles.

This can be said to be the discourse underlying the following text:

> The basic psychological function of roles is to provide the individual with a fairly specific model for interaction. It is a model in the sense that any role is defined in terms of its relation to other roles, as the role of 'parent', for example, is defined in relation to that of children. Each role is associated with what, for the moment, is best called norms of 'behaviour'.[1]

So it is that the writer can be said to conduct a covert interchange to establish a convergence of frames of reference so that the information he wishes to convey is made accessible to his supposed reader. To do this he has recourse to the kind of tactical procedures illustrated here whereby he anticipates the immediate reactions of the imagined second person addressee and so provides for the linear development of the discourse. But he also makes use of procedures of a more strategic kind to foreground or bring into focus the main points of his presentation and to distinguish them from information which is only intended to serve an enabling function. Such strategic procedures occur commonly in conversation, when they are generally used retrospectively to summarize or recapitulate the gist or upshot of what has preceded:

> What has emerged from our discussions, then, is ...
> So we are agreed that ...
> In short, the indications are that ...

Such procedures have been referred to by the ethnomethodologists as 'formulations' (Garfinkel and Sacks 1970, Heritage and Watson 1979). Apart from these retrospective procedures for formulating, however, the writer also makes use of prospective procedures to give *pre*formulations of what he intends to say:

> There are three points I wish to make: first ... second ... third ...
> The purpose of this paper is ...

Such devices make explicit in advance the hierarchical structure of the discourse and compensate for the absence of immediate feedback which in conversation allows for the structure to be monitored into shape through reciprocal interaction.

The discourse procedures mentioned so far are directed at providing for what I have referred to as accessibility. The writer may also need to take acceptability into account so that he does not project an image of dogmatic rectitude or insult the intelligence of his reader. Hence expressions like 'of course', 'perhaps' and the mitigating use of modality. However, the writer is not in a situation of actual physical confrontation and is under no immediate threat of reprisal should he cause offence by unwarranted trespass. Furthermore, whereas spoken interaction, no matter how formal, must inevitably involve individuals and expose them to the dangers of attack, written discourse is, with the exception of personal correspondence, not typically directed at individuals at all, but at groups. Writers are therefore less concerned with the protection of persons. Indeed, the problem of the writer is not so much to avoid conflict as to create conditions for an engagement, and to this end he will sometimes provoke reaction by flouting acceptability. Consider this example:

To see, we need light.

Such a statement invites the riposte:

You don't say. Now tell us something new!

But as the discourse develops it becomes clear that this is a deliberate ruse to engage our attention:

To see, we need light. This may seem too obvious to mention but it has not always been so obvious—Plato thought of vision as being due not to light entering, but rather to particles shot out of the eyes, spraying surrounding objects.[2]

I have characterized written text as the partial record of a discourse enacted by the writer on behalf of a supposed reader. This enactment involves the use of tactical and strategic procedures to convey a scheme or pattern of information which is a projection of the writer's world. His purpose is to induce the reader to recognize his territorial claim. If the actual reader is prepared to play the role that the writer has cast him in, then he will seek to recover the underlying discourse from the textual clues provided. In this case, in respect to the point made earlier about dominance and dependence in social behaviour, reading will be an act of submission. The reader, recognizing the authority of the writer and wanting to allow access to the information given, will adjust his own frames of reference to accommodate it. He will then allow himself to be directed by the writer and be content to keep to the course that has been plotted for him. He will follow the text like a script.

But the reader may not wish to submit to writer control in this way; he may not be willing, or may not be able, to accommodate the writer's conceptual scheme into the patterns of his own life space. Nor is he obliged to do so. In spoken interaction the co-operative imperative imposes constraints on freedom of action and will direct interlocutors towards accommodation and convergence (cf. Giles and Smith 1979). But the reader is not under such constraint. The text is there before him, dissociated from the discourse which created it, and so he can use it in whichever way best suits his purposes, free to disregard the discourse that the writer has enacted on his behalf. Instead of adjusting his scheme of things to accommodate that of the writer, he can project his own scheme on what he reads and change the direction of accommodation so that the text is adjusted to fit the patterns of his own significance. In this case reading is an act not of submission but of assertion.

Communication involves the transmission of information from one individual world to another, from one schematic setting to another. Negotiation is necessary to bring about the required adjustment so that there is an alignment of frames of reference. But in spoken interaction the very social nature of the activity, and in particular the acceptability requirement, calls for circumspection and compromise. The interlocutors, caught up in a social event, have to act in accordance with the requirements of social be-haviour, and the discourse that results represents not only the negotiation of meaning but also the management of interpersonal relations. The written text, on the other hand, is produced as the report of a discourse enacted in detachment from the immediacy of a social encounter and the reader, in like detachment, can choose to relate it to his own scheme of things in whichever way serves his purpose best. He may choose to be dependent and to adjust in submissive fashion to the writer's scheme, following the discourse development plotted for him. Alternatively, he may choose to be dominant and to assert the primacy of his own conceptual pattern, fitting textual information into it directly and short-circuiting the discourse process.

I am suggesting, then, that since the reader is not under social pressure to key his reactions into the structure of an actually occurring interaction, he is free to take up whatever position suits his purpose on the dominance/dependence scale, asserting his own scheme at one point, submitting to that of the writer at another, alternately using the text as a source of information and as the script of a discourse. But the positions the reader takes up will not be determined by the *interpersonal* factors that are so crucial in conversation, but by *ideational* factors (to use Halliday's terminology). That is to say, the reader's concern is to derive as much information as he needs from his reading so as to consolidate or change the frames of reference which define his particular conceptual territory. If he seeks to consolidate he will tend to be assertive, and if he seeks to change he will tend towards submission.

Whether the reader adopts an interpersonal attitude of submission or assertion, to achieve his ideational purpose he has to make a connection between the writer's frames of reference and his own. There has to be some coincidence of what Sanford and Garrod refer to as 'scenarios', which, as they point out, provide the basis for prediction:

> The scenario is an information network called from long-term memory by a particular linguistic input ... in all cases the basic principle is one of enabling the knowledge of the reader to be used in such a way as to allow for direct interpretation of entities or events predicted by his knowledge. To the extent that any text conforms to the predictions it is readily interpreted, to the extent that it does not, it will be more difficult to understand. (Sanford and Garrod 1981: 127)

The first circumstance mentioned here, where the text keys in closely with reader predictions, will encourage assertion. The second, where the text is relatively unpredictable, will require submission to the writer's discourse. But in both cases the aim is to relate what the writer says to a pre-existing scheme.

A consideration of reading as the ideational matching of frames of reference or scenarios requires us to shift our attention from the psychology of interpersonal relations to the psychology of perception. For the process of prediction which Sanford and Garrod refer to is engaged as much for the interpretation of visual images as for the interpretation of linguistically coded information. Thus Neisser makes reference to 'anticipatory schemata' which correspond to the scenarios of Sanford and Garrod:

> In my view, the cognitive structures crucial for vision are the anticipatory schemata that prepare the perceiver to accept certain kinds of information rather than others and thus control the activity of looking. Because we can see only what we know how to look for, it is these schemata (together with the information actually available) that determine what will be perceived... At

each moment the perceiver is constructing anticipations of certain kinds of information, that enable him to accept it as it becomes available. (Neisser 1976: 20)

The schema, then, like the scenario, is projected on to events which are then interpreted with reference to it. But clearly if actuality always fitted neatly into anticipation and predictions were always confirmed, then schemata would fossilize into fixed stereotypes and nothing would be learnt from reading or visual experience. Allowance, therefore, must be made for information to modify existing schemata. In view of this Neisser proposes a perceptual cycle whereby a schema directs the perceiver to explore reality by sampling the available information and modifying the original schema where necessary. Diagrammatically, the cycle is presented like this:

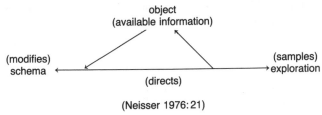

(Neisser 1976: 21)

It seems clear that the reading process can be characterized in terms of this perceptual cycle. The reader applies a schematic frame or scenario to the textual object, samples the information it represents, and makes whatever modification is necessary to incorporate information not previously accounted for into the structure of his knowledge. There are, however, complications. To begin with, the object to be sampled is itself schematically organized and so represents a structural order which the reader has to reconcile with his own. Where the two orders are similar, little sampling and modification will be required to make them congruent. Where they are different, the reader may choose to sample the text to make minimal modifications, thereby asserting the primacy of his schemata, or may feel the need for major schematic modification, and in this case the sampling will take the form of a submission to the writer's discourse, of which the textual object is a realization.

I have tried in this paper to indicate what seem to me to be the salient characteristics of reading as a communicative activity. Essentially they derive from the detachment of first person addresser and second person addressee and the consequent dissociation of text from discourse in written language use. This enables the writer to concentrate on accessibility and the reader to use the text for ideational purposes, sampling the information it offers without being involved in the management of interpersonal relations, and without having to process it as it emerges in real time. The reader is free to deal with it as a perceptible object. On the other hand, the text is the report of a discourse and so the interaction which originally informed it can be recovered as required by the reader assuming the second person role presupposed by the writer. Thus the reader is able to adopt the social attitudes of dominance and dependence to suit his own personal purposes in acquiring information without being troubled by their implications in social interaction.

So it is that the difficulties of reading, unlike those of conversation, have to do less with the negotiation of constraints than with the use of freedom. The reader can negotiate meaning on his own terms. His problem is to know what these terms should be on particular reading occasions. If he is too assertive, there is a danger that he may distort the writer's intentions and deny access to new knowledge and experience. If he is too submissive, he runs the risk of accumulating information without subjecting it to the critical discrimination necessary to incorporate it into the schematic structure of existing knowledge. In both cases, reading is deprived of its essential purpose since it does not result in the change of state which, as I suggested earlier, is a defining feature of the communicative process.

Notes

An early version of this paper was presented at the LEND Conference at Martina Franca, and published in Italian in the proceedings: *Educazione alla lettura*, Bologna: Zanichelli, November 1980. This revised version appears in Alderson and Urquhart, 1984.

1　Extract from Kelvin (1971).
2　Extract from Gregory (1966).

Discourse: schema, procedure, and sign

The papers in this Section elaborate on certain issues raised in the preceding Section and seek to show how they may be interpreted in reference to models of language knowledge and social interaction proposed by scholars whose interest in the pragmatics of language use arises from an assortment of different disciplinary preoccupations.

Paper 8 is principally concerned with the kinds of knowledge structure which the user draws upon in the discourse process and with the procedures used for the realization of abstract knowledge for actual communicative outcomes on particular occasions. It is both survey and synthesis. It attempts to fashion out of ideas from a variety of scholarly sources a conceptual pattern which imposes some order on the scene. An exercise in exegesis of this kind involves risks of misrepresentation, particularly in a field like pragmatics which has no agreed charts to define it, and no stable terms of reference. The purpose of this paper, however, is not precise topography: it is rather to produce something more in the nature of a sketch map for people concerned with the teaching of language, to give them some way of taking bearings on an area of enquiry which relates closely to their concerns. In this respect, this paper conforms to the principles of applied linguistics as outlined in Section One: it aims to make statements of relevance.

The second paper in this Section follows directly from a footnote in the first. Whereas Paper 8 focuses attention on what is required of the language user in the achievement of discourse, and is basically sociolinguistic in orientation, Paper 9 relates the discourse process to certain basic distinctions in semiotics. The central point made here is that the linguistic sign in the sentence, the linguist's traditional object of analysis, operates in a radically different way from the sign as realized in the utterances of language use. I use the term *symbol* to refer to the first and *index* to refer to the latter. In respect to the discussion in Paper 8, therefore, one can describe discourse as the use of procedures for converting systemic symbols into the indices of schematic meaning. In this way, the language user reverses the decontextualization process which (as is pointed out in Lyons 1972) is an aspect of idealization which the linguistic analyst imposes on data in order to isolate the sentence.

I have borrowed the terms *symbol, index*, and *icon* from C. S. Peirce and interpreted them, rather cavalierly, to suit my own convenience, although Peirce's formulation of the distinction does give some warrant to my interpretation. The terms, carrying the meaning I have pressed upon them, and the central concepts of schemata and procedure, as discussed in Paper 8, reappear in various configurations of argument in the papers which follow. They prove to be of service in clarifying issues in the description and teaching of literature (Section Four) and English for specific purposes (Section Five) and in course design and methodology for communicative language teaching in general (Section Six).

8   Procedures for discourse processing

Introduction

This is a working paper, which tries to impose some order on partial understanding. It is therefore a fugitive affair. Discourse analysis is a particularly busy area of enquiry, a field full of folk from all sorts of different academic backgrounds ploughing their own different, sometimes lonely, furrows. This paper attempts to provide a review of some of these various activities and to organize their findings into a coherent scheme so that we might better assess what relevance they have for the teaching and learning of languages. In particular it is concerned with work which contributes towards an understanding of the strategies or procedures that a language user employs in the actual discourse process.

The paper aims at making ideas in theory accessible for use in the practical domain of language teaching and learning. It begins with pedagogic issues and works its way through areas of research which seem to make some contribution to their clarification and resolution. The hope is that at the end of the paper we might have a clearer idea of what directions it might be profitable to take, and what distances we have yet to travel.

1   The pedagogic perspective

The subject of language teaching has generally been defined with reference to what is to be learnt rather than to the activities which promote the language learning process. Thus the content of language courses is commonly specified in terms of items and rules to be internalized as knowledge. How this internalization is to be brought about is considered to be the concern of methodology and in principle a separate matter. Typically, no implicational relationship is established between the syllabus, what is to be learnt, and the techniques used by the teacher for implementing it. Methodology is seen as a set of procedures for facilitating the transmission of course content through learner activities which are ancillary and not essentially a part of what is actually to be learnt (see Munby 1978: 217). The shift of emphasis towards a communicative characterization of content has not, I think, essentially altered this view of pedagogy. Learner activities, then, are thought of as a means to the acquisition of language under the direction of the teacher. They are not generally thought of as intrinsic to natural language behaviour as such and so as an essential element of the course which the learner has to master for himself if he is to be an independent user of the language he is learning.

Clearly the language learner has to acquire a knowledge of rules, of usage and of use, but he also has to acquire the ability to act upon his knowledge, to exploit it to achieve communicative objectives. The assumption underlying the separation of syllabus design from methodology seems to be that the acquisition of this knowledge is a process distinct from its use in communicative behaviour and so can be left to the ingenuity of pedagogic technique. The exploitation of such knowledge in the business of actual language use is then left to the learner to work out for himself. But recent research in first and second language acquisition represents acquisition as a function of language use in contexts of interaction, and indicates that a consideration of discourse provides some explanation for the development of first language systems in children (e.g. Bates 1976, Halliday 1975) and for the ordering of morpheme sequences in the interlanguage of second language learners (e.g. Hatch 1978). If this is so, it would seem reasonable to suppose that an investigation into the procedures that language users employ in the discourse process should provide us with a description of activities to be incorporated into course design: activities which while creating conditions for acquisition simultaneously develop the necessary ability for language use.

The position taken in this paper, then, and its claim to pedagogic relevance is that the conditions for language learning and the conditions for the effective communicative use of language are the same and need to be incorporated into a definition of what is to be learnt as learning objectives and not simply converted into pedagogic techniques as teaching aids. There is, I believe, a crucial distinction here so it would be as well to make it clear.

When learner activities are used by the teacher to facilitate the acquisition of language, the situations set up to serve as a context for such activities typically have two characteristics. Firstly, they are language dependent. This is a necessary consequence of their separate methodological origin: they have been brought in from outside the language content of the syllabus to help in its transmission. Secondly, their association with the language is correlational: a particular language form expressing such and such a communicative function correlates with certain situational factors. As a consequence of these characteristics, the language is represented as having self-contained meaning and language learning as being a matter of putting expressions in store ready to be issued when situations arise which will correlate with them. What this means is that these expressions are taught as sentences, exemplificatory devices, and not as utterances of natural language. For the utterances of natural language relate to the situations in which they occur in a radically different manner. Firstly, the direction of dependency is reversed: it is not the language which is serviced by the situation but the situation which is serviced by the language. Secondly, the association of situation and language is not correlational but complementary. In real life, situations occur which need to be resolved in some way by the use of language and the language user will conduct the business by exploiting language to clarify and change the situation according to his purpose. The situation constrains the selection of language but language also acts to extend and modify the situation: the relationship is complementary, with utterances and situational features providing for each other's inadequacies. But this transaction can only be achieved by language users entering into an *interaction* with each other whereby they seek to establish common recognition of the situational factors concerned. Situations are recognized and changed through human agency.

The meaning of sentences, that is to say of expressions which are correlated with dependent situational factors, is invariant and not open to negotiation. The meaning of utterances is always negotiable through interaction whereby the 'reciprocity of perspectives' (see Cicourel 1973) on a particular situation is established.

The purpose of this paper is to discuss what is involved in such interactive endeavour, assumed to be the essential principle in the process of language learning and language use.

2   The theoretical perspective

Text and discourse

Communication is called for when the language user recognizes a situation which requires the conveyance of information to establish a convergence of knowledge, so that this situation can be changed in some way. This transaction requires the negotiation of meaning through interaction. I refer to this negotiation as *discourse*. The term in this paper, therefore, refers to the interaction that has to take place to establish the meaning value of utterances and to realize their effectiveness as indicators of illocutionary intent. This interactivity is a necessary condition for the enactment of any discourse. In some cases, however, it may be overt and reciprocal, as in conversation, and in others it may be covert and non-reciprocal, as in much of written language (but see Holec 1980).

Discourse is a communicative process by means of interaction. Its situational outcome is a change in a state of affairs: information is conveyed, intentions made clear. Its linguistic product is *text*. This can be studied in dissociation from its source as a manifestation of linguistic rules, that is to say as a compendium of sentences. The extent to which recovery of discourse from textual evidence is possible will depend on how far the situational features which complement the recorded utterances are known to the receiver. In the case of reciprocal discourse, text is recorded by third person non-participant intervention, and subsequent recovery might well involve a difficult analytic operation using techniques for reconstitution or expansion (see Labov and Fanshel 1977: 49ff). In the case of non-reciprocal discourse, text is deliberately designed to facilitate recovery, but the very nature of such discourse allows the receiver to recover selectively according to his purposes. Since he is not himself an actual participant in the discourse recorded in the text (his participation having been assumed by proxy by the producer) he is relieved of the usual responsibilities of co-operation. Thus the reader can take short cuts and does not have to follow the route taken by the writer.

When considering procedures for discourse processing, then, a distinction needs to be made between activities engaged in the actual process of discourse development, and those which are engaged in recovering information subsequently from a textual record of a discourse already enacted by non-reciprocal interaction. The latter are likely to take their bearings directly from the desired situational outcome: that is to say, the reader will adjust his engagement with written text according to his purposes in reading.

Knowledge and functions of language

Discourse is the process whereby language users negotiate a 'reciprocity of perspectives' for the conveyance of information and intention. To do this, they draw on a knowledge of language and the conventions associated with its use in social contexts. Such knowledge is acquired to meet individual and social needs and so it is convenient to consider it under two heads.

First, language is learnt as a means of establishing a relationship between the individual and his environment and of providing, thereby, for personal security. Language offers the possibility of controlling the environment by providing the means of conceptualizing it in the categories of the language code. This is language in its essentially ideational function: it promotes thinking and allows for the fashioning of propositions. Halliday puts it this way:

> Language serves for the expression of 'content': that is, of the speaker's experience of the real world, including the inner world of his own consciousness... In serving this function, language also gives structure to experience, and helps to determine our way of looking at things, so that it requires some intellectual effort to see them in any other way than that which our language suggests to us. (Halliday 1970: 143)

One kind of knowledge, then, is ideational: a knowledge of how language serves as a device for forming propositions about the world.

Language is also learnt as a means of establishing a relationship between the individual and his fellow men. Social life depends on co-operation and this has to take place in accordance with all kinds of conventions for proper conduct. Language is not only learnt as a device for private thinking but also as a device for taking action and for engaging with other people in the business of social life. Again, Halliday puts it this way:

> Language serves to establish and maintain social relations: for the expression of social roles ... and also for getting things done, by means of the interaction between one person and another. (Halliday 1970: 143)

A second kind of knowledge is interpersonal: a knowledge of how language serves to perform social actions.

Halliday shows how these functions are reflected in the structure of the language system. Our concern here is how they are internalized in such a way as to retain their potential for use and how they are actualized as behaviour in the discourse process. It is important to note that the internalization of the ideational and interpersonal functions of language as *knowledge for use* is different from the knowledge that a language user has of the sentences of his language. It has been suggested that communicative competence includes linguistic competence in the Chomskyan sense (e.g. Canale and Swain 1980). This, I think, is misleading if the latter is conceived of as in some sense a separate component within the former. The language user knows his language as a formal system and can, under certain conditions when asked to play the role of analyst, demonstrate that knowledge by the composition and comprehension of sentences in isolation. There may also be occasions of communication failure when he will need to resort to this formal knowledge. But in the production and understanding of utterances, the user will typically draw on simpler conceptual schemes which mediate between a formal knowledge of the system and actual communicative behaviour. In this sense, communicative competence is a level of organization, developed from habitual performance, which represents a stage of preparedness of use. It would, after all, be surprising, if the procedures employed in the acquisition and use of language in discourse were not retained in the memory as a principle of organization ready for deployment when similar occasions arose. There seems no reason why a child, for example, should obliterate all traces of past experience, strip language of its contextual association and only store it in the form of abstract rules for sentence formation and lexical items as semantic isolates.

The view adopted in this paper is that apart from a knowledge of sentences the language user has at his disposal knowledge of certain executive operations which will realize meanings in use in the discourse process. The extent to which such operations are dependent on sentence knowledge, or how sentence knowledge derives from such operations are matters which call for further enquiry, but it is clear that discourse cannot simply be defined as 'language above the sentence' (see Winograd 1977: 65). Nor can we assume that stretches of language use which are isomorphic with sentences are the sole business of the grammarian, for these too are the realizations of the discourse process. In Goodwin (1979), for example, there is a demonstration of how a single sentence-like utterance is compiled as an interactive process. He observes:

> Sentences emerge with conversation. However, in traditional linguistics it has been assumed that the analysis of sentences can be performed upon examples isolated from such an interactive

process. In opposition to such a view it will be argued here that sentences in natural conversation emerge as products of a process of interaction between speaker and hearer and that they mutually construct the turn at talk. (Goodwin 1979: 97–8)

Goodwin, however, is not really concerned with sentences but with *utterances* which have formal sentential analogues. What he demonstrates is that utterances 'emerge as products of a process of interaction'. Only when such products are studied in dissociation from the discourse process do they take on the character of sentences. There is no opposition between this view and that adopted in traditional linguistics. It is just as confusing to try to account for sentences in discourse analysis as it is to try to account for utterances in models of grammar (cf. Sadock 1974, Leech 1977).

What is being proposed, then, is that there are levels of language organization which represent functional potential in states of preparedness for use which are drawn upon directly in the discourse process. Such levels enable the language user to form propositions and take interpersonal action without composing every expression *ab initio* by direct reference to linguistic rules. This level might be thought of as a set of adaptable idioms.

It would appear that Firth had something of this sort in mind when he set up the 'context of situation' as a level of linguistic analysis (Firth 1957: 182). This has been criticized on the grounds that it does not adequately account for sentence meaning (cf. Lyons 1966) but Firth seems to have had the utterance and not the sentence in mind and to be trying to work out rules of use. Consider, for example, the following passage:

The description of the context of situation by stating the interior relations of the constituents or factors, may be followed by referring such contexts to a variety of known frameworks of a more general character such as (a) the economic, religious, and other social structures of the societies of which the participants are members; (b) types of linguistic discourse such as a monologue, choric language, narrative recitation, explanation, exposition, etc; (c) personal interchanges, e.g. mentioning especially the number, age, and sex of the participants and noting speaker-listener, reader-writer and reader *or* writer contexts, including series of such interchanges; (d) types of speech function such as drills and orders, detailed direction and control of techniques of all kinds, social flattery, blessing, cursing, praise and blame, concealment and deception, social pressure and constraint, verbal contracts of all kinds, and phatic communion. (Palmer 1968: 178)

Characteristically, Firth does not demonstrate how the constituents of the context of situation—the relevant features of participants, the relevant objects and events, the verbal action of the participants etc.—might be referred to the frameworks he mentions, but it is clear that he anticipates here subsequent developments in speech act theory and discourse analysis. He himself says:

> The technical language necessary for the description of context of situation is not developed, nor is there any agreed method of classification. At this level there are great possibilities for research and experiment. (Palmer 1968: 177)

There are now some areas of research and experiment which can be referred to to give some formal shape to Firth's intuitions about a communicative function level of language organization. It is to these areas that we now turn.

3   Internalization and actualization of knowledge for use

A recognition that there exists an intermediate level of language organization is not new. It is presupposed for example in traditional studies of rhetoric and in the structuralist analysis of narrative (see Culler 1975, Scholes 1974, Hawkes 1977). The underlying structures postulated in such analyses can be related to the constructs proposed more recently by workers in Artificial Intelligence. Thus the motifs that Propp isolates from a variety of tales, the logical structure which underlies different versions of myth that Levi-Strauss talks about, the narrative grammar of Todorov can be seen as examples of what Schank refers to as scripts (Schank 1975) and Winograd as schemas (*sic*). Winograd, for example, speaks of schema as 'a description of a complex object, situation, process, or structure', and goes on to elaborate as follows:

> A schema contains 'context-dependent descriptions' of the component objects which make it up, and these can serve as variables in describing 'instances' of objects, situations, and structures, by analogy with it. A particular instance is described by referring to an appropriate schema and listing the specific differences between the standard information assumed in the schematic structure and the specific information relevant to the

instance. A single instance can be described by reference to more than one schema... They can be thought of as economical structures for storing memories of objects and events (including discourse events). (Winograd 1977: 72–4)

I will assume that the functional knowledge of language in communicative readiness, as distinct from the formal knowledge of language as a self-contained and separate system, is internalized as a set of schemas (or, as I will prefer to call them, schemata[1]) of the sort that Winograd proposes. Those which prepare ideational knowledge for use I shall refer to as ideational schemata and those which service interpersonal knowledge I shall refer to as interpersonal schemata. Our task now is to give some idea of what such schemata might look like and how they are actualized in behaviour on particular occasions, how specific values are associated with schematic variables in instances of use: in short what the activity of 'referring to an appropriate schema' actually involves.

In finding my way towards a clarification of what discourse processing means, then, I have the following sketch map in mind:

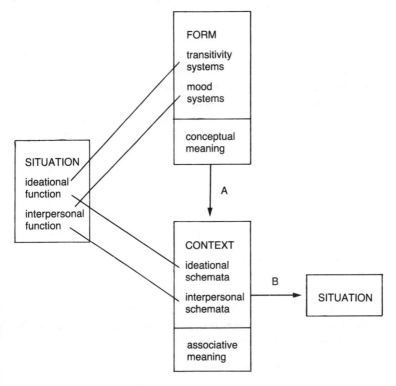

I have taken the Halliday term 'context' to refer to what I have spoken of as functional knowledge of language, language organized in preparation for use. The relationship marked A has to do with the extent to which it is possible to devise text or discourse grammars incorporating presupposition, illocutionary force, and so on; or if the two are to be regarded as separate levels of analysis (as proposed here), what correspondence rules need to be devised to relate them. Our concern in this paper, however, is with the relationship marked B between context and situation, the relationship between internalized schemata and their actualization in particular situations. It is the language user's activity in working out this relationship which creates discourse. Note finally that there is no link between form and situation: sentences have no existence in language use.

Schemata

I take it that one example of a type of ideational schema would be the 'frames' proposed in van Dijk (1977), and another would be what Sacks (1972) refers to as 'membership categorization devices'. Van Dijk first:

> ...a frame is an ORGANIZATIONAL PRINCIPLE relating a number of concepts which by CONVENTION and EXPERI-ENCE somehow form a 'unit' which can be actualized in various cognitive tasks, such as language production and comprehension, perception, action and problem solving. Thus in a RES-TAURANT-frame would be organized and conventional, i.e. general but culture dependent, knowledge that a restaurant is a building or place where one can eat publicly, where food is either ordered from a waiter/waitress or taken at a counter, etc. That is, a frame organizes knowledge about certain properties of objects, courses of event and action, which TYPICALLY belong together ... propositional knowledge from frames is necessary to establish the explicit coherence between sentences of a discourse, under the assumption that propositions belonging to a frame, and hence having a more general nature, need not be expressed in the discourse. This explains among other things that in a sentence like *We went to a restaurant, but the waitress was too busy to take our order immediately*, the noun phrase *the waitress* may be definite although no waitress need have been referred to by previous expressions in the discourse. (van Dijk 1977: 159)

Properties of objects etc. which typically belong together can be accounted for in terms of what Leech refers to as the associative meaning or communicative value of words (Leech 1974: 26–7). This can be distinguished from conceptual meaning, denotation and sense, which has to do with semantic relations within the formal system.[2] We are again in the murky area between form and context but it would seem that Halliday's separation of lexis as a level of linguistic organization within form (Halliday 1961, Halliday, McIntosh, and Strevens 1964) is hard to justify. Patterns of collocation, for example, (see McIntosh 1961, Halliday 1966) reflect typical co-occurrence in use and would appear to be a property of propositional frames, to be accounted for at the level of context.

Of course, the distinction between form and context is not a clearly defined one and, as I have said, the relationship between them is problematic. The formal system must in some way provide for the development of context schemata. The sense relation of hyponymy, for instance, provides for contextual synonymy or what Halliday and Hasan (1976) refer to as reiteration. Here the contextual function is derivable from the formal system in a straightforward way. In other cases the relationship is less evident. Consider the observation made in Sinclair and Coulthard (1975) about the discourse function of past tense, to the effect that utterances like:

Oh sorry—I just wanted to check a few points.
I was just wondering if you could have a look at this.

do not express propositions referring to past time but realize interpersonal meaning in achieving the effect of mitigation. Examples like this lead Sinclair and Coulthard to suggest that certain syntactic features might be transferred from grammar to discourse: that is to say (in the terms of my diagram) be dealt with within context rather than form. Recent work in Roulet (1980) on the linguistic realizations of politeness strategies (of the kind discussed in Brown and Levinson 1978) can also be seen as a demonstration of the context significance of formal items.

There is obviously a good deal of work to be done on the relationship marked A on the diagram. Our concern here, however, is with the relationship marked B. And this, as we shall see, has its own problems.

Van Dijk's concept of the frame is taken over from studies in artificial intelligence. Sacks's similar construct—the membership categorization device—derives from sociology. He points out that when hearing a child's simple story: 'The baby cried. The mummy picked it up', we understand the mummy to be the mummy of the baby, although there is no genitive marker to provide us with the cohesive link. As part of his explanation, Sacks suggests that the category 'baby' can belong to two devices: *family* and *stage of life*, other categories of the former being, for example, mummy and daddy and of the latter being child, adolescent, adult. In van Dijk's terms baby belongs to both the *family* frame and the *stage of life* frame. But now Sacks goes on to spell out what he calls rules of application which will enable the hearer to infer that baby in this case is to be related to the family frame. One such rule (called a hearer's maxim) runs as follows:

> If two or more categories are used to categorize two or more members of some population, and those categories can be heard as categories from the same collection, then: Hear them that way. (Sacks 1972: 333)

Now this would appear to be a knowledge construct of a somewhat different kind from that represented by the frame: it is not related to ideational structures but to the procedures required to infer particular instances of propositional meaning with reference to them. So they have to do with the relationship between context and situation in the diagram in that they serve the executive function of bringing internalized ideational schemata towards actualization, of activating knowledge to generate the discourse process. I will refer to them as procedures or procedural principles. These procedures are seen as mediating between functional knowledge organized for use, of which the frame is an example, and actual communicative behaviour on particular occasions. They are ranged, therefore, on a continuum of increasing specificity to particular situations and decreasing generality. I have preferred the expression procedure to that of strategy in reference to such mediating principles since they have a strategic character at the context end of the continuum but a tactical character at the situation end.

We have, then, something like the following picture:

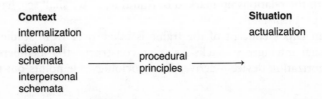

With reference to the ideational schemata associated with collocational patterns, for example, one might suggest a set of general procedures for the receptive processing of written discourse in something like the following way:

1 Focus attention on lexical items.
2 Assume that they are associated with each other in a typical or normal way.
3 If this procedure fails to make sense, shift attention to syntax.

There is some psycholinguistic support for the supposing that something like this goes on in the discourse process. Thus Slobin (1966) observes that 'non-reversible' passives as exemplified by:

The flowers are being watered by the girl.

are more readily understood and remembered than 'reversible' passives like:

The boy was hit by the girl.

The lexical pattern *flowers-water-girl* allows us to infer meaning without recourse to syntax whereas the pattern *boy-hit-girl* does not, since boys are as likely to hit girls as the reverse. Whereas syntax can be considered primary at the level of form, it would appear to have much less significance at the level of context: it seems to be a sort of emergency service to be invoked in cases when normal procedures do not work, when the co-operative principle (see below) proves, for some reason or other, to be unreliable. If this is so, then we need to reconsider the common pedagogic practice of concentrating on syntactic units, using lexical items simply as devices for exemplifying them.

Sacks refers to procedural principles by such terms as 'economy rule', 'relevance rule', and 'consistency rule' and it is apparent that they are, in effect (like my own simple effort given earlier), particular applications from the receiver's viewpoint of the maxims from the producer's viewpoint presented by Grice under the general heading of the 'co-operative principle':

Quantity Make your contribution as informative as possible. Do not be more informative than required.
Quality Do not say what you believe to be false. Do not say that for which you lack adequate evidence.
Relation Be relevant.

Manner   Be perspicuous. Avoid obscurity and ambiguity. Be
           brief, orderly, and polite.
(Grice 1975)

These Gricean maxims are not only engaged, however, in the actualization of ideational schemata. They are also brought into service for actualizing schemata relating to interpersonal knowledge. Examples of interpersonal schemata would be the sets of conditions defining illocutionary acts proposed by Searle (1969), or those specified in Labov (1970).

Both writers subsequently develop procedural principles to account for the way illocutionary meaning is realized in actual instances, rather as Sacks links up his collections with application rules for the realization of propositional meaning. In Labov and Fanshel (1977) for example we find both a *rule of requests*, which is an interpersonal schema, and a *rule for indirect requests*, which is procedural in the sense that it provides guidance as to how the conditions on requesting, internalized as a rule of use, are actualized on particular occasions. The rule of requests appears as follows:

> If A addresses to B an imperative specifying an action X at a time
> T and B believes that A believes that
>> 1a X should be done (for a purpose Y) (*need for the action*)
>> b B would not do X in the absence of the request (*need for the
>>   request*)
>> 2 B has the *ability* to do X (with an instrument Z)
>> 3 B has the *obligation* to do X or is willing to do it
>> 4 A has the *right* to tell B to do X
> then A is heard as making a valid request for action.
> (Labov and Fanshel 1977: 78)

A direct application of this rule yields unambiguous illocutions. There would normally be no problem about the interpretation of the action performed. There may well be a problem of acceptability, however: (B) may believe that (A) believes that a certain condition holds, but may nevertheless wish to challenge the belief as being erroneous:

> A Pick up the suitcase.
> B Who do you think you are? (challenging condition 4)

or

> B What do you think I am, a porter? (challenging condition 3)

It is in order to avoid the danger of confrontation of this kind that language users customarily resort to indirect methods for conveying their illocutionary intent, particularly, of course, when the illocution in question is threatening in some way (see below). In other words, language users draw on certain known procedures for realizing such rules under the normal constraints of social life. One such set of procedures is the Labov and Fanshel rule for indirect requests, which runs as follows:

> If A makes to B a request for information or an assertion to B about
>   a the existential status of an action X to be performed by B
>   b the consequences of performing an action X
>   c the time T_1 that an action X might be performed by B
>   d any of the preconditions for a valid request for X as given in the rule of requests
> and all of the other preconditions are in effect, then A is heard as making a valid request of B for the action X.
> (Labov and Fanshel 1977: 82)

Searle (1975) expresses the same sort of procedural operation in the form of a series of inferential steps.

Factors in the choice of procedure

Such procedural principles provide in general for the possibility of performing what Brown and Levinson (1978) refer to as a face threatening act with redressive action. But we are still some distance from actualization, and more mediating procedures are needed. The question arises, for example, as to which of the features of the situation (a), (b), (c) or (d) should be focused on and whether they should be referred to by assertion, or request for information, for a request for action to be effective on a particular occasion. The formula given above allows for sixteen possible outputs (cf. Labov and Fanshel 1977: 83). What are the situational factors which constrain the choice of one rather than another?

It would seem as if these factors have to do with the protection of what Brown and Levinson refer to as positive and negative face by the redressive action of mitigation. We are concerned here with the basic issue of territoriality. When someone engages in interpersonal behaviour, moves out of his private world, he necessarily invades another person's life space and leaves his own vulnerable to invasion. He needs, therefore, to encroach by stealth so that his interlocutor does not rebuff him, and to do this involves having a care for the self-esteem (positive face) and sense of personal rights (negative face) with which the interlocutor maintains his life space.

Labov and Fanshel deal with these issues in broad terms, whereas Brown and Levinson investigate them in detail. These enquiries are of importance because they lead towards an explicit formulation of factors controlling formality, a notion which has often been exemplified but not explained in previous discussion of language use (cf. Joos 1962, Halliday, McIntosh, and Strevens 1964). For our present purpose, however, we need to make certain general points to indicate the relevance of the matter for discourse processing.

Mitigation and solidarity

Labov and Fanshel point out that 'there are several general principles or tendencies that seem to determine whether a form is mitigating or aggravating' (1977: 84–5) and mention two in particular. The first is that reference to needs and abilities generally mitigates more than reference to rights and obligations and the second is that requests are more mitigating than assertions. We need to enquire into the reasons why this should be so in order to arrive at the underlying principles of procedural activity.

We should note, to begin with, that needs and abilities do not relate to the individual in the same way as do rights and obligations. The individual may need to carry out some action or other and may have the ability to do so without involving others. He cannot exercise a right or submit to an obligation without reference to social structure, without involving others by implication. Thus ability for example carries no implication of converseness: if I am able to do something this does not imply any inability on the part of others. Any one asserting a right, however, implies a converse obligation. Any reference to need or ability expresses a common individual condition: any reference to right or obligation, on the other hand, expresses an awareness of social inequality. The former pair of notions can be said to relate, therefore, to the dimension of solidarity, and the latter to the dimension of power in human relations (see Brown and Gilman 1960). But these dimensions are also evident in the second tendency that Labov and Fanshel mention. Thus a request invites the participation of the interlocutor and so provides for the possibility of solidarity through agreement, whereas an assertion makes no such provision, and an imperative, of course, explicitly denies the possibility and claims a position of power.

What I am suggesting, then, is that procedural principles for achieving illocutionary intentions should include a general instruction to the effect that if you are not certain of your power, as will often be the case, then you should ensure solidarity by appealing to common humanity, common interests, common knowledge, etc.

One advantage of this general principle is that it repairs certain inadequacies in the Labov and Fanshel account of mitigation procedures. They suggest that requests for information are more mitigating than assertions, with tag-questions coming in between. With regard to the linguistic form used, therefore, we have the following scale of increasing mitigation or, equivalently, decreasing aggravation:

Imperative	Dust the room!
Declarative	You will dust the room.
Tag-question	You will dust the room, won't you?
Interrogative	Will you dust the room?

However, this scale is not a reliable predictor of the relative mitigating effect of such forms of discourse. There are two further factors to consider.

Mitigating elements in the utterance

First, these forms can be accompanied by other elements in the utterance which can modify their effect. Intonation is the most obvious of these (see Brazil, Coulthard, and Johns 1980). Thus the imperative can be expressed in such a way as to approximate towards an appeal for co-operation, thereby shifting from the power to the solidarity dimension. Such shifts will often be supported by other devices for expressing solidarity, including the use of different forms of address. Consider the following:

Darling, dust the room!
Be a darling and dust the room!
Henry, be a darling and dust the room!
Dust the room, there's a dear!
and so on.

It seems clear that the whole question of the power and solidarity function of different terms of address is relevant here. Ervin Tripp has devised an algorithmic diagram of such rules of address (as operative in the U.S.A.) but is quick to point out that:

The diagram is not intended as a model of a process, of the actual decision sequence by which a speaker chooses a form of address, or a listener interprets one ... the task of determining the structure implicit in people's report of what forms of address are possible and appropriate is clearly distinct from the task of studying how people, in real situations and in real time, make choices. (Ervin Tripp 1972: 219–20)

That is to say, in the terms I have been using in this paper, Ervin Tripp's rules are intended as a type of interpersonal schema— formal items tagged with a functional label of contextual appropriacy. The question now is: under what conditions are particular forms actualized? Brown and Levinson point to their relevance in achieving positive politeness. One of the strategies they mention runs as follows:

Use in-group identity markers.
By using any of the innumerable ways to convey in-group membership, S (the speaker) can implicitly claim that common ground with H (the hearer) is carried by that definition of the group. These include in-group usages of address forms, of language or dialect, of jargon or slang, and of ellipsis. (Brown and Levinson 1978: 112)

Other strategies they mention are: (1) Notice, attend to H (his interests, wants, needs, goods), (2) Exaggerate (interest, approval, sympathy with H), (3) Intensify interest to H, and so on. These procedural principles indicate that there are very many more devices available for mitigation (and aggravation) than Labov and Fanshel seem to suggest. The question arises as to what more refined procedures can be specified which will bring us closer to actualization on particular occasions. When does one use strategy (1) rather than strategy (2) or (3) or (4)? Or are they in free variation across all contexts of use? I will return to such questions presently. Meanwhile we have to consider the second factor that makes the Labov and Fanshel scale of mitigation unreliable.

Preparatory and reparatory negotiation

The first factor not sufficiently considered by Labov and Fanshel, then, has to do with other elements within the utterance which can modify the 'standard' effect of a particular structure either to make it more mitigating or more aggravating. In general, I am suggesting that any device which appeals to solidarity will have a mitigating effect, and any device which denies solidarity will tend to aggravate, with the tendency increasing to the extent that such a denial openly invokes the power dimension.

The second factor to be considered has to do with the contextual location of the expressions concerned. Labov and Fanshel, rather curiously, seem to imply that certain degrees of mitigation are carried by expressions themselves and are unaffected by how they function in the discourse process. But it is surely unusual for illocutionary intent to be incorporated within a single utterance without preparing the ground, particularly of course in cases of face threatening acts. So it is that some utterances are more likely to function as preparation for the performance of an act and some as confirmation that the act has been performed. Thus an utterance of the form:

This room needs dusting.

is essentially preparatory, since it refers to one of the conditions that have to be established for a request for action to be valid (Searle does indeed refer to such conditions as preparatory conditions). But if all other conditions obtain by virtue of the situation, the utterance can, of course, be heard as a request. On the other hand, an utterance like:

You will dust the room, won't you?

can hardly be preparatory. It will generally carry the implication that the request for action has already been performed and so it serves as a confirmation or reminder. Whereas preparatory utterances seek to establish agreement on the existence of pre-requisite conditions for a particular act, confirmatory utterances seek to consolidate agreement that a particular act has been performed. The latter have the character of what the ethnomethodologists refer to as formulations (Garfinkel and Sacks 1970, Heritage and Watson 1979).

I will return to formulations presently. Meanwhile, however, we have to relate preparatory utterances to the more general discourse function of negotiation. I said that utterances of this kind are used to establish that the requisite conditions obtain for a particular act to be effectively performed. But the speaker does not only prepare the ground, he has to keep it under constant supervision and monitored to maintain its common character as the discourse progresses. Negotiation, therefore, involves preparation and reparation. Reparatory utterances are required to correct the course of an interaction, to clarify misunderstandings, to counter unforeseen reactions, and so on.

Negotiation, then, involves the establishment and maintenance of conditions which will facilitate the achievement of communicative purpose. Preparatory and reparatory utterances are used to ensure that the receiver is receptive to the information and intention that the speaker seeks to convey. They are, in other words, devices for achieving agreement, for establishing solidarity with respect to a particular piece of social business. Sometimes, of course, agreement will be a relatively straightforward matter—when interlocutors have a common world knowledge, common interests, and so on— but sometimes it will require protracted negotiation. It is the negotiation required to achieve agreement that provides the dynamic of discourse development. In this view, then, discourse is the use of language to achieve accord so that individual worlds can converge for some communicative purpose.

In the achieving of agreement, it would appear that a very general rule applies: the greater the imposition on the interlocutor, the more negotiation will be needed. The kind of imposition will vary: it may relate to the magnitude of the task the producer commits himself to or the receiver is required to carry out; it may relate to the potential threat to face or peace of mind, or to the strain on credulity.

Negotiation in written discourse

In written discourse, it would seem that preparatory utterances are generally less concerned with the protection of face and more concerned with engaging interest and establishing common frames of reference. This, of course, is not surprising, since written discourse is of its nature removed from the immediacy of reciprocal exchange. The writer conducts a simulated interaction and is not involved in an actual confrontation: he does not threaten to invade an individual's territory and his own is not vulnerable to attack in the course of the engagement. Often, in fact, his main problem is not to avoid casualties but to provoke a confrontation. So it is that we get openings like:

Men must organize.
(The first statement in the first chapter of a book[3])

Such a curt categorical assertion invites an immediate retaliation ('Why? What makes you so dogmatic?') and the writer is ready with a supporting statement which will repair the dissension he has deliberately provoked:

In order to obtain food and shelter, to guard against periods of shortage or misfortune, and to propagate their own kind, men are obliged to co-operate with their fellows.

In effect, what the writer does is to stimulate engagement with an assertion and then provide reparatory utterances which seek to convert it into a statement which the reader will accept. Another instance:

> India was one of the best governed countries in the world. Persons and property were safe. Thought and speech were more secure than in recent times. There was effective action to arrest famine and improve communications.[4]

Negotiation and formulation

The obvious disadvantage of preparatory utterances from the receiver's point of view (particularly in spoken discourse which has to be processed in flight) is that they may leave him uncertain about the producer's main point or purpose. Sometimes, of course, he will recognize the drift of the preparatory remarks and draw a conclusion before the producer is required to be explicit. On other occasions, the point or purpose will need to be drawn out from the negotiation in the form of a summary or recapitulation. This is where formulations come in. Whereas preparations lead to elaboration in the interests of interpersonal agreement, formulations lead to a reduction of the message to its basic essentials. The procedure is described by Garfinkel and Sacks as follows:

> A member may treat some part of the conversation as an occasion to describe that conversation, to explain it, or characterize it, or explicate, or translate, or summarize, or furnish the gist of it, or take note of its accordance with the rules, or remark on its departure from rules. That is to say, a member may use some part of the conversation as an occasion to *formulate* the conversation. (Garfinkel and Sacks 1970: 350)

Heritage and Watson (1979) distinguish two types of formulation: gists and upshots. The former are utterances which summarize and the latter those which draw a conclusion. Heritage and Watson offer the following extract from a face-to-face interview with the 'Slimmer of the Year' as an example of a gist formulation:

Slimmer   You have a shell that for so long protects you but sometimes things creep through the shell and then you become really aware of how awful you feel. I never ever felt my age or looked my age I was always older—people took me for older. And when I was at college I think I looked a matronly fifty.

And I was completely alone one weekend and I got
to this stage where I almost jumped in the river. I
just felt life wasn't worth it any more—it hadn't
anything to offer and if this was living I had had
enough.

Interviewer   You really were prepared to commit suicide because you were a big fatty...

(Heritage and Watson 1979: 132)

In this case, it is the receiver who produces the gist formulation as a
summary of the producer's single contribution, but it is easy to see
that the producer can himself formulate a gist and that such
formulations, from either interlocutor, can be introduced at any
point in a negotiation where either feels the need to establish
agreement. Typical linguistic markers of such formulations are *in
other words, in short, that is to say*.

As an example of an upshot formulation Heritage and Watson
give the following extract from a telephone interview with Conor
Cruse O'Brien:

O'Brien   The Dublin government is extremely concerned
er—especially about the growth in political sec-
tarian murders er—in Northern Ireland and the
er—government is anxious that all possible steps
er—be taken and to try to control this situation we
realize the extreme difficulty er—in doing it and
the government is prepared er—to co-operate in
every way in the er—pulling down of the various
violent er—organizations and gangs which exist on
both sides of the border.

Interviewer   You'd support Mr. Rees if he decided on er—
tougher security than he is instituting at present...

O'Brien   In general, yes.

(Heritage and Watson 1979: 135–6)

Again, it is obvious that upshots can be formulated by either
interlocutor in the course of a conversation when either feels the
need to draw a conclusion. There is one difference between gists
and upshots, however, that needs to be noted: it is that gists relate
to propositional meaning only, whereas upshots can also draw
conclusions about illocutionary intent. If the interviewer in the first
extract, for instance, had come out with a remark like:

> Interviewer   You confess that you really were prepared to commit suicide because you were a big fatty.

then this would have constituted an upshot formulation, since he would have drawn conclusions from the slimmer's remarks about their illocutionary character. If in the second extract, the interviewer had said:

> Interviewer   You undertake to support Mr. Rees if he decided on er—tougher security than he is instituting at present.

then this would have constituted a formulation of both propositional and illocutionary upshot. Typical linguistic markers of upshots are *thus, therefore, so*.

In written discourse, formulations seem to correspond to what rhetoricians have referred to as the 'topic sentence' of a paragraph. This can appear as an opening utterance (i.e. an orthographic 'sentence'), of course, and in this case the utterances which follow are reparatory in the sense I have been using the term: they provide for the conveyancing of the main point by acting upon the reader's knowledge and attitude. The varying placement of the topic sentence can be explained by reference to the writer's judgement as to whether and to what extent the reader needs to have the ground prepared, already has an open mind to what is to be said and so on.

At this stage it would seem appropriate for me to produce a formulation of the preceding discussion. The kind of procedural principles proposed by Labov and Fanshel do not seem to account for the negotiating procedures of a more tactical sort which are employed by language users whereby they achieve the general strategic objective of agreement, a convergence of ideational and interpersonal knowledge which will ensure the conveyance of information and intention. This, I have suggested, involves the appeal to solidarity in the selection of certain vocative expressions, the invocation of common attitude and interest and so on within the individual utterance, and the use of utterances to negotiate the grounds for such commonality and to focus on what is to be conveyed by formulation.

Two issues arise from the foregoing discussion. One concerns descriptive possibility: how far is the tactical manoeuvering I have referred to subject to specification in terms of procedural principle? There presumably comes a point of diminishing returns when it becomes self-defeating to try to account for the multifarious factors controlling actualization. The second question concerns pedagogic relevance. It does not follow that a more precise description necessarily will have greater pedagogic applicability then a more general one. Validity and utility of description have different conditions to meet. What their relationship is is a matter for applied linguistics to determine.

4   The descriptive issue

I have pointed out the gap between certain procedural principles and the business of actualization in particular instances. How far can one bridge the gap by specifying more tactical procedures relating to particular situations? In respect of ideational meaning, for example, Clark and Haviland (1977) point out how the general Gricean maxims are invoked in what they call the 'given-new contract'. They express this as follows:

> Try to construct the given and the new information of each utterance in context (a) so that the listener is able to compute from memory the unique antecedent that was intended for the given information, and (b) so that he will not already have the new information attached to that antecedent. (Clark and Haviland 1977: 9)

Such a procedural principle has, they say, to meet three requirements: appropriateness, uniqueness, and computability. These are readily met when given information has one and only one direct antecedent. But quite commonly, this is not the case. The speaker, or writer, chooses not to refer to direct antecedents. So under what circumstances does he choose to be indirect, to rely on conversational implicature? And having so decided, what constraints operate so that an appropriate, unique and computable relation is established by the choice of one cohesive device rather than another? Halliday and Hasan (1976) provide an exhaustive account of all such devices available in English, but which makes the most satisfactory 'cohesive tie' in a particular instance? Is there, for example, a procedure which goes roughly as follows:

If a second referent is brought in and intervenes between given information and its antecedent, express given information by a form which provides minimal differentiation between the competing antecedents.

What else controls the variation in the semantic content of 'proforms' so that propositional meaning is carried over from utterance to utterance? If there is no intervening referent which might interfere with the recovery of the given information, can one count on minimal reference being enough, no matter how attenuated the referential range might be? Is it not the case that referential identity has to be re-established by relexicalization to counter memory limitations? These and many other questions come to mind as warranting investigation in the hope that we might extend a range of procedures to the very verge of actualization. There is here plenty of scope for further research. The problem is to know when to stop: when the specification has to take so many conditional constraints into account that it gets lost in its own specificity.

The same observations may be made of procedural principles which are referred to in the actualization of illocutions. I have noted how Brown and Levinson's account extends what Labov and Fanshel have to say about mitigation and aggravation. But one can see how the account might be extended further. Consider the strategy relating to the use of address forms conveying ingroup membership. Brown and Levinson offer the following:

> honey.
> Bring me your dirty clothes to wash, darling.
> Johnny.

Even assuming that these address forms are in free variation as far as their mitigation value is concerned, one wonders whether their effect varies according to their position in the utterance. Do they function in exactly the same way if they appear initially?

Darling, bring me your dirty clothes to wash.

In the terms I have used earlier, initial position has a preparatory effect, whereas terminal position has a reparatory effect. Is it, then, another politeness strategy to be related to all the others that Brown and Levinson discuss? And if we take this and other additional features into account do we not simply sacrifice insightful generality at the strategic level in the quest for tactics which will bring us to a closer approximation to actualization?

One way of controlling detail of description is, of course, to invoke the notion of usefulness, in effect bringing in the principle of utility to define the scope of analysis (cf. Halliday 1964). The question then becomes: how detailed a description do we need of the procedures that are used in discourse processing in order to develop in our learners an ability to employ such strategies in using the language they are learning?

5   The pedagogic issue

Learners of a foreign language are already practised users of language and know how to apply procedures for discourse processing. What they do not know is the extent to which these procedures are also applicable in dealing with the foreign language, and what linguistic forms are used in their actualization. Conventionally it has been the latter area of ignorance which has been the focus of attention, on the assumption that once such forms are learnt, the learner will find out how to use them for himself. But if they are taught in isolation from their discourse function, the learner is presented with a model of language which does not correspond with acquisition or use and which cannot easily be associated with his own experience as a natural language user. In these circumstances the learner is denied access to his knowledge of how discourse works and is prevented from engaging in the learning process.

What seems to be needed (as suggested in Section 2 of this paper) is an approach to presentation which will encourage the learner to act on his knowledge. The question arises, of course, as to how far discourse procedures are universal and so transferable across cultures. Ethnographers have, as yet, provided no definite answer (compare, for example, Brown and Levinson 1978 and Ochs Keenan 1976). It seems a reasonable supposition, however, that the more specific the description of procedural principles is, the more involved does it become in the cultural differentiation between social groups: they in effect deal in increasing detail with particular ritual constraints on behaviour (Goffman 1976). For example, there are, as we have seen, certain general considerations that have to be taken into account in conducting a conversation which, as Brown and Levinson suggest, might be regarded as of universal application, as necessary conditions, indeed, for any social interaction to take place. One such consideration has to do with the managing of the initial invasion of privacy so that some kind of solidarity is achieved. The more particular procedures which are called upon to achieve this in telephone conversations, however, may differ quite widely even across cultures which in other respects might be regarded as quite closely allied, and which might indeed share the same language (cf. Schegloff 1972b; Godard 1977).

There will be occasions when it will be desirable to draw the attention of learners to the more specific and tactical procedures associated with particular situations. In the case just given, for example, an ESP course for hotel receptionists or travel agency staff would presumably wish to include instruction on correct comportment on the telephone. In general courses, too, which are meant to prepare learners for actual encounters with native speakers, it can be pointed out what can go wrong when the customary rituals are not observed, and here there is an opportunity of integrating cultural studies of the 'life and institutions' kind into a practical language programme. But learners cannot be pre-programmed for every possible situational eventuality. They need to know how to use the more strategic procedures for interaction so that they have the means of learning the more specific constraints on actualization as and when they feel that an adaptation to other cultural patterns of behaviour is called for. We cannot provide the learner with detailed scripts to follow: we can only give him a set of guidelines which will help him learn the parts he has to play.

But how is this to be done? I think we need to reverse the conventional direction of dependency in the presentation of language: instead of focusing attention on language items (whether these are conceived of in structural or notional terms) and then devising activities contingently to facilitate their acquisition, we might think primarily of activities which call for a contingent use of language and which necessarily involve the engagement of the sort of procedures discussed in this paper. Such activities would pose problems and would not, as is commonly the case with current pedagogy, provide solutions. Where one has language-dependent activities, the language is seen as the problem and the activities are used to solve it: where one has activity-dependent language, the reverse is the case.

The task for pedagogy in this view is to devise problems which will require learners to engage discourse procedures in some principled way so that they acquire language for use in the very learning process. Whether such problems would be brought in to effect the reversal of dependency after the first stage of course design has established a basic structural ordering, or whether the nature of the problems may itself provide a principle of sequential arrangement is an open question. There is at least a possibility, which is worth exploring, that problems might be organized along a dependency scale analogous to the scale of increasing complexity reflected in a structural syllabus. The methodologies of other school subjects would seem to presuppose such a scale, although curriculum studies do not seem to have given it explicit recognition, and these methodologies would appear to be a promising place to begin enquiries. And other school subjects, of course, deal in activity-dependent language. If such a scale could be established, it could provide for the development of language acquisition and use by procedures associated with a controlled exposure to language items and with their systematic but motivated repetition.

Notes

This is a revised version of a paper commissioned by the Council of Europe and written in April 1981.

1   There is, in the literature, a bewildering number of names used to refer to these mental structures: e.g. plans, frames, scripts, schemata. For an attempt to give some conceptual warrant for this terminological variety see de Beaugrande and Dressler (1981: Chapter 5, Section 16) and de Beaugrande (1980: Chapter 6). I have preferred the term schema (and the plural schemata) on the grounds that it seems to be the most neutral and also the most traditional (see Bartlett 1932).

2   One can express the difference between conceptual and associative meaning by making a distinction between the linguistic sign as *symbol* and the linguistic sign as *index*. The symbol, as the unit of analysis, denotes category types and contracts sense relations with other symbols as terms in linguistic systems. Its meaning, therefore, is self-contained and invariant. The index, as the unit of language use, directs the user's attention to a particular schema. It is, therefore, essentially referential and does not signal meanings by its own form but points to where meaning is to be discovered by interpretative effort. In this respect, the symbol is the systemic sign and the index the schematic one.

3   Extract from Banton (1965).

4   Extract from Galbraith (1977).

9   Types of linguistic sign in texts

In this paper I want to try to get at an understanding of what is involved in the use of language in texts by reconsidering the nature of the linguistic sign. And I want also to try to draw out what implications such an understanding might have for language teaching pedagogy.

My first move is to ask the basic question: What *is* a text? De Beaugrande and Dressler in their recent *Introduction to Text Linguistics* (de Beaugrande and Dressler 1981) define it as a 'communicative occurrence'. But I do not see that it can be an occurrence since it has no dynamism of its own but can only be activated by human agency. It does not itself communicate but provides the means whereby communication can be achieved. Indeed, de Beaugrande and Dressler would, in spite of their definition, appear to agree, since they point out that of the seven constitutive conditions of textual communication (viz.: cohesion, coherence, intentionality, acceptability, informativity, situationality, intertextuality) five are user centred and have to do not with the text itself but with its use in interaction. Texts, I would suggest then, do not communicate: people communicate by using texts as a device for mediating a discourse process. It is this process which is the communicative occurrence. Texts as such are simply a static configuration of linguistic signs which have to be interpreted in a particular way if they are to serve their mediating purpose.

This may seem like a quibble. But it seems to me that if this point is not made clear, there is a danger that we might suppose that text signals its own meaning, like the sentence. Certainly in language teaching there has been a tendency to make this supposition. Learners have been led to believe that there is a complete and single meaning in reading passages immanent in the language itself and recoverable by a close scrutiny of the text, and recourse to the dictionary where necessary.

Texts do not signal their own meaning as sentences do. But why not? They apparently use the same set of linguistic signs. Here, for example, are three sentences extracted from a text:

Popular colours were white and green.
They don't seem to care for the taste.
Mahogany was still expensive.

Presented like this with three separate sentences, you have no difficulty assigning meaning to each by simply engaging a knowledge of the syntax and semantics of English. You know what the word *colour* denotes and you know that it has a superordinate sense relation to the two hyponyms *white* and *green*. You know that past tense denotes past time and that it contracts a sense relation with other terms in the tense system of English, so you know that:

Popular colours were white and green.

has a different meaning from:

Popular colours *are* white and green.

And so with the other sentences. *They* denotes plural entities and is a term in the pronoun system, thereby contrasting in sense with *you, we, I*. You know the denotation of the lexemes *care for, taste*, and so on. So you have no difficulty with the meaning of:

They don't seem to care for the taste.

You know then what each of these sentences means as a combination of linguistic signs and you could produce a German translation if called upon to do so. So the meaning of these sentences is not a matter of dispute: it can be assigned quite simply by invoking a knowledge of the language system of English. And that meaning will, of its nature, be complete and fixed: it admits of no variation. But now suppose that I present these expressions to you not as sentences but as elements of text, as utterances, intending to mediate a common understanding between us. In this case, although you may quite legitimately claim that you know what the sentences mean, you do not have the slightest idea what I am talking about.

Popular colours were white and green.

Popular with whom, when exactly, and colours of what—paint, flowers, socks: it could be almost anything. Obviously in offering you this textual fragment I am failing dismally to conform to the Gricean co-operative principle (Grice 1975). My remark is uninformative and irrelevant. And the same of course is true of the other expressions. The textual elements fail to mediate. There is no communicative occurrence. Since the expressions could mean almost anything, they are virtually meaningless.

And yet the signs and their manner of combination would appear to be identical, in each case, whether they are construed as sentence or utterance. But appearances are deceptive. It is obvious that the linguistic sign in the sentence has a quite different mode of meaning from that in the text. Indeed, I want to suggest that it is a different kind of sign. In the sentence, the sign is a *symbol* which by virtue of its place as a term in the linguistic system contracts internal sense relations with other symbols and relates to the external world by the denotation of abstract types, or general classes of entities. In the text, on the other hand, the sign has to be interpreted as what I will call an *index* (cf. Lyons 1977b: 99–109). Its function is to indicate or point to where meaning is to be found beyond itself, and this meaning is achieved by the language user in following the directions which are indicated. Symbolic meaning is *virtual* and the concern of semantics. Indexical meaning is *actual* and the concern of pragmatics (cf. Cicourel on 'Indexical Expressions' in Cicourel 1973: 56, 87–8).

The receiver of a text, then, uses the sign as an index to refer him to areas of his own non-linguistic knowledge which may have been acquired before his encounter with the text or in the course of processing it. The sender of the text has the task of calculating how much information he needs to provide so that it meets the indexical needs of his interlocutor. If he provides too much, he will be accused of prolixity ('Yes, yes, I know; all right, I've got the point'). If he provides too little he will be accused of obscurity or even deliberate obfuscation ('What are you on about? I'm sorry, I don't quite follow ...').

In reciprocal discourse, as in conversation, interlocutors can, of course, overtly negotiate the convergence of knowledge to achieve the congruence of intention and interpretation necessary for the purpose of their interaction. In non-reciprocal discourse, however, in which readers and writers are engaged, or, for that matter, in which speakers address an attentive audience, the sole begetter of the text has to continually shift his perspective, take turns on behalf of his interlocutors and anticipate reaction, make assumptions about shared knowledge. This kind of vicarious discourse enactment is a tricky business. Life, however, is easier for the receiver of non-reciprocal discourse than for the interlocutor in reciprocal discourse because he is involved by engagement without participation. Not being responsible for textualizing the discourse, he can control the extent of this engagement in relation to his purpose or his interest. He can, if he wishes, skim the page, or switch off his attention to what the lecturer is saying and think of other things, or even go to sleep.

I shall return to this matter of participation and engagement a little later. For the moment I want to dwell a little on the question of knowledge, that elusive abstraction which passes between interlocutors through the mediation of the text. To avoid getting into the tangles of epistemology, we may cut a Gordian knot or two and say that knowledge is a set of cognitive constructs derived from experience, abstracted from particular instances. Its most obvious embodiment is the system of symbols in natural language and the rules for their combination. The linguistic symbol represents an abstract category of actual and particular instances. So it is that you know what a sentence means as an isolated string of symbols. But I want to suggest that knowledge also operates to organize experience at another and less analytic level, at the level of context as well as code, of the schema as well as the system. Consider, for example, this expression, presented this time as an utterance, an extract of text:

She does not take care of her nails.

We assume that what are being referred to here are *finger*nails. But why should we make such an assumption? Why does the expression not invoke with equal force the image of a female carpenter being reproached for not looking after the tools of her trade? There is nothing whatever in our systemic knowledge of symbolic meanings which constrains us to prefer the first interpretation rather than the second. So why do we associate nails with fingers and not with hammers in this expression?

We do so because we interpret the signs as being indexical of what we know to be a normal frame of reference. In our society, though not necessarily in others, female carpenters are uncommon, and so although there is nothing intrinsically wrong with the concept, it just does not enter into our customary scheme of things. It is this awareness of what is customary that I refer to as contextual or schematic knowledge: the knowledge we have of the accepted attitudes, beliefs, and practices which define what is normal, established, conventional, what are the standard patterns of experience. When we interpret a text we do so by recognizing that the linguistic signs are indexical of a particular pattern, a particular schema. So to understand the utterances in texts, to realize meaning in language use, we need to engage schematic as well as systemic knowledge. It is not enough to know the general symbolic meaning of signs, we need to discover their particular indexical meaning as well in actual contexts of occurrence. The interpretation of text is a matter of taking bearings from both systemic and schematic knowledge so as to achieve the indexical value of the signs.

With this in mind, let us return to the three expressions that I quoted earlier. Restored to its context, the first now appears as follows:

> Quite a lot of furniture was completely painted. Popular colours were white and green, picked out in gold. Adam's earlier style also included pieces elaborately carved and gilded all over.

The frame of reference is established as that of antique furniture. We are now able to realize the indexical value of *colours* as having reference to paint. We may not have sufficient schematic knowledge of antique furniture to be able to realize a specific indexical value for the past tense, but for those who do have such knowledge the reference to Adam would afford the necessary indication. Notice, too, that we can assign an appropriate indexical value to the word *pieces* as referring to pieces of furniture rather than, let us say, to pieces of sculpture or music.

The other expressions I cited earlier come from the same passage and we can make indexical sense of them in a similar way by relating them to the frame of reference projected by the text. In the case of the third expression, the association is straightforward:

> Mahogany was still expensive.

And contextualization now does enable us to realize the time reference. The passage continues as follows:

> Beech was the wood most usually used for furniture intended to be entirely coated with paint or gilt. It was also used as a cheaper substitute for satinwood, especially for legs. It is a good, close-grained timber, but very prone to attack by woodworm. In the late eighteenth and early nineteenth centuries, it was general practice to construct the frame of chair seats in beech and veneer them with mahogany. Mahogany was still expensive, although the heavy duty formerly imposed on its importation had been mitigated in 1747.

But what now of the third expression:

They don't seem to care for the taste.

It is not easy to imagine how this might fit into the schematic frame that the passage develops. And yet it does with no difficulty, as follows:

> This economizing on seat frames (i.e. making them of beech rather than mahogany) has had unfortunate results for us today. Mahogany is not much liked by woodworm. They don't seem to care for the taste, preferring a savoury morsel of walnut, elm, oak, pine, or beech.[1]

So what I am trying to demonstrate is the way that the writer exploits systemic knowledge, which he assumes to be shared by his supposed interlocutor, to project his schematic knowledge into text. He thereby converts linguistic symbols of fixed denotation into indices whose appropriate reference the reader has to realize in order to recreate the schemata in question. The writer assumes that there will be common ground to build upon, that the reader he has in mind will have some schematic knowledge of the furniture frame of reference, and will co-operate in the approved Gricean fashion by engaging it. The purpose of the interaction thus mediated through the text is to extend or elaborate this frame by bringing reader and writer knowledge into convergence.

The model of the communication process that I am trying to construct, then, looks like this. Interlocutors inhabit different individual worlds of knowledge and experience, but there are elements in common which provide the means of connection. One set of such shared elements is the language system and another is the collection of cultural patterns of normal practice and thought, what I have referred to as schematic knowledge. Communication is achieved when these elements are exploited to bring the different worlds into convergence, thus, for the interlocutors, extending the common ground of shared knowledge. This convergence is brought about by means of indexical realization whereby the language user computes the meaning of signs in texts by taking bearings on systemic and schematic knowledge. This taking of bearings is what the ethnomethodologists refer to as interpretative procedures (see Cicourel 1973). These procedures essentially involve the conversion of symbols into indices. If they are not engaged, then the text does not mediate and no communication takes place.

I want to turn now to pedagogic matters. I assume that to learn a language, in the sense of learning how to *use* a language effectively for purposes of communication, must entail the ability to use texts to mediate a transfer of information in the way I have outlined. This information may be essentially ideational in character and have to do with the propositional content, it may be essentially interpersonal and have to do with illocutionary intent. But in both cases, the conveyance of information brings about a change of state whereby two worlds of knowledge in varying degrees of correspondence are brought into whatever state of convergence is required of the interlocutors. I have argued that for this process of conveyance and convergence to take place, the interlocutors need to engage interpretative procedures whereby they plot meaning, as it were, by taking bearings on both systemic and schematic knowledge. The question now arises as to what kinds of texts are most likely to promote this necessary procedural ability in the learners.

First let us note, as I indicated earlier, that although all text is the trace of discourse interactivity, this interactivity may be realized overtly and reciprocally, as in face to face interaction where meanings can be jointly negotiated and where text is produced by direct participation; or interactivity may have to be realized covertly and non-reciprocally, where one interlocutor is in charge of constructing the text and the other is engaged as a non-participant, having to react, as it were, without responding and without being able to influence the development of the discourse. Let us call texts which are the immediate by-product of reciprocal interaction *participant* texts and those which call for non-reciprocal engagement *non-participant* texts.

The creation of participant texts in the classroom is not at all easy to achieve and we should be wary of counterfeits. The provision of formally appropriate responses to given cues, for example, does not produce text in the sense I have been using this term. In an exercise in a textbook currently in use in Germany, for example, learners are asked to study what are described as 'short conversations' and then to make up similar so-called conversations of their own. Examples:

Is the oil polluting the river now?
Yes, it is. It pollutes it all the time.

Is the government inspector visiting the factory now?
No, he isn't. He doesn't often visit the factory.

The activity here is directed at the teaching of systemic knowledge and not at the procedural exploitation of such knowledge to achieve meaning through text. These are pairs of spoken sentences and not conversation. Again, the familiar specimen dialogue associated with situations like the theatre, the post office, the railway station will generally be pseudo-text to the extent that it is non-negotiable. The learners are provided with ready-made correlations between system and schema so that no procedural work is required to achieve indexical value. In neither case do learners take any part in a discourse process so they make no contribution to a developing text: they simply follow a pseudo-textual script prepared in advance. This is not to say that sentence-pairs and specimen dialogues do not have a role to play in the teaching of language. Clearly they do, and an important one at that. But they do not constitute participant text. They do not involve the learner in the negotiation of indexical meaning. Nor do they involve him in what we might call the discourse management aspects of reciprocal interaction, in the recognition and use of linguistic signs not as indices of meaning but as *signals* of interactive function, which indicate that the interlocutor is bidding for a turn at talk, or shifting to another topic, or closing his contribution, and so on. So although exercises with pseudo-texts have their value in teaching language system, learners need to be involved in other activities as well as these, which will afford them the opportunity to participate in realizing the system as a communicative resource, and so to learn the use of indices in interpretation and signals in interaction. Such activities are difficult to devise because they have to create situations which call for negotiated settlement and which are based on some purpose which the learners will accept as worthwhile and warranting the interactive effort. The activities are, of course, intended to have a language learning *effect*, and it will often be necessary to ensure that they do by tactful teaching, but their *purpose* must carry conviction in its own right independently of this effect. Not otherwise is the learner likely to negotiate a satisfactory outcome through participant text.

The question of purpose arises too, of course, with non-participant text, but there it creates a problem of a rather different order. The text that results from reciprocal exchanges is, as I have said, jointly produced as a concomitant output from the discourse process itself. It is a co-operative enterprise which naturally constrains the interlocutors towards a common purpose. They do not always find it easy of course: they may indeed find themselves, as we say, at *cross* purposes. If they do they may try to repair the fault or if that fails they may make a schematic shift to another frame of reference where convergence is easier to achieve. So interlocutors may give up their discussion on existentialism or God and talk instead about the weather. If we find ourselves 'worlds apart' or 'not talking the same language' or 'not getting our message across'—all expressions which refer to the failure to meet the participant purpose of what Cicourel calls 'reciprocity of perspectives'—then in this event, we withdraw from this particular interaction and go and find somebody else to talk to.

Now in non-reciprocal interaction the text is entirely controlled by one interlocutor. He has his own purposes and he proceeds on the assumption that his addressee will accept them as his own. This enables him to enact a covert discourse, taking on the role of the addressee vicariously by a kind of unauthorized proxy, and supposing that the addressee will co-operate on his terms, and match interpretation with intention. But since non-participant text does not require co-operation in its production, it cannot compel us to co-operate in its reception. We engage with it on our own terms. If we choose to be submissive, then we can indeed fall in with the text producer's plans, and allow his purpose to prevail. But we may choose to be assertive and to impose our own purpose on the text, drawing out from it what want or need, and skimming over the rest. One can of course vary attention in this way during participation as well, one can 'switch off' during a conversation, but then control of the interaction is diminished. But with varying attention in the engagement with non-participant text, control is increased.

Now I want to suggest that the difference between submissive and assertive engagement can be related to Piaget's distinction between accommodation and assimilation (e.g. Piaget 1952). Submission typically occurs when there is considerable disparity between the schematic knowledge of the interlocutors and when the addressee is impelled for one reason or another to modify the structure of his knowledge so as to accommodate that of the text producer. Convergence is then, as it were, addresser controlled and its achievement naturally makes particular demands on what I have called the procedural ability to realize indexical meaning. Assertion, on the other hand, typically occurs when there is considerable overlap between initial states of schematic knowledge, so that new information can be readily assimilated into the receiver's existing conceptual categories. Convergence then is addressee controlled, and its achievement calls for less exertion of the procedural ability.

This is, no doubt, too neat, too simple, an altogether too

speculative scheme, but let me presume on your submissive engagement with my present text and point out that what I have said, if valid, creates a pedagogic dilemma in the use of texts for teaching language.

Most of our processing of non-participant text is, I would suppose, of an assertive kind. We generally read, for example, about things we are familiar with and what is prepared for us by the agents of mass media is designed to be easy to assimilate into our customary categories of reality, easy to fit into the slots of our schematic knowledge. So if we want learners to approximate to normal or 'authentic' behaviour in their use of a foreign language, we should presumably encourage them to process text assertively. But then if they do they will not be effectively using text to develop their procedural ability, which is, paradoxically, most actively engaged by submission, when the text records information which is not familiar and which has to be interpreted by schematic accommodation. If, however, one then chooses texts which are schematically remote from the learners' knowledge, on the grounds that they will encourage the learning of procedures, one runs the serious risk of undermining motivation since such texts will tend not to relate to the learners' interests or practical concerns.

This dilemma must be faced up to in any discussion about the use of texts in language teaching: indeed, I think it lies at the very heart of language teaching pedagogy in general. It cannot be simply solved, as some people would seem to imply, by appeal to the notion of authenticity. Certainly *I* cannot claim to have found a solution. But what I would like to do, still counting on your submission, is to let loose a hare which I think might just be worth chasing.

There is a kind of text, of an intrinsically non-participant kind, which its producer uses to create schemata which are not intended to be conceptual structures of conventional reality and cannot therefore in principle be conveyed intact to the receiver but must always be subject to some interpretative accommodation. I refer to literary texts, and in particular to lyric poetry. Here the linguistic signs do not strictly speaking refer, since there is no established schema to refer to. Rather they represent a unique patterning of reality and take on the character of yet another kind of sign: the *icon*. The mode of meaning in literature is, I think, essentially not one of indexical reference but of iconic representation, and its realization depends upon an understanding of how the systemic resources of the language are exploited to create unconventional schematic configurations. Such an understanding must obviously place a heavy reliance on procedural work. And yet since these represented schemata of literature do bear a resemblance to the schemata of normal knowledge referred to by means of conventional text, they are not remote from the experience of the receiver and so although there can never be convergence, there can be, and must be, a basis for comparison. Literature, like myth, creates an alternative, counter-reality by the reformulation of the familiar. What is represented must be recognized as a version of the world of conventional reference.

This then is the hare I want to let loose among you. It may be that by a judicious use of literary texts alongside conventional ones we may resolve the dilemma I mentioned and help learners towards the procedural ability they need to be effective users of the language they are learning. But even if it turns out that the hare is too elusive to capture, the chase may lead us through terrain that is well worth exploring.

But meanwhile, let me review, in summary, the terrain that I have been travelling, rather errantly, in this paper. Texts are used to mediate interaction whereby two worlds are brought into convergence. This mediation cannot be achieved simply by issuing tokens of linguistic symbols: to do this is only to demonstrate systemic knowledge. It can only be achieved by interpretative procedures which establish correspondences between systemic and schematic knowledge and thereby convert symbols (which denote) into indices (which refer). Communication is thus achieved through text by a realization of indexical value. When the states of schematic knowledge of two interlocutors are initially in close correspondence, then the need for procedural work is diminished, since indexical realization is relatively easy to achieve. Conversely, when schematic states are far apart, considerable demands are made on procedural negotiation to bring them together. There is a problem for pedagogy here. If we want to develop procedural ability in the learner, then it would seem logical to do so through texts which are schematically remote, but then the learner is likely to be less disposed to engage with the texts since by the same token they are also likely to be remote from his interests and purposes. In view of this, it might be worth considering using texts in which signs functioned not as indices referring to conventional schemata, but as icons which represented schemata which, though comparable with familiar patterns of reality, are unique and need to be procedurally created. This was my hare. Apart from the symbol, index, and icon,

I mentioned a fourth type of sign: the signal. This is used in the business of maintaining or managing the interactivity itself, of organizing the actual participation or engagement in the discourse process. Signals indicate shifts of speaker turn, changes of topic, and so on: they organize the immediate conveyancing of information and intent. Knowing how to use them is a matter of interactive rather than interpretative procedure.

Traditionally, language teaching has focused attention on the linguistic sign as symbol, on the development of systemic knowledge. This, as I have tried to indicate, is a necessary but not a sufficient condition for the understanding of language in use. If learners are to acquire the ability to achieve meaning through the language they are learning, then a further condition has to be met. They need to be engaged with texts, whether they participate or not, so as to mediate purposeful interaction. They need, in other words, to develop interpretative and interactive procedures for the realization of the indexical and signalling functions of linguistic signs in texts.

Notes

Paper presented at the Annual Conference of the German Association of Applied Linguistics (GAL), Cologne, September 1982, and published in the proceedings, Kuhlwein 1983.

1 Extract from Philp (1962).

The use of literature

The term 'use' here, as in Section Two, is deliberately ambiguous. I intend it, on the one hand, in the sense of language use, as distinct from usage. Papers 10 and 11 are in particular concerned with use in this sense and seek to identify the distinctive characteristics of literature as a kind of discourse. But I also intend the term to mean usefulness, or utility, and Paper 12 attempts to indicate how literature can be put to the service of practical language teaching pedagogy.

Paper 10 restricts its attention to poetry. It was originally prepared for a varied audience of linguists, literary scholars, and language teachers and its purpose was to establish points of reference on which these different interests might converge by showing how certain central theoretical issues in linguistics can be interpreted to have a crucial bearing on an understanding of the nature of poetry. It is an attempt to provide a conceptual framework within which literary criticism and linguistics might co-exist in co-operative amity, and, more importantly, within which a principled approach to the teaching of literature might be formulated.

The other two papers in this Section can be seen as developing from this first one, but in rather different ways. Paper 11 discusses conventional uses of language as compared with the deviant uses in literature in terms of the difference between reference and representation, which are modes of meaning realized by the use of indexical and iconic signs respectively. This paper, then, elaborates on the theme of Paper 10 by referring it to issues raised in the papers of the preceding Section.

Paper 12 develops certain pedagogic implications arising from the arguments of the preceding papers. The main theme here is not the use (in the sense of utility) of language in the teaching of literature, but the way in which literary uses of language can contribute to the effective teaching of language. Whether one sees language as ancillary to literature or the reverse, the meaningful relationship between them to be exploited by pedagogy depends on a recognition of the nature of literature as language use, as outlined in Paper 10 and further expounded in Paper 11.

The papers of this Section are meant to be understood in a way which leaves the ambiguity of 'use' unresolved. For the ambiguity in effect incorporates a belief which informs the argument in all of these papers: that literature cannot be effectively taught unless it is conceived of as a kind of language use and that it is because it is a kind of language use that it can be put to effective use in the teaching of language.

10   The deviant language of poetry

'To circumscribe poetry by a definition', says Samuel Johnson in his
Lives of the Poets 'will only shew the narrowness of the definer.'
Nevertheless I intend to take that risk and try, concentrating on
lyric poetry as the paradigm case. Such attempts have been made
before of course and I simply follow the great tradition, or if you
prefer it the common pursuit. '... words set in delightful proportion ...' (Sidney), '... the very image of life expressed in its eternal
truth ...' (Shelley), '... the spontaneous overflow of powerful
feelings ...' (Wordsworth). And more recently Ezra Pound: 'Poetry
is a composition of words set to music. Most other definitions of it
are indefensible or metaphysical.' Whether this applies to the
definition I shall offer I must leave it to you to judge.

Whatever else literature may be, we will agree that its effects are
achieved through the medium of language. And here we encounter
our first difficulty. The term is ambiguous. On the one hand it may
refer to the underlying system of common knowledge, *langue*, and
on the other to particular realization of this knowledge as instances
of behaviour: *parole*. F. W. Bateson provides a recent reminder of
this distinction:

> *Langue*, you will remember, is the speech system, the vocabulary,
> accidence and syntax that a speech group learns, adjusts and
> stores away in its individual memories for use when required. ...
> *Parole*, on the other hand, is the particular speech act ...

He then goes on to say:

> The literary artefact ... is *parole*. (Bateson 1961: 74, quoted in
> Butler and Fowler 1971: Extract 285)

Since linguists from de Saussure onwards have been essentially
concerned with *langue* (the argument runs), what they have to say
is of limited relevance to the student of literature. For 'he' (the
student of literature) 'is concerned only with *la parole*, a series of

individual communicative acts, individual applications of the code.'
(Hough 1969: 104)

It should be pointed out perhaps that nowadays the linguist's
attention is not focused so fixedly on *langue* as it has been in the
past. There is an increasing interest in aspects of *parole* and a
concern to account for those 'particular speech acts' and the
'individual communicative acts' that Bateson and Hough refer to.
The linguist can no longer be kept at bay by the observation that
the literary artefact is *parole*. But *is* it *parole*? On closer investigation, the answer seems less than self-evident.

Consider, for example, how one would characterize the following expressions:

The door is strange to be unlocked.
Slept Rip Van Winkle twenty years.
He saw not the beautiful lady.
I to him turn with tears.
It sads me in my heart to leave you.
When will you your round me going end?
There looked a strange man through the window.
When will you under be my roof?

If these were produced by a foreigner, one would be disposed to say
that he lacked command of the language, and that what he comes
out with is 'not English'. So these would be characterized as
instances of *parole* which are referable to some linguistic system
other than that of English. Such a system would be an unstable
interlanguage, a transitional *langue* of a kind, though dissociated
from any established social domain of use. But what if these
expressions were produced by native speakers of English competent
in the standard language? One might counter the question by
saying that they wouldn't be, unless the speaker in question were
temporarily incapacitated by some condition which induced mis-
takes in performance—affected by fatigue or drink or drugs, or
crazed with care or crossed in hopeless love: involuntary distortions, correctable by sober reflection. But then what is one to say
about the following:

God with honour hang your head,
Groom and grace you, bride, your bed
With lissome scions, sweet scions,
Out of hallow'd bodies bred.

Each be other's comfort kind:
Deep, deeper than divined,
Divine charity, dear charity,
Fast you ever, fast bind.

Then let the march tread our ears:
I to him turn with tears
Who to wedlock, his wonder wedlock,
Deals triumph and immortal years.
(G. M. Hopkins: 'At The Wedding March')

One must suppose that the distortion is deliberately fashioned for an effect. One does not react by accusing Hopkins of incompetence and correcting his English. Now consider another of our examples:

When will you your round me going end?

But how do we react to precisely the same syntactic deviation in the following lines (Hopkins again):

When will you ever, Peace, wild wooddove, shy wings shut,
Your round me roaming end, and under be my boughs?
When, when, Peace, will you, Peace?
(G. M. Hopkins: 'Peace')

It will not now do to say: 'What he really means is: "When will you ever ... stop roaming round me and be under my boughs"', because this normalization does *not* mean the same as the original. Hopkins' syntactic arrangement is, we must suppose, a deliberate act of artistry designed to achieve a particular meaning.

By now you will be suspecting that all of the examples of deviant expressions I have provided are taken from poetry.

Slept Rip Van Winkle twenty years.   (Longfellow?)

The door is strange to be unlocked.   (Dylan Thomas?)

In fact all the others are attested instances of learner error and are taken from a compendium of such errors entitled *The Gooficon* (Burt and Kiparsky 1972).

We cannot then judge by appearances. An error is taken as evidence of deficient competence in the language and calls for correction. A deliberate literary deviation on the other hand is taken as evidence of more than common mastery—after all poetry is (according to Coleridge) the best words in the best order. Yet we cannot distinguish between them as far as their outer form is concerned. Only when we know their origin do we know whether to deplore or praise.

So it is that if a foreign learner ventures to use the language creatively, with deliberate intent—'The march,' he might say, 'The march treads our ears'—he is likely to be condemned for his innovation. That's not English. But then why does it suddenly become English when it appears in a poem by Hopkins? The *parole* of the learner is the projection of an interlanguage which represents a different kind of *langue* from that of standard English. Then it is surely the case that the *parole* of the poem is also the realization of a different kind of *langue*. The literary artefact, we might say in reply to Bateson, exists precisely because it is NOT *parole* in any straightforward sense. It is in a way. But again in another way, it is not, since it does violence to accepted rule.

It is in a way; in the sense that it is recognizably related to the system of a particular language: a poem in English, no matter how curiously wrought, is not mistaken for one in French or Swahili or any other language. On the other hand, the language items are not simply projected as tokens of established linguistic types. Often, there are no types that they can be tokens of, as we have seen. This is not to say that deviation from the rules of the linguistic system is a necessary or a sufficient condition for poetic effect. But whether or not language items in the poem conform to type, they always contract relations with other items within the context and so create significant regularities over and above those required by the language system from which they derive. They are significant because they signify. The phonology of English, for example, requires no alliteration, assonance, rhyme, or metric measure in message forms but these sound patterns are used in poems to fashion a design of sound which combines with syntactic and lexical arrangements to create a code for the occasion. And elements in that extempore code take on a particular meaning value accordingly.

Consider an example. The word *river*. Its signification appears in the *Shorter Oxford Dictionary* as follows:

> *river* A copious stream of water flowing in a channel towards the
> sea, a lake, or another stream.

But when the word is worked into the language patterns of poems it takes on meaning as a feature of their design, just as familiar and commonplace objects become a part of the configuration of colour and form in a painting, and so acquire a particular significance.

Never did sun so beautifully steep
In his first splendour valley, rock or hill;
Ne'er saw I, never felt a calm so deep!

The river glideth at his own sweet will:
Dear God! the very houses seem asleep;
And all that mighty heart is lying still.
(Wordsworth)

The river sweats
Oil and tar
The barges drift
With the turning tide
(Eliot)

Five miles meandering with a mazy motion
Through wood and dale the sacred river ran,
Then reached the caverns measureless to man,
And sank in tumult to a lifeless ocean ...
(Coleridge)

From too much love of living,
From hope and fear set free,
We thank with brief thanksgiving
Whatever gods may be
That no life lives for ever;
That dead men rise up never;
That even the weariest river
Winds somewhere safe to sea.
(Swinburne)

In each case the word takes on a different value in the unique frame of reference created by the internal patterns of language within the poem.

But it is always the case, it might be objected, that words take on particular referential value when they are used in context, when they appear in *parole*, no matter how commonplace. So *river* might on different occasions refer to the Thames, the Amazon, the Cam; might be associated with bridge building, military manoeuvres, romantic assignations, and so on. This of course is true. Words are variables which take on different values in context. But these values are established by the normal operation of syntax and so are explicit projections of the conventional code. There is an accretion of particular attributes but *the* river remains *a* river, a token of a type, always and only a copious stream of water. In poetry this is not so. Here there is no simple accretion but a fusion of distinct category types to create a new category for the nonce. The river is not only a copious stream, it is also the deep calm of nature, or grease and sweat, or a mysterious movement in dreams, or the weariness of life. And all this because the word fits into place in a unique pattern of language in the poem, a pattern of sound and lexical association and syntactic form created by arrangements which have no dependence on the conventional functioning of syntax. The river that glideth at his own sweet will, the river that sweats oil and tar, the sacred river five miles meandering with a mazy motion, the weariest river that winds somewhere safe to sea are not just different instances of the same thing, they are also quite different things because they appear in different contextual designs. These designs constitute a secondary code, as it were, independent of the primary code of the language system as such.

In conventional discourse, the form that the message takes other than that dictated by syntactic rule does not matter to its meaning. Paraphrase leaves it unaltered. But in poetry it does matter and when it is changed the meaning changes also. No paraphrase is possible. This is because one is translating from a contextually determined code which has no generative power outside the message form of the particular poem.

I am suggesting, then, that in a poem we have two co-existing systems locking into each other so that terms take on two values simultaneously. Sometimes these values may be consistent one with the other, sometimes they may create a conflict which has to be reconciled. Conflict occurs for example in the occurrences of *river* we have been considering: in the conventional code the word has the feature of inanimacy but in the code of the poem it is animate: the river glideth at his own sweet will, the river sweats, the weariest river. Contradictions impossible in the ordinary world are fused here and reconciled. So what we have is a double structure, of *parole* which is also *langue*, of *langue* which is also *parole*, neither one nor the other, and yet both. A paradox, an anomalous hybrid. No wonder Empson remarks that 'the machinations of ambiguity are among the very roots of poetry' (Empson 1961: 3).

My use of the expression 'double structure' to refer to this unique convergence of linguistic patterning in poetry is in a way an act of deliberate provocation. The term already has a well-established sense in linguistics. But the way in which this sense differs from what I intend by the term is, I think, of particular significance for the definition of poetic discourse. In linguistics, double structure refers to the fact that the units at the phonological level only function internally within the language system itself to form higher level units. Sounds have no direct executive function in the expression of meaning in language use. In consequence they are not themselves meaningful but only provide the means for forming units which are: words. Thus the substantial character of a word (the sounds of which it is composed) does not determine its denotation or the sense relations it contracts with other words. The relationship of sound and meaning is of its nature arbitrary. We return to de Saussure. For him the arbitrary relationship was one of two 'primordial characteristics' of the linguistic sign, and represents one of the two basic principles of language. But in poetry this principle is not operative. As we have noted, sounds are fashioned into designs which *are* meaningful: the patterns of language are significant beyond their function of realizing the rules of the conventional code, and this is why there can be no transposing into a different message form by paraphrase without radical alteration of meaning. So it is that the double structure of poetry, the convergence of patterns, necessarily depends on the denial of double structure as a primordial characteristic of the linguistic sign. Poetry operates on a fundamentally different and contrary principle from that which informs conventional language use.

I said that de Saussure pointed out the arbitrary nature of the linguistic sign as one of two primordial characteristics or basic principles of language. The other one does not apply to poetry either. It is the *linear* nature of the signifier. The importance of this principle, says de Saussure, equals that of the first principle: 'the whole mechanism of language depends upon it' (de Saussure 1966: 70). But the whole mechanism of poetry depends in large part on the undermining of the principle. For poems are not simply linear. Their very appearance on the page, their rhyme scheme, their rhythmic shape are devices for overcoming the limitations of linearity determined by syntax so that we are presented with a series of pattern units, with each one finding its place in the overall arrangement. This is a consequence, of course, of the transfer of the principle of equivalence from the paradigmatic to the syntagmatic axis of language (see Jakobson 1960). Once this transfer is made and equivalent items are actually realized within the message form itself, then they will inevitably project a two-dimensional design which transcends linearity.

Not surprisingly, this curious mode of language use calls for an adjustment to our customary reading habits. We would normally reject the form of the message as waste product, once it had served its purposes of conveyance, so as to extract the conceptual gist. The reading of poems, however, requires a conservation of message forms by recurrent acts of focusing so that the forms are realized as parts of the design as a whole,

> where every word is at home
> Taking its place to support the others ...
> The complete consort dancing together ...
> (T. S. Eliot: *Little Gidding*)

The words of a poem are arranged like notes in music or steps in a dance: they appear in a succession but create a depth in harmony and movement, as if the co-ordinates of spatial relations were transposed into temporal arrangement. One can now appreciate the force of Ezra Pound's definition of poetry as 'a composition of words set to music'.

The double structure of poetry denies the principle of arbitrariness and creates a two-dimensional mode of expression which transcends the principle of linearity. Poetry is a deviant kind of discourse which exploits the resources of conventional language in order to develop contradictory quasi-systems of its own, systems compounded of both *langue* and *parole* which derive from a disruption of normal linguistic principles. But to what purpose? What is the point of such topsy-turvy activity?

It follows from their very nature that these contradictory nonce systems are only valid for the occasion for which they were created. They generate no messages outside the poem. They are useless for any further purpose. Conventional kinds of discourse, conforming as they do to normal linguistic principles, fit into a continuity: they are located in ongoing social life which is serviced by the conventional code. When I speak or when I write I do so in response to some requirement and I anticipate some consequence: my discourse is located in a contextual continuum and it has to conform to rule so that it may mediate my involvement in ordinary social interaction. But poetry is not and cannot be part of a continuum in this way. It is essentially dislocated from context, set aside: it presupposes no previous or existing situation outside that created by itself, it anticipates no continuation. It exists apart, complete in itself, self-contained within its own pattern. And no matter how fully our minds may be *engaged* by the situation created by a poem we can never be *participants*: it exists in a different plane of being. Consider this example:

> She walks in beauty, like the night
> Of cloudless climes and starry skies,
> And all that's best of dark and bright
> Meet in her aspect and her eyes ...
> (Byron)

Who e'er she be, we should note (thinking of Crashaw) this is an impossible she, for, contrary to standard rule, the definite personal pronoun here refers to no definite person. We do not know at the end of the poem who is being described. And since she appears in a poem it would not be proper to ask, as Byron would no doubt be the first to agree. And now, another lady:

> That's my last Duchess painted on the wall,
> Looking as if she were alive. I call
> That piece a wonder, now ...
> (Browning)

It is indeed a wonder, since, though pointed out to us if it were present before our eyes, the picture is not there. It only exists, for all its immediacy, within the confines of the poem, closed off from contact with the world. It belongs to a quite different dimension of reality fashioned within the poem itself. There is no recourse to, and no need of, any circumstantial evidence provided by context.

The peculiar convergent system of poetic expression functions to realize speech acts which cannot occur in normal discourse: an identification which has nothing to identify:

> That's my last Duchess painted on the wall.

A summons to someone who has no existence:

> Come into the garden, Maud. (Tennyson)

Or, rather more lustily, from Ben Jonson:

> Come my Celia, let us prove
> While we may, the sports of love ...

A poem, then, proclaims its independence of contexts which normally condition our understanding of discourse, and instead fashions its own convergent double structure to compensate for this severance of connection. As a result, it realizes speech acts which have no validity in ordinary language interaction. What Searle (1969) refers to as 'normal input-output conditions', essential requirements for communication, just do not obtain. How can one characterize remarks addressed to entities which are of their nature non-participant third person things: nightingales and cuckoos, the west wind and a Grecian urn, daffodils and the lesser celandine, quite apart from less evocative vocatives, such as this from Wordsworth:

Spade! with which Wilkinson hath tilled his lands.

and this from William McGonegall (poet and tragedian):

O Beautiful railway bridge of the silvery Tay.

And what are we to make of speech acts supposedly *performed* by such entities: we are addressed by a hawk roosting, a windmill, a corpse, a cloud, a brook:

I come from haunts of coot and hern.

What kind of speech act is that? None that we know of, or can know of outside the imagined and dissociated context of the poem (see Widdowson 1975).

So there can be no commitment to truth or to the normal conditions of communication in poems, because there is a deliberate distortion of the means for discharging such a commitment. Poetry, as Graham Hough has observed, 'exists within a parenthesis, as it were, distinguishing it from actual discourse'. It is not like real language. And yet, as Hough goes on to point out:

Within the parenthesis all the effects that have been observed outside it are still active. (Hough 1969: 28)

The words carry with them their ordinary language meanings, together with the aura of association that surrounds them because of the contexts of their most common occurrence. And these effects are indeed still active. Cuckoo and celandine, wind and river retain their reference to familiar phenomena, and remain tokens of shared experience. But their occurrence in the designed message form of the poem make them mean something more, for they appear as part of an unfamiliar pattern, dissociated from the company they would normally keep, and so they take on a strangeness. They are familiar because of the presupposed context they carry with them from normal use, and unfamiliar because of the actual context in which they find themselves.

This 'dissociation of sensibility' based on a dissociation of sense by displacement of context is, I think, what art in general seeks to achieve. A mass of twisted metal removed from its normal setting in the scrap yard and placed on a pedestal in a public square forces a reconsideration of stock responses and makes appeal to our aesthetic sense. So does a can of Campbells' soup isolated from the supermarket shelves and put in a frame, and fire-bricks set out symmetrically in the Tate Gallery. They meet the necessary conditions for art.

But this shift from normal patterns of occurrence would in ordinary circumstances simply cause confusion. We cannot live in a world where categories are unclear, where contraries combine, where there is no security in an established order sustained by the conventional language. Dislocation, disorientation, derangement: that way madness lies. But the chaos is recast into a different form in the patterns of the poem. The rhyme, the metrical arrangement, the whole design reassembles the dislocated elements into an alternative order held in momentary balance in the pattern of the poem itself. Poetry, like the god Siva, is both destroyer and creator simultaneously.

From the Swiss linguist Ferdinand de Saussure to the Indian god Siva: a tortuous route, you may think, and a tenuous connection. But it seems to me that we cannot understand the aesthetic effect of poetry without recognizing what kind of discourse it is, and the nature of its deviance from normal language. Poems, I have argued, represent unique language systems in which the regularities of *langue* and *parole* converge, systems which are linguistic paradoxes in that they are based on a denial of the primordial characteristics of arbitrariness and linearity and have no power to generate other messages. They express, therefore, what no other use of language is capable of expressing: a kind of converse reality, a different existential order in another dimension of experience, a fugitive paradox held for a moment outside ordinary time and place. And since no other use of language can convey this, it seems best to leave the last word to a poet:

> Only by the form, the pattern,
> Can words or music reach
> The stillness, as a Chinese jar still
> Moves perpetually in its stillness ...
> Here the impossible union
> Of spheres of existence is actual,
> Here the past and future
> Are conquered, and reconciled. ...
> (T. S. Eliot: *Four Quartets*)

Note

Paper presented at Wolfson College, Cambridge, February 1981. Published in *ELT Documents* 115.

11 Reference and representation as modes of meaning

What I want to do in this paper is to enquire into the nature of literary discourse and to try to establish in what respects it differs from discourse of a conventional kind. For it seems clear that literature *does* differ from customary uses of language in quite fundamental ways. To begin with, the Gricean co-operative principle (Grice 1975) would appear to be in abeyance. Literary writers do not, for example, seem to set much of a premium on perspicuity, but often seem studiously to avoid it. They are not, either, bound by any commitment to the truth of what they say; they are concerned only that it should be convincing. And yet if there is no co-operation on the part of the reader, then no meaning can be made out of literary text. It would seem that in reading literature we are required to enter into a different kind of contractual agreement from the one we subscribe to in normal communicative circumstances. What then are the co-operative principles that control the functioning of literary discourse? If we do not read a lyric poem in the same way as a set of fire instructions, or a novel in the same way as an historical treatise or a textbook in sociology, then what is the difference in the way we interpret the linguistic sign in each case?

The first move I want to make in the consideration of these questions is to press into service certain semiotic distinctions made by Peirce (Peirce 1931: 58; discussed in Lyons 1977b: I). Peirce develops an elaborate and somewhat bewildering system for the description of signs, but within his system, and central to it, is a classification of three kinds of relationship between sign and object (between signifier and signified) which is of particular epistemological significance since it accounts for ways in which reality is conceptualized and therefore brought under control by the imposition of order. These three relations are realized by three modes of signifying, three categories, if you will, of mediators of meaning: the symbol, the index, and the icon.

Now Peirce's own description of the distinctive features of these sign–object relations is not entirely clear and I do not know how closely my own interpretation would accord with his intentions. But for the purposes of my own exposition, it is convenient to characterize these different modes of signifying as follows.

The icon functions by virtue of a relationship of resemblance between sign and object. Though by nature a conceptual entity, the sign bears recognizable traces of perceptual experience. The index functions by virtue of a relationship of implication between sign and object. So whereas the icon signals a representational relationship, the index signals a referential one. The symbol, to complete the triad, functions by virtue of an arbitrary agreement that the sign should stand for an object: it has no perceptual warrant but exists only by a kind of conventional conceptual contract. The relationship here is one of denotation.

Defined in this way, symbolic and iconic signs are both co-extensive with objects to which they relate, and so in some sense incorporate them. The index, on the other hand, separates sign and object. The sign directs attention away from itself and serves as a clue to where the object is to be found elsewhere: it does not signal meaning by virtue of its own form. Reference, we may say, implies inference: representation and denotation do not. It follows that the index is dependent on a context to provide it with something to point to. The symbol and the icon, on the other hand, carry within them their own conditions for meaning and are in this sense context free.

Let me now turn from semiotics in general to that branch of it called linguistics, the study of the linguistic sign. As defined by de Saussure, and the linguists following in his wake, this relates to reality in the manner of the symbol: the signifier is an arbitrary form which bears no resemblance to the object to which it relates. It denotes by convention. But we should notice that the linguistic sign is given symbolic status as a result of the linguist's idealization of language use, whereby he removes it from its natural context of occurrence (see Lyons 1972). Separated thus from its contextual connections, the sign is then shown to contract relationships with other signs as terms in the system, rather than with other signs as object indicators. In this respect, the linguist isolates the symbol artificially by methodological contrivance. For in its natural surroundings, the linguistic sign functions not as a symbol but as an index. It is exploited by non-ideal speaker/listeners (and writer/readers) to connect with context and therefore to refer.

Context is not to be thought of as an undifferentiated mass of

amorphous reality but as a set of schemata which define conven-
tionalized patterns of experience. More than thirty years ago, Firth
referred to his concept of 'context of situation' as a 'schematic
construct to apply to language events ... a group of related
categories at a different level from grammatical categories but
rather of the same abstract nature' (Firth 1957: 182). Over recent
years the concept has made a reappearance under different
terminological guises—script, plan, macro-structure, frame,
scenario, schema (see de Beaugrande 1980: Chapter 6, de Beaugrande and Dressler 1981). Although they differ in detail, all of
these can be seen as variants of Firth's original formulation of
context, even though he gets no credit for it.

In language use, then, the linguistic sign is interpreted indexically
as a means of engaging with the schematic constructs of context.
Where these constructs have to do with recurrent frames which
organize propositional content, the indexical interpretation results
in the achievement of reference.

And it is, let us note, an achievement. For although the symbol
denotes in its own character, the index can only refer when it is
interpreted in relation to particular contexts. A common way of
demonstrating this is to present passages of language which are
symbolically clear but indexically obscure. Like the following,
quoted in Bransford and Johnson (1972):

> The procedure is actually quite simple. First you arrange things
> into different groups. Of course, one pile may be sufficient,
> depending on how much there is to do. If you have to go
> somewhere else due to lack of facilities that is the next step.
> Otherwise you are pretty well set. It is important not to overdo
> things. That is, it is better to do too few things at once than too
> many ... etc.

This passage presents no difficulty at all as far as symbolic
meanings are concerned: you know, I will assume, what the lexical
items *procedure, thing, pile, group*, and so on denote. If you do not
know, you can always find out by recourse to a dictionary:

Procedure: regular order of doing things.
Group: number of persons or things gathered or placed to-
         gether, or naturally associated.
etc.

What you do not know is what these lexical items are *referring* to.
You cannot interpret them as indices, so you do not know what the

passage is about. Although it is cohesive as text, it is incoherent as discourse. Only when a context or frame of reference is provided can you make satisfactory sense of it: only then can you realize the indexical value of the signs. In this present case, the context is provided by a title: *Washing Clothes*.

The index, then, is the linguistic unit of language use. Once it is realized through interpretation, reference is achieved. But reference must presuppose something, some object, some entity to refer to, something that can be identified as having independent existence. If we cannot discover the object which the sign relates to, then there is no indexical relationship and the expression fails to refer for us: it can then only be understood symbolically as a device for denotation.

This is the key to the famous philosophical puzzle about the King of France and his baldness (or wisdom, in an alternative version). The puzzle goes like this. Suppose that somebody here and now were to come out with the expression:

The King of France is wise

or

The King of France is bald.

We would agree that the expression is in some way meaningful—it is not just gibberish or gobbledygook. The linguistic signs are present and correct, as it were, and the expression is therefore significant. But how can it be meaningful, when we all know that there is no King of France, wise or foolish, bald or hairy? How can it be significant when there is nothing in reality that answers the description it offers? (See the discussion in Strawson 1950/68.) By invoking the distinctions I have been making, we can say that if the expression is understood as a sentence, then it is significant symbolically and it denotes a state of affairs which is not required to correspond to reality. If each symbol has a conventional denotation and relates to the other symbols in a manner sanctioned by syntactic rule, then the resulting expression is a significant sentence and can be understood as such. If, however, we take this expression as an utterance, as an instance of language use, then the case is quite different. Because now we require of the expression that it should be *indexically* significant, that it should refer; and if there is nothing for it to refer to, or if it refers to something we know to be non-existent, then it is indexically defective. In other words, the expression is significant as a string of symbols and is meaningful as a sentence by virtue of its denotation, but it is not significant as an utterance because its indices indicate no corresponding object and so it fails to refer.

Taken as a sentence, then, this expression has the same character as those which appear in textbooks of linguistics and language teaching. For example:

Sincerity frightens the boy
The dog looks terrifying
The farmer kills the duckling
The book is on the table
The cat is on the mat.

We may call up the shade of Firth again at this point. He was particularly scathing about examples such as these. He comments:

'I have not seen your father's pen, but I have read the book of your uncle's gardener', like so much in grammar books, is only at the grammatical level. From the semantic point of view it is just nonsense. (Firth 1957: 24)

I would argue that such examples are symbolically well formed as sentences and so from the semantic point of view are *not* nonsense, if by semantics we mean, as linguists generally *do* seem to mean, the study of symbolic significance. The problem with such examples is that although the definite article and the simple present tense would naturally lead us to an indexical interpretation in relation to some context of shared knowledge or some context of immediate situation, these expressions in these cases actually direct us into a void. There is nothing beyond the expression to refer to. It is from the *pragmatic* point of view that they are nonsense. They are well-formed as sentences, but deviant as utterances.

But of course expressions of this kind are not intended to be interpreted as utterances. We are supposed to suppress our natural language instincts and simply process them as sentences. And the same condition is imposed on language learners when they are presented with similar expressions in the classroom. They are not encouraged to ask inconvenient questions like: '*Which* dog looks terrifying, and where is this dog in question, and which boy are you talking about, and what is the point of the information you are providing?' These are inadmissible questions because they have no bearing on the significance of the symbols in their syntactic settings. But they are questions which are naturally prompted by the signs in these expressions considered as utterances, since it is precisely questions like these which mediate the indexical relation and lead to a realization of reference.

There are occasions, however, when expressions of the kind we have been considering *are* intended to provoke interpretation and are not just presented as sentences. If I were to say:

The King of France is bald.

I could be telling a story, as I would be if I said:

The king is in his counting house counting out his money,
The queen is in the garden eating bread and honey ...

In this case, the signs are not meant to denote, since the intention is to call up a particular state of affairs. But they do not refer either, since there is nothing in the immediate context for them to refer to. What we have here are signs of the third kind that Peirce distinguished: the icon. Their function is not to denote or refer but to represent. And representation is the mode of meaning of literature.

The essential condition for reference is that there should be something to refer to, some object, entity or whatever within a context separate from the sign. To put the matter in another way, the index has to have something to point to. With representation, context is necessarily created by the signs themselves and there are no objects, entities or whatever other than those iconically rep-resented by the signs. Reference is of its nature context-dependent, but representation, like denotation, signals self-contained meaning. It follows from this that whereas the same reference can be achieved by a variety of indexical expressions—you can point at the same thing from different directions—meanings which are denoted and represented will be locked within particular forms so that when the form changes then different meanings will be signalled.

This brings us to another celebrated philosophical puzzle. This time it concerns the planet Venus. This is called both the morning star and the evening star. This being so, one might argue, then 'the morning star' and 'the evening star' are phrases which have identical meaning (see Lyons 1977b: 197–8). So why is it that the expression:

The morning star is the evening star.

is meaningful and informative, whereas the expression:

The morning star is the morning star.

is a meaningless tautology?

The answer in relation to the present discussion is that the phrases 'the morning star' and 'the evening star' considered as strings of symbols have different denotations: the entry for 'morning' in the dictionary will be quite distinct from the entry for 'evening'. But the phrases considered indexically are used to refer to the same object. And the point of actually saying:

The morning star is the evening star.

would be precisely to indicate that the difference in denotation is to be disregarded and that the two phrases are indexical of the same referent.

In conventional language use, then, the indexical interpretation of signs in utterances will commonly lead to the neutralization of differences which are, from a denotation point of view, significant. The index, if you will, takes precedence over the symbol. But in the use of language in literature, these denotation differences are carried over and converted into different representations. In literature, in other words, it *does* matter whether the writer chooses 'the morning star' or 'the evening star': they *represent* different entities. Consider, for example, the occurrence of the two expressions in the following lines:

1   The world's great age begins anew,
    The golden years return.
    The earth doth like a snake renew
    Her winter weeds outworn;
    Heaven smiles, and faiths and empires gleam,
    Like wrecks of a dissolving dream.

    A brighter Hellas rears its mountains
    From waves serener far;
    A new Peneus rolls his fountains
    Against the *morning star*.
    Where fairer Tempes bloom, there sleep
    Young Cyclads on a sunnier deep.
    (Shelley: *Hellas*)

2   Sunset and *evening star*,
    And one clear call for me!
    And may there be no moaning of the bar,
    When I put out to sea,

    But such a tide as moving seems asleep,
    Too full for sound or foam,
    When that which drew from out the boundless deep
    Turns again home.
    (Tennyson: *Crossing the Bar*)

In Shelley's lines, the star is associated with exuberance in the vision of renewal, the dawning of a brave new world. In Tennyson's lines, it is associated with resignation to the ending of his days. The distinction in denotation between *morning* and *evening* is given full representational force. So it is that every denotation distinction can be pressed into use as a representation by the literary writer and the distinctions are significant and cannot be disregarded as if they were simply referential variants. Referential expressions in conventional discourse can be recast into a different form without loss of significance, but the representational expressions of literary discourse cannot. To paraphrase a poem, for example, is to shift from a representational mode of meaning to a referential one and to destroy its essential character. Poems can be rewritten as different poems in a different language but they cannot be translated.

The iconic signs of literature, then, are in this respect like the symbolic signs of the language system: different forms directly signal different meanings, without connection with external context. They resemble indices, however, in that they are meant to be interpreted as use, they are meant to provoke the kind of reaction which would be inadmissible in a consideration of symbolic meaning. Consider, for example, the following expressions:

The sun is warm.
The sky is clear.
The sea is calm.

Taken as sentences, we may note that these expressions exemplify the same structure of definite noun phrase, copula verb, and predicative adjective. Their denotation is clear. We seek no referential meaning; the normal indexical function of the definite article is held in abeyance. But it happens that these expressions also appear as first lines in poems:

The sun is warm, the sky is clear.
The waves are dancing fast and bright,
Blue isles and snowy mountains wear
The purple noon's transparent might ...
(Shelley: *Stanzas written in dejection near Naples*)

The sea is calm tonight.
The tide is full, the moon lies fair
Upon the straits ...
(Arnold: *Dover Beach*)

The expressions now take on a different character. We have to interpret them as utterances, as instances of language use, and to do this we have to realize them as representations. This involves the engagement of procedures we would normally apply to conventional referential uses of language (What is being talked about here? Why is that mentioned? What is the point in saying that? and so on). But these procedures are directed now not at recovering meaning in context outside the sign but in creating an internal context within the poem. The procedures have to seek significance therefore in denotational distinctions and in sign patterns over and above their normal referential function.

Literature, then, represents realities other than those conventionally referred to by creating unique schemata which confer upon signs an additional dimension of meaning. The signs that are thus, as it were, iconically transmuted may be linguistic, as they commonly are in poetry, where metre, rhyme, alliteration, assonance, lexical and syntactic equivalences serve to fashion superimposed patterns of significance. In this case the icon derives from the symbol. In fiction the signs are commonly those which have a standard referential significance and figure in conventional schemata: here character, characteristics, roles, events, and so on are fashioned into the underlying patterns of narrative structure. In this case, we might say, the icon derives from the index.

The reading of literature, the realization of its representational mode of meaning, calls for the deployment of interpretative procedures, not for the discovery of meaning in context, but for the creation of contexts which define their own significance. As a consequence, the conditions for conventional indexical communication are no longer in force; the Gricean co-operative principle is suspended. The maxim of quality, for example, does not apply.

We do not expect of literature that it should be true, but only that it should carry conviction. Indeed if we interpreted it as being true, we would be treating it as reference and not representation and would thereby be denying its literary character. The maxim of quantity is, again, continually flouted. Literary writers say more than would be necessary by referential effectiveness: why does Shelley go on about the sea, the sky, the sun in such a long-winded way instead of coming straight to the point and say he is feeling sad? And literary writers say less than would be referentially acceptable, leaving us deliberately in the dark about their intended meanings and in general making a virtue of ambiguity.

Representation, then, as I have tried to characterize it in this paper, is a curious, hybrid mode of meaning. On the one hand it requires us to focus on the form of the signs, as if they were symbols, and on the other it requires us to engage interpretative procedures as if these signs were indices. Thus literature forces us into a reappraisal of the nature of both sign and object, provides us with a fresh perspective on both language and life. Hence its value as a force for renewal in the individual and in society.

But it has its utility too in the more pedestrian and practical business of language teaching. If it is the case, as I have argued, that representation calls for a concentration on the formal features of signs as if they were symbols, but also requires that they be interpreted as language use, as distinct from usage, as if they were indices, then one might suggest that literature might be used to mediate between a structural and communicative orientation to language teaching. There is no time to explore this possibility now (see Paper 12), but let me leave you with this observation: the following expressions:

He came back into the kitchen.
The cock is crowing.

could both appear in a conventional language lesson, read off from a substitution table as well-formed sentences. But the first begins a story by Somerset Maugham and the second begins a poem by Wordsworth. And all sentences are potentially representations in the same way. If this is so, then is there not a good reason for realizing this potential in the classroom so that learners can both learn the symbolic meaning of signs and develop interpretative procedures for subsequent referential use? I hope that my attempt to clarify the nature of denotation, reference and representation as modes of meaning will make you feel that this question is one that is well worth pondering. And might lead you to believe, as I do, that there is a case for reinstating literature to a legitimate place in the pedagogy of language teaching.

Note

Paper presented at the annual Conference of the Finnish Association of Applied Linguistics (AFinLa), Oulu, November 1982. Published in the AFinLa Yearbook 1983.

12   The use of literature

There was a time when literature was accorded high prestige in language study, when it was assumed that part of the purpose of language learning, perhaps even the most essential part, was to provide access to literary works. There was a time when it was assumed, furthermore, that the actual process of learning would be enlivened and indeed facilitated by the presentation of poems, plays, and prose fiction. But that time is past, and now literature hardly figures at all in language programmes. It is linguistics rather than literary studies that prevails as the informing influence. Here poetry sometimes makes a brief appearance but only to provide examples of deviant linguistic data. The term 'literature' occurs quite frequently in the writing of linguists but it usually refers only to disquisitions on predicate raising, embedded clause deletion, deep case categories, and the like: deep matters no doubt, but not always profound. A far cry from *The Mayor of Casterbridge* and the *Odes* of Keats. 'The old order changeth, yielding place to new...'

But what are the arguments against the inclusion of literature in language courses? First, there is the matter of purpose. It can be argued that literature contributes nothing to the utilitarian objectives of language learning. The current obsession with needs analysis and cost effective accounting which parades as pedagogy lends weight to this argument. Literature has no practical uses and so it is useless. What is the point of teaching it to people who are looking to the language they are learning to meet academic and occupational needs? *The Scarlet Letter* will be of no earthly use to students on business correspondence courses. Students of botany will get nothing specific to their purpose out of poems on birches or daffodils or the lesser celandine. There is no need of literature in courses designed to meet the demands of practical utility.

'O reason not the need', we might cry, as did King Lear when his daughters hounded him with similar arguments.

O reason not the need. Our basest beggars
Are in the poorest thing superfluous;
Allow not nature more than nature needs,
Man's life is cheap as beast's...
(II 4)

There is more to life than safe investment of effort. Language
learning is surely not simply a part of *training*, an element in
actuarial estimates and the calculations of manpower needs. Surely,
we might murmur wistfully, it should also have something to do
with *education* as well? And is this not where literature comes in
with its humanizing influence, its revelation of the hidden significance of everyday life, its celebration of language, indeed, as the
expression of 'the glory, jest, and riddle of the world' of 'exulta-
tions, agonies, and love and man's unconquerable mind?' Perhaps.
But one has to concede that such counterarguments are unlikely to
be listened to in the busy din of the pedagogic production line.

But there are other arguments against the inclusion of literature.
These have to do not with the *purpose* but the *process* of learning.
Thus it is pointed out that literature is a potentially disruptive
influence in the well-ordered world of the carefully controlled
language course. Since creative writers do not compose by reference
to a checklist of graded words and sentence patterns, they produce
language complexity out of sequence, thereby creating nothing but
alarm and despondency. Imagine a class being coaxed into the
learning of a certain sentence pattern:

Can Margaret open the door? Yes, she can.
Can Mary cook the dinner? No, she can't.

Imagine such a class suddenly confronted with something like:

Can a storied urn or animated bust
Back to its mansion call the fleeting breath?
Can honour's voice provoke the silent dust
Or flattery soothe the dull cold ear of death?
(Thomas Gray)

Yes it can? No it can't? Storied urn? Animated bust? What place do
these grotesque obscurities have in the tidy simplicity of classroom
language in the language classroom?

Of course you would not normally be so perverse as to choose
texts of such complexity. It is possible to select literature which is

more easily accommodated within a graded language course. However, there is always likely to be some lack of fit between the two, so there is always likely to be some danger of disruption. It is safer to resort to the usual means of dealing with non-conformity: suppress it.

There is another reason for taking such a course of action. Literature introduces complexity where it is not wanted, so offending against the principle of strict control. That is bad enough. But it also offends against another cardinal principle of conventional language teaching: the principle of correctness. Consider again the case of the storied urn. These lines surely exhibit a structure which would not be counted as correct if it were used by learners:

Can storied urn or animated bust
Back to its mansion call the fleeting breath?

Can Margaret back to its kennel call the dog?

Can John back to the library bring the book?

This calls for correction:

Can John bring the book back to the library?

Can Margaret call the dog back to its kennel?

Can storied urn or animated bust (whatever they may be) call the fleeting breath back to its mansion?

And so order is restored and we return to the conventional world.

But to adjust literature to conform to regulation standards is to destroy its character. 'Touch it and the bloom is gone', as Lady Bracknell put it. Literature, and poetry in particular, has a way of exploiting resources in a language which have not been codified as correct usage. It is, therefore, misleading as a model. So not only is literature likely to be disruptive by its quantitative lack of control, it is also likely to be subversive by its qualitative lack of correctness. It has no place in an approach to teaching that insists on the gradual accumulation of correct linguistic forms.

So it is that literature is judged not only to be irrelevant to purpose, the ends of language learning, but also detrimental to process, the means of achieving them. Guilty on both counts and banished.

But then an interesting and paradoxical development follows. Having got rid of literature, materials writers proceed to invent their own. Textbooks are full of fiction. Mr and Mrs Brown, son David, daughter Mary pursuing the dreary round of their diurnal life, breakfast, lunch, tea, and supper, father reading his newspaper in the sitting-room, mother in the kitchen, the children in the garden, the cat on the mat, 'God's in his Heaven, all's right with the world'.

There are occasional excursions. We follow their adventures at the theatre, at the railway station, in the post office, and from time to time, daringly, at the disco. Here they are at the restaurant. Actually this is the Miller family, son Jimmy, daughter Barbara, but the names do not matter: they are the same familiar pasteboard figures. So here they are on stage in a dramatic sketch entitled *This Isn't Tea*!

Barbara Run, Jimmy!
Jimmy Where?
Barbara To the empty table!
Jimmy Which table?
Barbara The big table!
Mrs Miller The square table!
Jimmy Is this it?
Barbara No, not the round table. That's a small table. Run to the square table.
Mrs Miller Sit down! Sit down! Jimmy! That's the table!

The apparently half-witted Jimmy is eventually directed to the desired table, but the problems of the Miller family are not over yet.

Man Excuse me. Is this your table?
Jimmy Yes, it is.
Man Oh!
Mr Miller Waiter!
Waiter Yes, sir?
Mr Miller Are these cups of coffee or cups of tea?
Waiter Tea, sir.
Mrs Miller No, they aren't. They're cups of coffee.
Waiter Sorry, sir. Those are your cups of tea.
Barbara Yes, these are their cups of coffee and those are our cups of tea.

It is well nigh impossible to sort out what is going on in this travesty of interaction. But it doesn't matter anyway, since the dialogue operates only as a device for displaying language structure. Learners are meant to read and indeed to enact this charade in all seriousness, it is not supposed to be funny, or even remotely entertaining. Students solemnly participate without being humanly engaged.

So much for textbook drama. And now for prose fiction. A story entitled *Walking in the Park*.

Penny and Kate are walking in the park. It is a big park with tall trees and a small lake. Penny is looking at the birds. The birds are flying over the lake. It's a small lake with boats on it. Kate is looking at a plane. It is flying over the houses. They are big houses with many windows.

Not so far a walk of great intrinsic interest. But now other human figures appear on the scene, our pulses quicken:

Three small boys are playing football and a man is looking at them. They are playing with a small black ball. One boy is standing between two trees and his friends are kicking the ball. Now the man is playing with this dog. He is a thin man with long legs. He is throwing a ball and the dog is running after it...

How are we to characterize texts of this sort? They resemble literature in that they represent a non-verifiable reality existing in a different plane of being from everyday life. The Millers at the restaurant, Kate and Penny in the park are literary in that they appear in a setting which creates its own time and space. They are here but not present, now but not *in* the present.

These cups of coffee.
These cups of tea.

This bread I break was once the oat
This wine upon some foreign tree
plunged in its fruit...
(Dylan Thomas)

Which cups? Which bread? Which wine? Where? Nowhere. There is no external referent; the language makes its own.

Penny and Kate are walking in the park.

The trees are in their autumn beauty
The woodland paths are dry
Under an October twilight, the water
Mirrors a still sky...
(W. B. Yeats)

The act of referring creates the fact referred to. The expression is not a report but a representation. The park, the trees, the woodland paths, the lake, the still sky, the boats, the houses with many windows all appear in the middle distance of illusion, actual but not real, before our very eyes. A conjuring trick.

So these textbook creations are cast in a literary mode in that they relate to no context other than that of their own devising, cut off from reality, self-contained, so that the language naturally draws attention to itself.

The writers of such materials may claim that their efforts are simulations of reality in simple language, dealing as they do with ordinary everyday events in restaurants, railway stations, parks, and post offices. But they are not simulations at all; they are dissimulations. For although the texts may exhibit simple usage and the events contained within them be commonplace to the point of paralytic banality, if we treat them as sorts of language *use*, the kind of discourse that results is not commonplace at all. Dreary, uninspired, though they may be, plodding their weary way along graded sequences; nevertheless, *considered as discourse,* they have the essential character of literature.

I am suggesting, then, that language which is meant to have the implication of discourse is necessarily cast in a literary mode if it detaches language from its social setting and so represents meaning as a function of language itself without dependence on external context. Consider another example:

He really was an impossible person.

Here is a linguistic expression. As a sentence displaying correct usage of English it might keep company with other sentences exhibiting the same structure:

He really is an impossible person.
She really is an impossible person.
She really is a delightful person.
She really was a delightful person.

and so on. Each of these is, as a sentence, complete, correct, self-contained, and because we recognize their status as samples on display, we do not seek to make sense of them as instances of language use. It would not be appropriate to ask who this person is who is impossible or delightful, or why we are being given this information. If our students were to ask such questions in the middle of a structural drill we would think it impertinent, in both senses of that word, and we would very quickly put them in their place.

Teacher He really was an impossible person.
Pupil Who do you mean, sir?
Teacher Shut up and just repeat the sentence.

Sentences are not intended to provoke natural language reactions; they force the learner into compliant participation and they are not meant to engage the learner at the level of language use. The discourse potential is suppressed. But if such expressions *are* treated as language use, then they inevitably take on a literary quality. There is in fact a story by Katherine Mansfield which begins with these very words:

He really was an impossible person.

Like the sentence, this is isolated from context. There is nobody outside the text that the pronoun *he* could refer to. But because this is clearly intended as a serious *use* of language and not just a display of usage, we *do* engage with it as discourse. Who is impossible? Why is he impossible? And in what way is it significant? Why are we being told this? As an instance of language use, this statement naturally provokes questions of this kind and since they cannot be answered by *external* reference, our attention is projected forward into the detached *internal* reality of the fictional world. We read on:

He really was an impossible person. Too shy altogether. With absolutely nothing to say for himself. And such a weight. Once he was in the studio he never knew when to go, but would sit on and on until you nearly screamed, and burned to throw something enormous after him when he did finally blush his way out . . .
(*Feuille d'Album*)

So now we know why he is impossible. But what is this about a studio? Is the narrator an artist then? And what is his or her relationship with this impossible person? We read on.

He really was an impossible person.

Understood as a sentence this precludes further enquiry. It signifies, but has no significance. But as a meaningful use of language, though deprived of any reference to external context, its meaning potential can only be realized as literary discourse. In this sense, every piece of language that appears as a sentence in structural presentation and practice is potentially a piece of prose fiction. Or potentially a poem. Consider the following expression:

The dog is lying by the door.

If you focus your attention at the usage level, you are not inspired to ask which dog or which door, or why the situation should provoke any comment in the first place. It is just a sentence. Here is another one:

The cat is sitting on the chair.

So I am, you assume, demonstrating a particular structure: definite noun phrase subject, present continuous tense, prepositional phrase.

The pen is lying on the floor.

Your assumption seems to be borne out: lexical variations on the same structural theme, as if read off from a substitution table, an array of paradigmatic equivalences. Next one:

There is contentment in the air.

But wait: that cannot be right: it doesn't conform to pattern. What's going on? We go over the sentences again:

The dog is lying by the door
The cat is sitting in the chair
The pen is lying on the floor
There is contentment in the air.

What emerges now is a poem. Not perhaps one which is likely to win the first prize in the Guinness Poetry Awards, but a poem nonetheless. And you engage a very different mental set towards it. You assume, since there is no access to the outside world, that each line, now no longer a sentence, is meant to interrelate with the others to create an internally coherent meaning, that the situations represented in the first three lines are intended in some way to relate to the one represented in the fourth line; that the dog, the cat, the pen are meant in some way to express contentment, and so on. In short, you engage procedures for interpretation, you negotiate meanings. Consider another example:

The cock is crowing.
The cattle are grazing.

As they stand here, these expressions have no value as use, since they key in with no context: they are sentences, formal isolates with no implication of utterance. But they can take on value as elements in literary discourse by figuring in patterns of language which create internal conditions for significance, as they do in this poem by Wordsworth.

The cock is crowing
The stream is flowing
The small birds twitter,
The lake doth glitter,
The green field sleeps in the sun;
The oldest and youngest
Are at work with the strongest;
The cattle are grazing
Their heads never raising;
There are forty feeding like one!

Like an army defeated
The snow hath retreated,
And now doth fare ill
On top of the bare hill;
The ploughboy is whooping—anon—anon:
There's joy in the mountains;
There's life in the fountains;
Small clouds are sailing,
Blue sky prevailing;
The rain is over and gone!

The cock crowing, the cattle grazing now appear as figures in a pattern and so we assume that they have some significance. And so we set about making sense of the expressions by referring them to other parts of the discourse in which they occur. We may conclude that their significance is slight. This after all is not a poem that conveys any great apocalyptic message. It probably would not win any poetry prizes either. But since the language is *used* there is some significance and *some* stimulation to discover what it might be. Sentences about cocks and cattle or about anything else for that matter have no significance at all.

That's all very well, you may say, but you are forgetting Penny and Kate and the walk in the park. The teacher does not just present isolated sentences; he fits them together into a text to tell a story. We do not just have 'Penny is looking at the birds'. We also have 'The birds are flying over the lake' related to it, followed by 'It's a small lake with boats on it'. Wordsworth's birds twitter, these fly over the lake. His lake glitters and this one has boats on it. But apart from these trivial matters of detail, what's the difference? Discourse in both cases.

No, not discourse in both cases. And here we come to the central issue in the argument. The pedagogic presentation of language as separate sentences and in texts of the *This Isn't Tea!* and *Walking in the Park* variety are like literature because they dissociate language from the link with social context that normally provides it with its value as use, so that meaning has to be created by means of language itself. Unlike literature, however, pedagogic presentation of this sort does not realize the meaning potential of language to create alternative contexts of reality; it simply manifests language usage, puts it on show disposed in a way that makes minimal demands on thought. So learners are not supposed to engage with what is presented at the level of language use at all. If they did, if they converted these texts to discourse, they would recognize them as a farcical distortion. At least I hope they would. It is a disturbing thought that learners of English might actually believe that the English-speaking peoples spend their time in cretinous conversations stating the obvious about cups of coffee and the shape of restaurant tables. But fortunately for our national image, learners do not relate to these texts in this way. They simply pay attention to the language, as they are directed to do, and suppress their natural instincts. They accept that what they are being given is for display purposes only. Text with no implication of discourse.

This is why, when we take them out of the textual display case of conventional pedagogic presentation within which they are enclosed and confront them at the discourse level, the Millers at the restaurant and Kate and Penny in the park are so ludicrous. They are fictional, literary figures. As such we would generally expect them to carry conviction as characters, instead of which they are stereotypic dummies, humanoids mouthing sentence patterns. We expect events represented in fiction and drama to reveal something of significance which we can recognize as a kind of reality beyond realism, reconstituted from the commonplace of everyday life. Instead, in the interests of display, we have a stultifying insistence on what is ordinary and insignificant. An apotheosis of the commonplace.

So the pedagogic presentation of language, of the sort I have illustrated, does not exploit the possibilities of creativity that are opened up by a dissociation from context. Literature, on the other hand, does. And creativity is a crucial concept in language learning. I am not using this term in the diminished Chomskyan sense, to mean the cybernetic process of sentence generation. There is an abundance of that in language teaching. I mean the human capacity for making sense, for negotiating meaning, for finding expression for new experience in metaphor, for refashioning reality in the image of new ideas and new ideals. There is very little provision made in language teaching for creativity of this sort, and therefore very little recognition of the human capacities of the learner. Indeed, the insistence on strict control and correctness means that the learner is cramped into conformity, 'cabin'd, cribb'd, confin'd, bound in'. When he does break out from the confinement he has been sentenced to by producing creative expressions, these are condemned as errors and the learner is forced back into corrective custody. Deprived, one might almost say, of his human rights.

For the use of language and the acquisition of language are essentially creative processes. Apart from certain relatively fixed and predictable routines that only require habitual conformity, all uses of language involve the imaginative construction of meaning *ex tempore*, referring to routine not as a *script* but as a *prompt*. They involve the subtle deployment of problem solving procedures in the process of making sense. Making sense: the very expression indicates the creative character of ordinary language activity. The kind of pedagogic display I have been referring to is fundamentally deficient because it represents language as entirely a matter of routine and in some degree, therefore, it is bound to diminish the human stature of the language user. There are no problems to solve by negotiation, because meanings are made explicit within the text and carefully prepared for easy assimilation. The learner is therefore not engaged at all at the discourse level. There is nothing to engage with. Everything is ready made and there is no scope for making sense. Using material like this to develop language ability is rather like trying to produce artists with kits of painting by numbers.

Of course, it can be argued that learners already know how to use language because they have experience of their own mother tongue. But this presentation of language as scripted routine, this close confinement and control, do not give the learner a chance to act upon his experience. If he is ill-advised enough to make the attempt he will, as I have already noted, expose himself to peremptory correction. The learner does not have native speaker privileges in this respect. If the native speaker comes out with an expression not sanctioned by convention, his innovation is applauded as evidence of mastery. If the learner does the same, his innovation is deplored as a deficiency, an error, a sort of involuntary spasm of interlanguage. But creativity is not the sole prerogative of the native speaker.

The tendency of pedagogic presentation, then, is to idealize language by reducing it to routine. Literary idealization, on the other hand, involves particular emphasis on procedures. This is a necessary consequence of dissociating discourse from an immediate social context. Dissociation of language for display purposes leads to text which represents language as essentially a matter of routine. Dissociation of language for literary purposes leads to discourse which represents language as essentially a matter of creating meaning by procedures for making sense. This is its central relevance to language teaching: it calls for an intensive use and a heightened awareness of just those procedures which have to be engaged whenever people are involved in the learning and using of natural language.

> He sits not a dozen yards away ...

Who? Where? What do you mean? This opening of a short story by H. G. Wells, like that of Katherine Mansfield considered earlier, immediately creates a problem to be solved, and since there is no external context we can depend on, our interpretative procedures are put on special alert.

> If I glance over my shoulder, I can see him. And if I catch his eye—and usually I catch his eye—it meets me with an expression—it is mainly an imploring look and yet with suspicion in it... (*The Truth about Pycraft*)

Where are these people sitting? Why is the look an imploring one? Why suspicious? We are engaged at the discourse level; we infer, anticipate, adjust, interpret. In short, we make sense as we go along.

> She was sitting on the veranda waiting for her husband to come in for luncheon ... (Somerset Maugham: *The Force of Circumstances*)

> There were four of us—George, and William Samuel Harris, and myself and Montmorency. We were sitting in my room, smoking and talking about how bad we were—bad from a medical point of view I mean, of course ... (Jerome: *Three Men in a Boat*)

> It was now lunch time and they were all sitting under the double green fly of the dining tent pretending that nothing had happened ... (Hemingway: *The Short Happy Life of Francis Macomber*)

And we read on, caught up in the discourse, involved in creating a world with language, and learning language at the same time as we use it in the realization of another reality. Far from being diminished, human experience is extended.

As with prose fiction, so with poetry. There has been a good deal of investigation over recent years into the interpretative procedures that have to be used to infer the underlying coherence in everyday conversation. Poems set problems of interpretation which make appeal to the same procedures but simply require them to be more intensively and more consciously applied, because, again, we cannot count on an external context to provide us with clues.

> She tells her love while half asleep ...

Who are you talking about? What is the point in telling us this?

> She tells her love while half asleep,
> In the dark hours,
> With half-words whispered low:
> As earth stirs in her winter sleep
> And puts out grass and flowers
> Despite the snow,
> Despite the falling snow.
> (Robert Graves)

Remote though it may seem to be from the practical use of language so close to the heart of current pedagogy, poetry calls for the same sort of creative accomplishment as is necessary in the understanding of the most ordinary and practical conversational exchange. Poetry is useful language because it represents language use, textual display is not because it doesn't.

The useless language of the textbook can have some pedagogic value as a device for demonstration and it can provide repetitive practice for the subconscious assimilation of linguistic forms. These advantages should not be denied. But the problems it poses are internal linguistic problems and not problems outside language which language is needed to solve. So this typical textbook language cannot of its nature develop the procedural activity so essential to language use and learning. Literature, of its nature, can. It can contribute significantly to both the process and the purpose of learning because it is a significant use of language.

But this is not to say that we should throw off all constraint, replace our course books with copies of *Paradise Lost* and *Finnegan's Wake* and confront our students with the baffling obscurity of the storied urn and the animated bust. We still have the responsibility to provide guidance by the careful selection and presentation of literary texts so that their potential as discourse for developing learning can be realized.

But until the case for a reprieve of literature has been accepted in principle, we cannot make a start on its rehabilitation in practice. This is why, to use a deliberate ambiguity, I appeal against the sentence. And this is why I have tried to argue today for the use of literature as a relevant resource in the process and the purpose of language learning.

Note

Paper given as a plenary address at the TESOL Convention, Detroit, March 1981, and published in Hines and Rutherford 1982.

SECTION FIVE
English for specific purposes

The argument in all three papers in this Section develops as an enquiry into the common assumption that what typifies ESP, and distinguishes it from English teaching in general, is that its courses are designed to a specification derived directly from a description of the required target repertoire, and so can exactly define the language that the teachers need to deal with.

Paper 13 points out that to design courses only with reference to terminal needs, to what the learners will eventually have to do with their language, leaves out of account their transitional needs as actual learners. The goals of learning can be specified by a description of the competence to be achieved, but the process of achieving can only be accounted for by reference to some theory about how people learn. The paper discusses, in appropriately tentative fashion, certain ideas about cognitive style which seem to have a bearing on this question. It suggests that to the extent that different cognitive styles are informing influences on the methodologies of academic subjects, then course design for ESP in these areas might, in following a process orientation, use these methodologies as a primary source of reference. The paper also suggests that a process-oriented approach to course design will of its nature allow for the achievement of terminal purpose by its very provision for transitional means of learning.

This suggestion is taken up and elaborated on in Paper 14. This seeks to show that the more precise a specification is, in the exact itemization of language forms, functions and skills, the further removed it becomes from the actuality of language use. It argues that only through an engagement with the negotiation of meanings in discourse can learning effectively take place. The process of discourse enactment and the process of learning are seen as essentially the same, so that provision for the former, as is required if learners are to achieve their terminal purpose, is accounted for in

provision for the learners' transitional needs. The further point is
made that since this process cannot be directly specified, it cannot
be directly taught: it can only be carried out by the learner going
beyond the confines of course specification and converting teacher
input to his own use.

Paper 15 places the issues raised in the other papers in this
Section in a general education context. It suggests that degree of
specification in the knowledge and skills to be learned corresponds
to points on a training—education continuum, and also relates this
continuum to the model of discourse outlined in Section Three.

Although the papers in this Section are nominally concerned with
ESP they naturally bring in considerations of much wider import
which have to do with the principles of language teaching in
general. They therefore prepare the ground for the section which
follows. One might add that it is not the least of the benefits that
ESP has brought to our profession that its widespread institutional
acceptance has challenged us to enquire into the pedagogical
justification for its existence, and this in turn has involved a
consideration of more general issues relating to the teaching and
learning of languages.

13 Criteria for course design

The work that has been done on the teaching of English for Special or Specific Purposes (ESP) has generally been predicated on the following assumption: if a group of learners' needs for the language can be accurately specified, then this specification can be used to determine the content of a language programme that will meet these needs. Thus, if, for example, we can specify what students of economics need to be able to do with English by analysing their textbooks or what waiters need to be able to do with English by analysing their interaction with patrons, we can devise custom-made courses of English that incorporate the results of the analysis.

This assumption of the necessary determination of course content by the learner's requirement for the language seems to underlie remarks in Halliday, McIntosh, and Strevens (1964), where mention is made here of 'English for civil servants; for policemen; for officials of the law; for dispensers and nurses; for specialists in agriculture; for engineers and fitters'. The authors go on to say: 'Every one of these specialized needs requires, before it can be met by appropriate teaching materials, detailed studies of restricted languages and special registers carried out on the basis of large samples of the language used by the particular persons concerned. It is perfectly possible to find out just what English is used in the operation of power stations in India: once this has been observed, recorded and analysed, a teaching course to impart such language behaviour can at last be devised with confidence and certainty' (Halliday et al. 1964: 190).

A more recent expression of this assumption, illustrated by a detailed demonstration of how it might be put into practice in ESP course design, appears in Munby (1978). The epilogue to that work contains the following statement: 'This book has been concerned with language syllabus design. More specifically, the contention has been that, when the purpose for which the target language is required can be identified, the *syllabus specification is directly derivable from the prior identification of the communication needs* of that particular participant or participant stereotype' (Munby 1978: 218 [italics added]).

It seems reasonable enough to assume that a specification of language needs should define the language content of a course designed to meet such needs. My purpose in this chapter, however, is to argue that such an assumption is mistaken, at least as far as English for Academic Purposes (EAP) is concerned, and to suggest alternative criteria for course design.

The first point to be noted, perhaps, is that the expression 'learner needs' is open to two interpretations. On the one hand it can refer to what the learner needs to do with the language once he or she has learned it. This is a *goal-oriented* definition of needs and relates to terminal behaviour, the ends of learning. On the other hand, the expression can refer to what the learner needs to do to actually acquire the language. This is a *process-oriented* definition of needs and relates to transitional behaviour, the means of learning. It is the first of these interpretations which is favoured in current ESP work. The basic belief is that which seems to be expressed in the quotation from Halliday *et al.* just cited: once the language the learners will have to deal with is described, then teaching courses can be devised with confidence and certainty by directly applying this description. Thus it is the ends that determine course design. The means, apparently, must shift for themselves.

This goal-oriented approach follows a well-established tradition. Its most familiar manifestation is in the early work on vocabulary selection that served as the basis for the structural syllabus. Here the basic procedure was to delimit the content of the syllabus in terms of linguistic items by reference to primary criteria like frequency, range, and coverage, all of which served to define what it was supposed the learner ultimately ought to acquire as terminal behaviour. Factors like learnability and teachability, which relate to means, were only adduced as contingent considerations for making minor modifications to the basic course design. This procedure has been subject to much critical discussion (e.g. Mackay 1965, Widdowson 1968) and more recently Wilkins has pointed out its limitations as a preliminary to his own proposals for what he claims to be a radically different approach. The approach he proposes however is, with respect to the two kinds of orientation I have mentioned, not really different at all. It is important for my argument here to demonstrate why not.

Having given an outline of the principles of vocabulary control, Wilkins reports, with approval, an observation made in Reibel

(1969) to the effect that '.... what is happening here is that we are taking the language behaviour and the language knowledge that we aim to produce in our learners, we are analysing the linguistic components of the desired performance and isolating its units. We are then teaching the units piece by piece so as to get back to the very position from which we started...' (Wilkins 1976: 5).

Now it emerges from subsequent discussion that Wilkins's objection to this procedure is not that it allows goal-oriented needs to determine course design but that the kind of linguistic components that are specified represent only a part of the language knowledge and behaviour that the learner needs to acquire eventually. His criticism of these criteria for defining course content is essentially that they operate on the wrong kind of unit: they isolate forms rather than functions and so develop grammatical rather than communicative competence. But the principle of allowing goal-oriented needs to determine the content of a course is retained as fundamental to the approach. This principle is stated quite explicitly in the following passage:

> The process of deciding what to teach is based on considerations of what the learners should most usefully be able to communicate in the foreign language. When this is established, we can decide what are the most appropriate forms for each type of communication. The labelling for the learning units is not primarily semantic, although there is no reason why the structural realization should not also be indicated. A general language course will concern itself with those concepts and functions that are likely to be of widest value. In the same way, in the provision of a course for a more specialized language learner, the limitation is on the types of content that he needs to express and not on the number of structures he needs to know or the situations in which he will find himself. In short, the linguistic content is planned according to the semantic demands of the learner. (Wilkins 1976: 19)

The innovation here lies in the redefinition of learning units as 'concepts and functions' rather than as structures, but the units themselves are still seen as derivable from desired terminal behaviour. It is still assumed that syllabus content must be determined by the goals rather than the process of learning.[1] Wilkins's reference to specialized language learners returns us to the main theme of ESP. The point he makes here is much the same as that made by Halliday *et al.*: with ESP one can be more precise than one can be with 'general' language courses in the specification of what language the learner will eventually have to cope with. The difference again lies in how this language is to be characterized. Halliday *et al.* think in terms of *what* English is used and speak of 'restricted languages' and 'special registers.' Their attention, therefore, is focused on linguistic forms whose incidence can serve to identify different varieties of English usage. Wilkins, on the other hand, thinks in terms of *how* English is used for the expression of concepts and the performance of functions whose incidence can serve to identify different varieties of English *use*. With reference to distinctions I have suggested elsewhere (e.g. Widdowson 1977) the view taken by Halliday *et al.* (and those of similar persuasion, like Crystal and Davy 1969) leads to a description of language variety as *text* defined as the way a particular language is manifested when it is put to particular purposes. Thus statements about the frequency of the passive or certain modal verbs in written scientific English are statements about text. The view taken by Wilkins (and those of similar persuasion) leads to a description of language variety as *textualization*, defined as the way a particular language realizes the concepts and functions of a particular type of discourse. Thus statements about how the passive or certain modal verbs in English are used to conduct scientific analysis and exposition are statements about the textualization in English of scientific discourse.

There are, then, two ways of describing a particular variety of English identified as the terminal goal of a particular group of learners. One way is to describe it as register: this involves making statements about its formal properties as a type of English text. The other way is to describe it as rhetoric: this involves making statements about the English textualization of a type of discourse, of a mode of communicating. It is in adopting this second mode of description that Louis Trimble and his associates have made their very considerable contribution (e.g. Lackstrom, Selinker, and Trimble 1970, 1972; see also Swales 1974) and there seems little doubt that this is the more profitable line to take, accounting as it does for the communicative functioning of language. Furthermore, such a description can be used to adduce aspects of the methodology of academic·subjects and so can be made relevant to a process-oriented approach. More of this later. For the present, the point I wish to make is that whether we describe text or textualization, register, or rhetoric, if we assume that our language description must directly *determine* course content then in both cases we adopt a goal-oriented approach to course design and focus attention on ends rather than means. I have said that this is a mistaken thing to do. It is time to give some substance to this assertion.

If one allows the description of the language-to-be-acquired to determine course content, whether this is done in terms of linguistic forms or communicative functions, then one assumes an equation between teaching and learning. By this I mean that one assumes that what is to be learnt must be expressly and explicitly taught. Yet we all know that learners have an irritating tendency towards independent action and will frequently follow their own patterns of learning behaviour in spite of the teaching patterns imposed upon them. These expressions of self-assertion are commonly characterized as errors. The term itself indicates that we interpret these expressions as evidence that learners learn *less* than they are taught, and our usual reaction is to try to restore the equation by more teaching. But of course we can equally well take these expressions as evidence that learners learn *more* than they are taught. As is now widely recognized, although these peculiarities of learner language may indicate a failure in teaching in that they deviate from the presented norm, they are also evidence of the learner's capacity for developing creative learning processes of his or her own.

It seems to me that the pedagogic equation, upon which the goal-oriented approach to syllabus design depends, must be wrong because the two sides of the equation are essentially different in kind. The teaching side can be expressed as a kind of product, a collection of formal or functional units to be stored away in the mind as knowledge. The learning side can be expressed as a kind of process, a set of strategies for making sense. In the classroom what commonly happens is that the teacher busily tries to change the learner's process into a product and the learner busily tries to change the teacher's product into a process. The teacher attempts to get the learner to put the language data in store and the learner keeps on converting it into energy to drive his or her own acquisition strategies.

Thus a fundamental conflict is created between what the learner needs to do in learning on the one hand and what the learner needs to have acquired after learning on the other. A goal-oriented approach focuses on the latter and makes what I believe to be the mistaken assumption that what the learner has to acquire necessarily has to be taught directly. The irony of the situation is that in trying to place his or her product the teacher inhibits the very process that would enable the learner to eventually acquire it.

What, then, is the alternative? I want now to consider what I have called a process-oriented approach, one concerned with transitional behaviour and the means of learning.

To begin with, such an approach rejects the pedagogic equation and accepts from the outset that the language data given to the learner will not be preserved in store intact but will be used as grist to the mental mill. Hence the language content of the course is selected not because it is representative of what the learner will have to deal with after the course is over but because it is likely to activate strategies for learning while the course is in progress. In principle, therefore, it is possible to conceive of an ESP course containing very little of the language associated with the special purpose so long as the language that it *does* contain is effective in developing the ability to achieve the special purpose after the teaching is over. In practice, of course, this facilitating language will often correspond quite closely in some respects to that of the special purpose because of the likely correspondence between what the learners need the language for and the ways in which they will acquire it. This point is closely related to the observation I made earlier about the potential relevance of a rhetorical description of language variety. I shall return to it presently. For the moment it is enough to note that if one avoids presenting *The Grapes of Wrath* and *The Mayor of Casterbridge* to students whose goal is to read engineering textbooks it is not because these novels are unrepresentative of engineering English but because we judge that they are not likely to engage the interest and to activate the learning strategies of such students and so would not have the necessary facilitating function.

Whereas the goal-oriented approach, then, focuses on the selection of language by reference to the ends of learning, allowing the means to be devised *ad hoc*, the process-oriented approach focuses on the presentation of language by reference to the means of learning and allows the ends to be achieved by the learner by exercising the ability he or she has acquired. The first approach assumes that the completion of a course of instruction marks the completion of learning and that all that is left for the student to do is to apply this ready-made knowledge. The second approach assumes that learning will continue beyond the completion of instruction since the aim of such instruction precisely is to develop a capacity to learn: it does not itself realize any special purpose but provides the learner with the potential for its realization.

If one follows a goal-oriented approach one needs to take one's bearing from models of linguistic description, since these will define the units of course content. A process-oriented approach, on the other hand, can only be pursued by reference to some idea about how people learn. There is, of course, a vast literature on this subject and this is not the place to review it, even if I felt competent to do so. What I would like to do, however, is to direct attention to certain recent work on different cognitive styles that, tentative though it is, promises to have some relevance to ESP course design.[2]

I want to consider first a distinction made in Pask and Scott (1972) between two types of learners: the serialist and the holist. The strategy adopted by the first of these is to follow a direct route, proceeding step by step, and avoiding digression and irrelevance. The holist's strategy, on the other hand, is to advance on a broad front, allowing access to all manner of information that might help him or her to find the way. Pask and Scott express the difference in rather more technical terms: 'Serialists learn, remember, and recapitulate a body of information in terms of string-like cognitive structures where items are related by simple data links: formally, by "low order relations." Since serialists habitually assimilate lengthy sequences of data, they are intolerant of irrelevant information unless, as individuals, they are equipped with an unusually large memory capacity. Holists, on the other hand, learn, remember and recapitulate as a whole: formally, in terms of "high order relations"' (Pask and Scott 1972: 218).

One might suppose that the terms *serialist* and *holist* could refer to alternative learning strategies within an individual's repertoire that are freely selected as appropriate to a particular learning task. But this is apparently not the case: Pask and Scott produce experimental evidence that indicates that there is a distinct difference in individual ability to deal with holist and serialist tasks. We are led to the conclusion that what we have here are two different kinds of competence. The pedagogic significance of this seems clear. If a teacher uses serialist methods he or she will inhibit the learning of holist pupils and vice versa. One might suppose that a solution to this dilemma would be to develop a methodology that combines serialist and holist procedures, thereby providing pupils with an equal opportunity to learn according to their natural cognitive tendencies. The difficulty with such a proposal is that one thereby imposes an unnatural programme on the teacher, since he or she will be inclined to teach according to his or her particular cognitive style and the lessons are unlikely to be very effective if the teacher is forced to do otherwise.

We appear to have arrived at an impasse. I have said, approvingly, that a process-oriented approach to course design uses language data as a means of activating learning strategies. Clearly this activation can only occur if the manner in which the language is presented is in accord with the cognitive style of the learners. But how can it be in accord with different cognitive styles, which may indeed be mutually incompatible? As far as I can see, there are only two ways round this problem. One is to design language programmes that will in some way provide for parallel development corresponding to the different styles. Here one runs up against the problem of the teacher's style, which I referred to earlier. The alternative is to separate the holists from the serialists and provide them with different programmes altogether. This latter looks to be a hopelessly impracticable proposition, particularly if it turns out (as seems likely on the face of it) that a much more delicate distinction between styles will be needed. However, in the ESP context, especially where the purposes refer to academic study, it may be that this is a natural and necessary course to take.

The grounds for this belief lie in the likelihood of different types of learner separating of their own accord to follow distinct lines of academic enquiry. There is some evidence to suggest that this does indeed happen and that there is a correspondence between disciplines and cognitive styles. Such evidence is to be found, for example, in the research recorded in Hudson (1966). Hudson also makes a broad distinction between two types of learner: he calls them convergers and divergers, and he defines them with reference to types of intelligence test. A typical question in a conventional intelligence test requires the subject to select from a restricted range of alternatives. Hudson gives the following example:

Brick is to house as plank is to ... orange, grass, egg, boat, ostrich.

And he comments: 'The victim knows that there is one solution which is correct, and his task is to ferret it out. His reasoning is said to *converge* on to the right answer.'

Instead of restricting the subject to a choice from a closed system, however, one can set an open-ended task and so invite a 'creative' response, as in the following example:

How many uses can you think of for a brick?

Hudson comments: 'Here, the individual is invited to *diverge*, to think fluently and tangentially, without examining any one line of reasoning in detail' (Hudson 1967: 50).

Now it seems to be the case that, as with the case of serialist and holist strategies, these two modes of mental operation are not equally accessible to all individuals. Some perform well on conventional tests and badly on creative tests and are naturally convergent in cognitive style, while others do the opposite and are naturally divergent.

What is of particular significance for the present discussion, however, is that convergers and divergers appear not to be evenly distributed throughout the student population but tend to cluster according to subject. Floyd, in an admirably clear exposition of research on cognitive styles, summarizes the findings of Hudson's work with open-ended tests as follows:

> ... Hudson had hoped that these open-ended tests would cut across the arts/science distinction and give some reflection of the boys' brightness. In fact, the opposite occurred. Scores on open-ended tests provided a very good measure of the arts/science split. Arts specialists tended to be divergers, weaker on intelligence tests than open-ended tests, whilst the scientists went the other way. In Hudson's sample between three and four divergers went into history, English literature and modern languages for every one that went into physical science; and between three and four convergers did mathematics, physics and chemistry for every one that studied arts subjects. Classics appeared to belong with physical science, while biology, geography, economics, and general arts were studied by convergers and divergers in roughly equal proportions. (Floyd 1976: 46)

It is not clear how far the cognitive styles distinguished by Pask and Scott can be set into correspondence with those of Hudson. It does seem however that serialists and convergers are alike in preferring precision and rational control and in their inclination towards the exact sciences, whereas holists and divergers share a common preference for wider networks of association and for imaginative excursion and incline towards the arts and the social sciences. At all events, the possibility emerges that the methodologies of different disciplines can themselves be characterized in terms of cognitive styles, being formalizations of different ways of resolving problems and of conceptualizing and controlling reality. If this is so, then it becomes feasible in principle to design programmes of English for academic study to accord with the learners' cognitive bias because the learners have already grouped themselves by the process of a kind of natural selection in their choice of subject specialization. Thus, a process-oriented approach to the teaching of English to, let us say, physical science students would adopt predominantly serialist/convergent type procedures of presentation. A course for social science students, on the other hand, would adopt procedures of a predominantly holist/divergent kind. All this sounds plausible enough. But how, the opposition might ask, does one set about discovering such procedures? For it must be recognized (and is recognized by the scholars I have referred to) that a good deal of research has yet to be done before different cognitive styles can be isolated and defined with confidence. And it would seem unlikely that such definite distinctions between serialists/holists and convergers/divergers can be maintained. In these circumstances the best one can do, I think, is to design EAP programmes by direct reference to the methodologies of subjects concerned on the grounds that these must of their nature incorporate the cognitive styles associated with their particular areas of enquiry.

Returning to the observation I made earlier, we can now see why it is that in respect to English for academic study what the learners need the language for may closely correspond to the ways in which they will acquire it. Both relate to the particular combination of cognitive styles that define the methodology of the subject of their specialization. So if one allows this methodology to determine the methodology of the language teaching, then one will necessarily be developing strategies in learning that will be applicable to later study. One can also see, I think, why it is that a description of the language to be learned as textualization is to be preferred to one that characterizes that language as text. It is because the discourse that is textualized must, as a particular mode of communicating, also correspond to the cognitive styles that characterize the subject. The difference between a goal-oriented and process-oriented approach lies in the way such a rhetorical description is used. The former uses it directly as a determinant of course content, an area of language to be selected and expressly taught. The latter uses it as evidence of ways of thinking that might indicate how language is to be presented so as to engage the appropriate cognitive styles. Of course, it may turn out in particular cases that the content of a course draws quite extensively on the description, but with process orientation it will do so not because it represents the language to be learnt, but because it is effective in activating the process of learning.

There is, I think, some reason to suppose that a process-oriented approach based on the principles I have tried to outline here would, by satisfying the cognitive needs of the learners, guarantee the eventual attainment of the desired terminal behaviour. The means imply the ends and transitional and terminal behaviour are simply different points on the same learning continuum. Whereas, as I have suggested, a goal-oriented approach creates a conflict between what the learner needs to do in learning and what he or she needs to have acquired *after* learning, a process-oriented approach based on subject methodologies contains no such conflict because these needs converge in the learning process itself.

All this may sound reasonable enough, but of course no problem has been solved. Things are never as neat as a turn of phrase can make them seem to be. For one thing we clearly need to know more about varieties of cognition: on the one hand, pedagogy, and indeed the very possibility of social life, depends on establishing styles of thinking across individual differences; on the other hand, people are unlikely to fall into neat binary divisions. We need to know more, too, about the cognitive style constitution of different methodologies and to investigate particular ways in which they can be exploited by language teaching procedures. All I wish to suggest here is that we should consider academic purposes in terms of learning processes reflected in specific methodologies rather than as static goals defined as language knowledge. To do this is not to solve an old problem but to restate it in different terms so that it can be approached from another direction.

Notes

Paper first presented at the TESOL Convention, Mexico City, April 1978, and published in revised form in Selinker, Tarone, and Hanzeli 1981.

1 It could be argued (a point made by Devon Woods) that the structural syllabus in fact focuses on process rather than goal since its proponents did not really suppose that the language presented constituted terminal behaviour but only the basis for its ultimate acquisition. I am not so sure about that. Why, if this is so, did frequency, range, and coverage figure so prominently as criteria for course content? And why was success generally assessed by reference to achievement as a measure of knowledge rather than by reference to proficiency as a measure of ability?

The truth of the matter is, I think, that the structuralists never really got their criteria clear and so their kind of syllabus contains a basic contradiction (discussed in Widdowson 1968): it was designed by reference to goals but is essentially only justified by reference to process. In both structural and notional syllabuses, at any rate, the assumption is that whatever later learning might take place after the course, it can do so automatically from accumulated knowledge, either of structures or notions.

2 My attention was first directed to this work by Althea Ryan, when she was conducting research in the Department of Linguistics, University of Edinburgh, on the relevance of cognitive styles to language teaching. This work was supported by the Hornby Trust and Oxford University Press.

14   ESP and the curse of Caliban

My text for this morning may seem as remote from ESP as it is possible to be: it is from Shakespeare's *The Tempest* Act I Scene 1 Line 353.

Prospero to Caliban/teacher to pupil:

> I pitied thee,
> Took pains to make thee speak, taught thee each hour
> One thing or other: when thou didst not, savage,
> Know thine own meaning, but wouldst gabble, like
> A thing most brutish, I endow'd thy purposes
> With words that make them known.

Caliban, however, is not a very appreciative pupil. He replies:

> You taught me language, and my profit on't
> Is, I know how to curse. The red plague rid you
> For learning me your language.

Learning me your language! He is not a very accomplished pupil either. I shall come back to this confusion of *teach* and *learn* a little later. For the moment let us note that although Caliban is somewhat deficient in accuracy, he seems to have acquired a considerable fluency in the language—particularly when it comes to cursing. But although Caliban may consider this his profit, it was certainly not Prospero's purpose in teaching. What, then, was his purpose? The answer seems quite clear. Earlier in the scene, Prospero is talking to his daughter Miranda:

Prospero	We'll visit Caliban, my slave, who never Yields us kind answer.
Miranda	'Tis a villain, sir, I do not love to look on.
Prospero	But, as 'tis, We cannot miss him; he does make our fire, Fetch in our wood, and serves in offices That profit us. What, ho! Slave! Caliban!

Again the profit motive or profit motif. But Prospero's profit and Caliban's profit are in clear contrast. We can be fairly sure that Prospero's purpose was a specific one: to teach Caliban language so as to make him a more effective slave: ESP.

But the pupil proves to be difficult. He has ideas of his own, and these include having designs on Miranda. He has other purposes, so the teaching fails. But he does learn how to curse. How, one wonders, has he managed to do that, since one must assume that cursing did not figure as a function in Prospero's language course. The teaching fails because it does not achieve the specific purpose of subservience; but Caliban succeeds in learning (or acquiring) the language suited to his needs as an individual. He refuses to be confined by the ESP prescribed for him—thereby risking confinement of a different kind: being pegged within the knotty entrails of an oak.

Caliban and Prospero are fictional figures: one is a monster and the other a magician. But they have their counterparts in our workaday world, and they provoke questions of particular relevance to ESP. Consider, for example, this matter of confinement. ESP is generally practised on the basic assumption that it is both desirable and feasible to delimit the language to be learned to match a specification of learner requirements. But is such a delimitation desirable? It may give language teaching a certain air of cost-effectiveness, but does it not also reduce the learner to a kind of commodity? Does it not also imply that his opportunity is delimited to the confines of the particular role for which the language has been specified? ESP could be interpreted as a device for keeping people in their place.

Suppose, for example, that you wished to teach a specific English course for waiters. You might first investigate the language behaviour required of waiters: *Good evening sir, madam. Can I help you? Might I recommend the halibut* etc. You then incorporate this behaviour into a teaching programme with the intention of turning out English-speaking waiters. If you succeed in keeping to the exact specification, you will produce a set of clones: tokens of the same stereotype all programmed to behave alike like robots. There will be no possibility of your waiter expressing any personal idiosyncrasies of behaviour, no chance of witty chat or repartee. Furthermore, your waiter cannot use his English to change his position in life: he has been specifically programmed to fulfil that purpose and not any other. 'O brave new world that has such people in't.'

But of course you are unlikely to succeed in delimiting language behaviour in this way. Employers have employees, but teachers do not have teachees; they have learners and what learners do is, as Prospero discovered, not entirely predictable. No matter how precisely you specify what is to be taught, the learner will always tend to defy its limitation. Indeed if he does not he will not have learnt anything at all. Sometimes this learning of more than is warranted by teaching will look like deficiency. This is the case with the so-called errors that learners commit—commit: the very word implies a misdemeanor, an offence against the established order. But these expressions which do not conform to our rules of conduct are of course evidence of an extension from what has been taught. They are teachee failures, but learner achievements.

So pedagogic experience tells us that teaching and learning are not converse terms. 'There needs no ghost come from the grave to tell us this.' What is not so obvious is what should be done about it, particularly in the case of ESP, which seems to depend on learners being confined to teaching specifications. As in other areas of human activity, one is tempted towards the simplicity of extreme solutions. On the other hand one might insist on the primacy of teaching and try to force the learner into submission so that he becomes a model teachee. On the other hand, one might insist on the primacy of learning and try to reduce the role of the teacher to virtual insignificance.

The first alternative seems particularly pernicious nowadays and one might be inclined to think that its unacceptability is self-evident. But we should be careful of complacency. It is always possible to devise ways of reducing individual initiative to the point of unthinking conformity. There are types of pedagogic and political systems that specialize in it. I had better draw back from the brink of indiscretion and give another literary example. We are still in touch with Caliban and Prospero because the example is from Aldous Huxley's novel *Brave New World*. Here we are introduced to a new teaching technique called hypnopedia (not to be confused with suggestopedia), or sleep-teaching:

A small boy asleep on his right side, the right arm stuck out, the right hand hanging limply over the edge of the bed. Through the loud grating in the side of a box a voice speaks softly.

'The Nile is the longest river in Africa and the second in length of all the rivers of the globe. Although falling short of the length of the Mississippi-Missouri, the Nile is at the head of all rivers as regards the length of its basin, which extends through 35 degrees of latitude...'

At breakfast the next morning, 'Tommy,' someone says, 'do you know which is the longest river in Africa?' A shaking of the head. 'But don't you remember something that begins: The Nile is the...

'The-Nile-is-the-longest-river-in-Africa-and-the-second-in-length-of-all-the-rivers-of-the-globe...' The words come rushing out. 'Although-falling-short-of...'

'Well now, which is the longest river in Africa?'

The eyes are blank. 'I don't know.'

'But the Nile, Tommy.'

'The-Nile-is-the-longest-river-in-Africa-and-second...'

'Then which river is the longest, Tommy?'

Tommy bursts into tears. 'I don't know,' he howls.

Tommy does not learn anything because all he does is to put the teaching input in store without converting it into cognition. But this, you will say, is an extreme, and a fictional extreme to boot. This sort of thing is remote from the real world. I am not so sure. In Bloom's *Taxonomy of Educational Objectives* reference is made to something similar, to an occasion when Dr. John Dewey asked a class: 'What would you find if you dug a hole in the earth?'

Getting no response, he repeated the question; again he obtained nothing but silence. The teacher chided Dr. Dewey, 'You're asking the wrong question.' Turning to the class, she asked, 'What is the state of the center of the earth?' The class replied in unison, 'Igneous fusion.'

And if we search our consciences, shall we not find that we have ourselves been guilty of similar attempts to reduce learners to the status of teachees, obediently submissive to the patterns we impose on their behaviour? There have been times when we have tried to drive out the devil error by means of the incantation of drill with the rigour of the Inquisition: so the orthodox practice of accuracy has been imposed and fluency stifled. And we have at times insisted (have we not?) on the response which exactly matches our expectation and teaching input, allowing no plausible or natural alternative. Answer in complete sentences (so that I can be sure that you have taken in what I have been teaching you). All too often we have had our students dancing on sentence strings like marionettes manipulated by the master puppeteer. Dancing, as it were, to habit formation.

I exaggerate, of course. But the point I wish to make is plain enough, and I think worth pondering on. It is that given the lack of correspondence between teaching and learning, there will always be the temptation to balance the equation by adopting or devising what appear to be more effective *teaching* techniques for controlling behaviour and directing it towards specific objectives. There will always be the temptation, in other words, to try to change learners into teachees.

The other alternative looks more acceptable and seems to be coming into current fashion. Instead of insisting on the primacy of teaching you insist on the primacy of learning. You alter the grammar of the classroom so that the subject of the verb *learn* is in the agentive case and you simultaneously alter the sociology of the classroom so that there is a reversal of rights and obligations. The teacher now adapts his behaviour to learner requirements, and not the reverse. It is now he that has to conform and so become in a sense, I suppose, a learnee.

We should note that this enticing prospect of individual freedom is not without its problems too. It is based, for one thing, on the assumption that learners have the will and capacity to take the initiative required of them, and of course if they do not have these qualities then the opportunity for initiative will itself, paradoxically, become an imposition. There is the assumption, too, that learner regulated activity necessarily leads to more effective learning and that all teacher intervention which changes the course of learner tendency is interference and has negative effects in that it prevents and does not promote achievement. I am not so sure. One senses in this a sort of Wordsworthian reverence for the untutored mind which it would be wise to treat with circumspection. What if the learner, by reason of natural disposition or cultural conditioning, needs the security of control and confinement: he may welcome constraint and may not feel like an unwilling prisoner:

Nuns fret not at their convent's narrow room;
And hermits are contented with their cells...

And what if the learner cannot adequately structure his own learning activity but needs to have it organized for him? Left to his own devices, Caliban might never have known his own meaning, might have continued to gabble like a thing most brutish. He might never indeed have learned how to curse.

But having noted the temptation of excess we will agree, I think, that the learner must be allowed some room for independent manoeuvre: the problem is to know how much and of what kind. The very nature of learning precludes it from being a simple reflex of what is taught. To try to confine the learner to a restricted repertoire of behaviour and furthermore to determine the route he must take to obtain it will be an attempt on his identity as a human being which he is likely to resist. But then what kind of control is the teacher to apply? What principles of course design is he to follow which will guide the learner towards his own effective initiative?

These are questions of concern to TESOL in general of course, and the subject of much current debate. But they have particular significance for ESP, because on the face of it, it looks as if ESP is bound to lead towards a pedagogy of teacher imposition. It is after all apparently based on the assumption that once a particular restricted repertoire has been specified as the target objective representing the purposes for which the language is being learned, then this specification will determine what is to be taught. If the teaching works, then the learner will, at the end of the course, have obtained the repertoire he requires. The formula for this pedagogic alchemy would look like this: target needs equal teacher input equals learner intake equals target needs. I have already said that it seems to me that this sort of equation is impossible and that attempts to make it balance can only lead to undesirable pedagogic consequences. So what is to be done with ESP? Again temptation beckons towards an extreme position: reject it, write it off, abandon the band wagon. But it would be as well to consider it more closely before being quite so dismissive.

It may after all be possible to conceive of ESP in a somewhat different way—in a way which allows for the reconciliation of teacher and learner roles we are looking for. I believe that there is such a possibility and in the remainder of this paper it is my own specific purpose to explore it.

There are, I think, two questions about ESP which are quite fundamental and which we should enquire into with some care. The first has to do with target needs and how they might be specified. What does it mean to specify a restricted repertoire? The second question has to do with the relationship between such a specification and the design of a teaching programme. How is it to be actually implemented as pedagogic practice? The first question is concerned with how one goes about describing language behaviour and the second with how one goes about developing language *learning* behaviour. It turns out, I think, that the two questions are closely related. But I anticipate.

First the matter of specification. What is one being specific about in ESP? The claim is that one is providing a description of the English required to carry out certain academic or occupational activities. What does this involve? It might involve the identification of specialist vocabulary. We could say, for example, that the English required for students of physics will include words like *neutron, magnet, force* and *gravity*, as distinct perhaps from *crouton, magnum, fork* and *gravy*, which are words identifiable as belonging to the English required of the waiter. Similarly the English of accountancy will include *credit, debit*, and *limited liability*; that of medicine *urinate, amputate* and *rheumatoid arthritis*. One might then wish to supplement this qualitative account with a quantitative statement of word frequency. This in turn will reveal the common occurrence of certain closed system function words, of certain tense and aspect forms and so on, and from here one would naturally be drawn to an investigation of the grammatical properties of different registers of English. And so one might discover without too much surprise perhaps that the English used by waiters, the restaurant register, manifests a high proportion of interrogative sentences, that the English of science exhibits a preponderance of passives. And so on.

What then does all of this tell us? It tells us that, in conducting their business in English, people in certain occupations and academic disciplines typically favour certain words and certain structures. It tells us nothing whatever about their purposes in producing such forms. We are left to draw our own intuitive conclusions about that. It is important to recognize, I think, that to describe a variety of English in terms of lexis and grammar alone is to describe the linguistic by-product of communicative behaviour and not the behaviour itself. What we get is an account of different varieties of usage, different manifestations of the language system which can be used to identify but not to characterize kinds of behaviour. Linguists and language teachers may achieve their purposes by manifesting language in this way, but ordinary human beings in the normal traffic of everyday affairs do not: they put it to use as a handy device for getting things done.

Well now, if this is so, perhaps we should aim at characterizing kinds of language as particular ways of doing things, not as manifestations of linguistic forms but as realizations of communicative functions. So we might focus attention, for example, on the sort of activities which constitute the waiter's daily routine. He has to greet customers on arrival: *Good evening, sir, good evening, madam*; he has to ask and respond to questions: *Would you care to see the wine list? Would you recommend the prawns in aspic?* He has to suggest: *Would you like to try the haggis on rye?* and so on. Similarly, we might specify certain functions for the student of physics: he has to define, classify, describe, generalize, exemplify and so on. And so we shift our attention from linguistic forms as such and concern ourselves with the communicative functions they are typically used to realize. In this way, we characterize areas of ESP as specific repertoires of communicative competence.

But unfortunately things are not so simple. A consideration of the acts that people perform with their language advances us, I think, some way towards an adequate account of communicative competence, but it stops short of the desired destination. Because what it yields remains a description of successful *outcomes* of a process but not the process itself. We take a corpus of language and analyse it into items and although these may be functional ones like description, explanation, suggestion and not formal ones like interrogative and conditional, they remain items nonetheless. The labels may be different but we still attach them to finished products.

A description of the particular speech acts (or notions or functions) associated with a field of occupational or academic activity is still, then, a *post hoc* description of language text, the spoken or written result of the *discourse* which represents the actual communicative process. We recognize such acts or functions as the consequences of a successful negotiation of intended meanings. But how is success achieved? How is meaning negotiated? What does the communicative process involve? These are momentous questions. But let me try to sketch out a rough sort of possible answer. Something along these lines.

The act of communication involves the conversion of abstract knowledge into actual behaviour. When I open my mouth to speak, reach for my pen to write, I have certain information to convey for some purpose or another and I have a knowledge of certain rules of conveyance which I assume is shared by the person I am addressing. These are rules of usage and rules of use which enable me to formulate what I have to say and to associate my intention with conditions for effective social action. So I know the rules for framing propositions and I know the rules for providing these propositions with an intended illocutionary force. But the actual realization of these rules on particular occasions presents problems.

An example. I wish to invite a colleague to dinner. That is my intention and I know that there are certain conditions which have to hold for an invitation to be effective. One of them has to do with his availability, so I might first try and establish that:

Are you doing anything on Friday?

Now how is he to react? I am asking him to provide some information but he does not know why. Perhaps I intend to involve him in extra work, or to make another tedious attempt to convert him to Christianity. So at this point he will be inclined to be cagey:

Well, I'm not sure. Nancy may have plans.

He may actually not be sure what sort of information I want:

I'm teaching the M.A. in the morning.
No I mean in the evening.
Oh! Well I'm not sure...

Perhaps he *does* recognize my utterance as the first move towards an invitation to dinner and is not sure whether another necessary condition holds on this particular occasion: viz. that the prospect is a pleasant one. He may be an enthusiastic gourmet, a fanatic of French cuisine who knows that our religion forbids alcohol and imposes a strict vegetarian diet of boiled cabbage. Perhaps he already has something to do on Friday but may want to know whether what I propose is an improvement.

So both of us are engaged in negotiating the realization of what I want to say and my purpose in saying it. We know the rules but we have to work out how they are to be applied on this particular occasion, we have to employ interactive procedures to achieve our objectives. Every instance of language use presents us with problems of this sort of varying degrees of complexity, which have to be solved by tactical manoeuvring. If I want to describe something to you, I have to establish common ground so that my description makes sense. If I want to give you directions, then I have to take bearings first on your knowledge of the locality. If I want to insult you, I must find out first where you are vulnerable.

This is what I mean by discourse: the process of negotiating meaning by interaction. And communicative competence means the ability to enact discourse and so to exploit a knowledge of rules (usage and use) in order to arrive at a negotiated settlement. It is essentially a capacity for solving problems, not a facility for producing prepared utterances. So if we are going to specify a restricted repertoire, it should be represented as a range of problem solving strategies, involving the contingent use of language, not a collection of items.

What would the relationship be between a specification so conceived and the design of a teaching programme? We come to the second question I posed earlier. If you specify target objectives in terms of linguistic forms or communicative functions, you are left with the difficulty of knowing what to do with them. You have extracted these items out of a corpus of language. Now you have to put them back into whatever corpus you feel might be appropriate for teaching purposes. This can result in the most curious hybrids: examples of language which manifest the categories of your analysis but which have very little implication of utterance, obviously designed for display purposes only.

The croutons are in the soup.
I have a magnet.
There is a neutron in the atom.
The surgeon amputates the limb.

ESP. But the specific purpose here is the teaching of language as an exercise in its own right. The fact is that forms and functions only have *extra*linguistic significance, only take on communicative value, when they figure as elements in purposeful negotiation. When they are isolated from this setting, they simply create their own problems: they do not contribute to the solving of any.

The advantage of focusing on the discourse-developing strategies of problem solving is that in this way we preserve the specific purpose of forms and functions. At the same time, we provide for a natural transition from specification to teaching. For it seems to me that learning in general can be understood as the developing capacity for solving problems of one sort or another, of which the different subjects in the school curriculum can be seen as alternative formulations. The procedures used in the learning process do not seem to me to be essentially distinct from those used in the process of discourse enactment. Every use of language, I have argued, involves the exploitation of what one knows for clarifying and solving the problem posed by a new situation, this activity itself serving to extend our knowledge. Language use promotes acquisition just as acquisition promotes use: the relationship is reciprocal. So it is with discourse and learning. Every act of discourse engages the learning process and every act of learning engages the discourse process.

I would argue from this that a specification of target repertoires in terms of problems which will activate discourse-processing strategies simultaneously provides a basis for effective pedagogy. What the learner will eventually have to do with his language and the learning process required for achieving this objective are one and the same thing: a capacity for using language to negotiate meaningful solutions. In this view of the matter, learning is a function of normal social behaviour which is facilitated by formal instruction but which develops to be independent of it. The teacher's task is to create conditions which will make him unnecessary: he has to preside over his own declining influence.

But creating such conditions is a tricky business, which is why it cannot be left to the learner's own unaided efforts. It is here, I think, that ESP is at an advantage. For particular areas of language use can serve as a source of *types* of problem which the learner will recognize as pertinent to his concerns and which are therefore likely to engage his interest and his learning. The teacher's task is to identify and analyse these problem types so as to represent them in a range of activities which require the contingent use of language. Thus an ESP course for prospective waiters would include problems involving repair strategies for clearing up misunderstandings, ways of coping with varying role relationships and so on. A course for physics students would include problems in logical inference, in information transfer from one mode of communication to another and so on. But these activities do not confine the student to a narrow repertoire of behaviour since although of particular significance for his specific purposes, they call for strategies which activate language learning and use in general.

In ESP, then, the particular problems which are likely to appeal to learner interest and to activate learning can be derived from a consideration of specific purposes. Specification of such purposes, then, becomes a guide not primarily to the selection of language but to the manner of its presentation. The direction of dependency changes: instead of selecting language first and then casting about for ways of presenting it, one would focus on presentation first and then select according to its requirements. Specification becomes a principle of pedagogic methodology. In general TESOL, of course, where there are no specific purposes and so no particular problems on offer, the task is to find an alternative source of supply. I have suggested elsewhere that one possibility worth exploring is the methodology of other subjects on the school curriculum, all of which are, after all, concerned with the development of problem solving strategies associated with different aspects of reality ranged on some scale of increasing complexity. Here, I would have thought, is a potential source that would repay some prospecting. If we were to strike it rich, then all TESOL might become ESP. An intriguing thought.

Meanwhile, there is, I think, one important contribution that ESP (conceived of in the way I have proposed) can make to the common cause of TESOL in general. It suggests a way of effacing the division between what happens in the classroom and what happens outside. It offers an alternative to the usual pedagogic practice of reducing reality to a simulated microcosm in which students are ascribed roles which rehearse them for their later encounter with situations in the real world. In the approach to ESP I have outlined, the focus of attention is not on situations as such but on the type of conceptual and communicative problems that they represent, and the solving of such problems will engage strategies which apply to both language acquisition and language use, both within the classroom and in the world outside. The underlying role is always the role of language learner or, equivalently, of language user. There is no distinction between the rehearsal and the real performance.

But now my own performance must close. Time for the curtain. And it seems appropriate to bring back Prospero and Caliban for a final appearance. For Prospero seems to articulate the basic aim of ESP:

> I endow'd thy purposes
> With words that make them known.

But who decides the purposes and who decides how they should be endowed with words? Prospero, the traditional pedagogue, assumes that it is his decision and that Caliban, that shapeless monster the learner, gabbling like a thing most brutish, must simply submit to his direction. But Caliban has a mind of his own and succeeds in learning where the teaching fails. And the teacher Prospero is cursed for his pains. Only a story you will say, a work of fiction. Perhaps: but also a useful parable.

Note

Paper presented in plenary session at the TESOL Convention, San Francisco, March 1980. Subsequently published in Fisher, Clarke, and Schachter (1981).

15 English in training and education

Let me begin with a commonplace remark: students who come to the United States, or to Britain for that matter, for purposes of training and education need to know English. This is not a statement which is likely to cause much contention, or indeed to excite much admiration for my acuity. But commonplaces always conceal complexity to create the illusion of certainty, and this one is no exception. There are difficult issues I think lurking beneath this simple proposition which call for careful enquiry. There are two, in particular, that I want to consider on this occasion.

One of these issues arises from the question: what does it mean to say that foreign students need to know English?

The second arises from the question: what is training and how is it different, if indeed it is, from education? Are these different concepts, or are they simply the same concept dressed up in different terms?

I believe that both of these issues, and the way they are related, have an important bearing on a proper understanding of the activity which goes under the name of English for Specific Purposes (ESP): an activity which is directed towards the provision of English for people who need the language as a means of achieving their occupational and academic purposes. ESP has over recent years achieved institutional status without any very definite constitution in the form of an agreed set of principles. There is a suspicion, even, in the minds of some people that ESP is a kind of vast confidence trick practised on the ESL profession, so that one begins to feel a little furtive about expressing an interest in it. I hope that what I shall have to say might be of some help in clarifying its status as an area of enquiry and practice in the general field of English for Speakers of Other Languages.

So much for the preamble. Let us now get down to business. Two issues confront us.

First: what does it mean to know a language? One answer, familiar enough to those acquainted with the work of grammarians, is that to know a language means to know the meaning of linguistic signs and the rules for their permissible combination in sentences. But is this the kind of knowledge we are talking about when we say that students need to know English to follow their courses of instruction?

Consider an expression in English:

The liquid passed down the pipe.

What does this mean? In one respect the answer is obvious. You know what the words LIQUID, PASS, PIPE denote. You know that *ed* is a past tense morpheme denoting past time. Furthermore, since you know your syntax, you know that this is a correct combination of signs, whereas other combinations, for example:

The liquid pass down pipe.

or

The liquid down the pipe passed.

are not correct. So your knowledge of English enables you to recognize that the expression:

The liquid passed down the pipe

is correct, and it enables you, too, to assign it a meaning.

But of course I have presented this expression to you out of the blue, in detachment, out of context, and you naturally suppose it to be a *sentence*, only a sentence, and you treat it accordingly, as a device for exemplifying the system of English. You assume that I am *citing* the expression, and not actually *using* it to convey relevant information. If you supposed that I *were* using this expression in the normal business of communication, you would be entitled to be mystified. Which liquid? I see no liquid. Pipe? Where? And why is he providing us with this pointless piece of intelligence? The passing of liquid down a pipe has in itself no bearing whatever on my theme. Students need to know English and the liquid passed down the pipe. Education and training are different concepts and the cat sat on the mat. These are correct sentences, and as sentences they have meaning, but they are quite incoherent and indeed meaningless as utterances, as instances of actual language use.

Knowledge of English enables us to assign meaning to symbols and their combination in sentences. But we cannot necessarily understand what people mean *by* utterances by simply invoking this knowledge. For utterance meaning is not directly signalled by symbols: it can only be achieved by human agency whereby each sign is treated as an *index*, a pointer, a direction to be followed. To understand an utterance we have to use the linguistic signs as indicators to where meaning is to be found in the context of the immediate situation of utterance, or in the context of our knowledge and experience. The symbols of the sentence carry their meaning with them. The indices of the utterance draw our attention to where meaning might be found outside themselves, and direct us to conjure up a situation, a state of affairs, to which they could conceivably refer.

In language use, meaning, then, is achieved by indexical and not symbolic means and must engage knowledge other than a knowledge of the language system. Indeed it is difficult for a natural language user to avoid indexical interpretation, even when he is presented with what appears to be a sentence, an abstract construct in isolation. Consider again this expression:

The liquid passed down the pipe.

Why is it that we understand the pipe referred to here as a length of tube, rather than a device for smoking tobacco or a musical wind instrument? There is nothing in our knowledge of the syntax and semantics of English which would prevent such an interpretation. The reason that these alternative possibilities do not spring to mind is that the association of liquid and pipe calls up a familiar frame of reference, is indexical of a conventional schema.

Or, again, consider the expression:

They were working at their tables.

There is no difficulty in assigning *symbolic* meaning to this as a sentence. But it is difficult to make sense of it as an utterance because the pronoun *they* gives us very little to go on. They? Who? It provides us with no definite indexical direction to follow; we cannot associate it with any particular frame of reference or familiar schema. So we cannot know what kind of table is being referred to here: mathematical ones or kitchen ones, restaurant or roulette. There is no way of knowing. If, however, we were to provide a more specific value for the pronoun, we are then able to take schematic bearings and make sense of the utterance:

The children are working at their tables.
The waiters are working at their tables.

Again, there is nothing in the semantics, in the symbolic signification of these expressions that prevents us from calling up images of
children setting out place-mats and cutlery, or of waiters calculating their tips or their tax returns, or of either group taking part in a
carpentry competition, or working part-time as croupiers in a
gambling casino.

But these rather unusual scenarios do not come immediately to
mind. What we do is to use the linguistic signs in the utterances to take
bearings on the most familiar, the most plausible, state of affairs.

The Oxford English Dictionary provides the following denotation for the word MEAT:

The flesh of animals used for food.

Here are two expressions in which the word appears:

The butcher sliced the meat.
The waiter sliced the meat.

You understand MEAT in the first of these expressions as referring
to *raw* meat, on a slab, whereas in the second utterance you will
understand this sign differently as referring to meat which is
cooked, on a plate. So you recognize that we have here two distinct
indexical meanings because the signs direct your attention to two
distinct frames of reference. But there is no difference in *symbolic*
meaning, no change of denotation. And the engagement of a
particular frame of reference sets you on course to make sense of
what might follow:

The waiter sliced the meat. It smelt delicious.

A familiar state of affairs unfolds in the mind. A restaurant table,
steaming comestibles, the festive chink of wine glasses. But what
about:

The butcher sliced the meat. It smelt delicious.

This, on the other hand, calls up a strange, even perverted picture of
ghastly surrealism and ghoulish appetites. A vision of vampires and
eaters of the dead.

Or to turn to less macabre images, consider the homely
expression:

The tailor made the coat.

The symbolic meaning of MAKE, as recorded in the Oxford Dictionary, appears as follows:

'construct or produce by combining parts or putting materials together; form or shape from materials; bring into existence...'

But this denotational knowledge is not sufficient for us to realize the *indexical* meaning of MAKE in the context of this particular expression as having to do with the measuring, cutting and stitching of cloth, and as making reference to an operation which has very little resemblance to that which is referred to by the same sign, MAKE, in the following expression:

The potter made a vase.

The tailoring of cloth and the moulding of clay are entirely different processes, yet both can be referred to by the same sign because the sign can be indexical of quite different frames of reference.

There are occasions, of course, when a particular utterance is indexical of two equally plausible frames of reference and then we have a case of pragmatic ambiguity, and misunderstanding arises. There is an instance of this in a recent British television commercial. Two men are sitting next to each other in an aeroplane: one is obviously a Texan and the other, just as obviously, has the rather effete appearance of an artist. The following exchange takes place:

A Do you work in oil?
B Watercolour, actually.

A clear case of double exposure or indexical confusion.

What I wish to demonstrate by these examples is that meaning in language use is not simply the projection of our knowledge of what the symbols of English denote in isolation or in combination. It is achieved by realizing the indexical value of elements in the utterance and we do this by taking bearings on our knowledge of familiar frames of reference, what I will call *schematic* knowledge, as well as on our knowledge of the formal elements of our language, what I will call *systemic* knowledge. Meaning in language use, in other words, is a function of the relationship between what we know of our language and what we know of the world.

Now there are some uses of language where there are close correspondences between systemic and schematic elements, where there are routine formulae to follow which in effect efface the difference between symbol and index. In the English used for air-traffic control, for example, there is a highly restricted repertoire of expressions designed to convey precise information and to avoid any possibility of misunderstanding. This language is in effect a repertoire of routine formulae, of fixed system–schema correlations. It is obviously necessary that this should be so. The language is required for a strictly utilitarian purpose, and it would be positively dangerous if it were otherwise. We do not want the pilot of PAN AM Flight 123 coming in to land at Seattle to ponder on the meaning of messages by working out system–schema relations as the runway looms up before him. He needs to simply apply the required formulae in the same routine way as he checks and adjusts his instruments.

But most uses of language are not like this. They cannot so conveniently be reduced to formula. They involve us in the use of procedures for mediating between systemic and schematic knowledge, alternately taking readings from one and from the other so as to plot our communicative course. When we say, or write anything, we do not put our meanings into verbal packages like groceries. We provide only a collection of clues to be followed. We leave implicit what we suppose can be inferred from common knowledge and we count on shared assumptions, shared beliefs, shared frames of reference to extend and supplement the signs and so realize their indexical value. And at the receiving end, we have to read, and listen between the lines, where the dialectical process of system–schema interaction actually takes places. In normal circumstances, an engagement in language use, then, is an exercise in problem solving which cannot be anticipated in advance by the simple expedient of learning a set of formulae. There are, as I have said, some uses of language which are formulaic, where system and schema are in close correspondence. The airline pilot and air-traffic controller can be trained in the application of such formulae, and there are occasions in general language use when we lock in to preprogrammed routines of a formulaic kind: greetings, farewells, service encounters and other recurrent common rituals of everyday life. But where a gap opens up between system and schema so that *ex tempore* negotiation is necessary to relate them by taking readings from each and reconciling their differences, then something other than training is called for.

But what, then, is called for other than training? And what, anyway, do I mean by training? I come now to the second issue that I mentioned at the beginning: the difference, if there is one, between the concepts of training and education.

I would want to argue (and indeed I shall argue in what follows) that a valid distinction can be made between these concepts and, furthermore, that such a distinction can be associated with the distinction I have already drawn between system and schema. But notice first that what I am doing here nicely illustrates the points about language use that I have just been making. I am creating indexical meanings for these terms *education* and *training* within the schematic framework of this present discussion. In another frame of reference, it might well be convenient to consider them as in free variation, as synonymous expressions. In zoological discourse, it is necessary to make a terminological distinction between insects like bees and grasshoppers and arachnids like spiders and scorpions, but it would be perverse pedantry to insist on the distinction in the framework of ordinary conversation. The precise zoological term for a bee or a scorpion is not likely to be of much interest to you when you have been stung by one.

So there is no warrant in the dictionary for the distinctions I wish to make. The relevant entries in the Shorter Oxford Dictionary appear as follows:

Education: ... the systematic instruction, schooling or *training* given to the young (and, by extension to adults) in preparation for the work of life.

Training: ... The action of train. To instruct and discipline generally; to *educate*, rear, bring up.

These records of symbolic meaning conflate the two terms: to educate means to train and to train means to educate. But in the schema I am in the process of devising it is quite legitimate as a normal practice of language use to make an indexical distinction. And that is what I now propose to do.

I want to suggest that training is directed at preparing people to cope with problems anticipated in advance and amenable to solution by the application of formulae. Training in this sense is orientated towards specific aims. But education, as I conceive it, is not. Rather it is directed at developing general intellectual capacity, cognitive sets, attitudes, dispositions which, it is supposed, can be subsequently brought to bear to deal with any eventuality that may arise. Education in this sense has a general, not a specific, orientation. It follows from this that training fails if the output behaviour of those subjected to training does not match the input instruction. Trainer and trainee are converse concepts, as their morphology implies. But there is no such direct reflexivity in education: here teaching and learning are not converse activities.

The instructional input is intended to be converted into something other than itself, transformed into general principles which transcend the particular subjects of instruction. The trainer produces trainees. The teacher does not produce teachees.

Now it seems to me that this distinction between training and education can be reasonably related to the system–schema distinction. The two issues with which I started converge into one.

A knowledge of system is a knowledge of abstract principles and a knowledge of schemata is a knowledge of how these principles are realized in actuality in recurrent and familiar situations. The purpose of training, presumably, is to bring the two into as close a correspondence as possible so as to establish formulae which can be applied without reference to theoretical principles whenever a problem arises. When I ask an electrician to come to the house to repair a fault in the wiring, I do not expect him to arrive with a textbook of physics under his arm. Whatever physics he needs to know will have been incorporated into his formulaic practices and he will only know as much of physics as is required in handling the plugs, switches, fuses and so on in electrical circuits. Outside his role as an electrician he may of course know a good deal about physics, or about politics, computers, microbiology or Byzantine art. But that is a different matter. Training for particular kinds of task does not diminish the general potential of the human mind. Being an electrician does not preclude you from writing epic poetry if the spirit moves you to do so. It is, of course, possible to impose training on aspects of human life which are more properly the concern of education. But that too is a different matter.

The purpose of training, then, I suggest is to establish close formulaic links between areas of theory and practice, between system and schema, so that problems can be accounted for by the application of formulae with minimum adjustment. The purpose of *education*, on the other hand, is to allow for a disparity between theoretical system and practical schemata, and to provide for the general procedural ability to mediate between the two and to solve problems by referring back to principles and checking them against particular situations. Education, in other words, is in the business of developing the ability to negotiate solutions to problems that do not correspond in any obvious way with pre-existing formulae.

But here I must sound a cautionary note. The distinction I am drawing is a *conceptual* one and is not meant to imply that there is in reality a sharp division between training and education *programmes*. Courses of instruction will vary in orientation and in primary emphasis and will incline towards training or education as end points on a spectrum. So although it seems to me to be reasonable to define training as being directed at the achievement of specific aims by means of formulae which fix system–schema relations in advance, in actual practice, of course, training programmes, no matter how tightly constrained, will have to allow for *some* flexibility in the application of formulae, *some* provision for occasions when negotiation is needed to arrive at a solution.

Similarly, although I would wish to define the *concept* of education as relating to theoretical principles and to procedures for interpreting these principles into a range of unpredictable applications, there is likely in practice always to be some necessity to provide formulae. There are, after all, in what the dictionary calls 'the work of life' certain things which are straightforwardly a matter of routine, and do not need to be subjected to the analysis of abstract thinking every time they occur.

In one of his lesser known travels, Swift's Gulliver arrives on the flying island of Laputa and finds that the people who live there get so lost in abstract cogitation that they need servants to bring them back to reality by tapping them on the ear or mouth with inflated bladders like balloons filled with small pebbles or dried peas. Gulliver goes on to remark:

> Their houses are very ill built, the walls bevil, without one right angle in any apartment, and this defect ariseth from the contempt they bear to practical geometry, which they despise as vulgar and mechanic, those instructions they give being too refined for the intellectuals of their workmen, which occasions perpetual mistakes.

The problem of the Laputans, clearly, is that they are suffering from an excess of education untempered by elements of training: abstraction has taken over entirely from actuality. When practical things are to be done, they remain buried in thought, paralysed by cogitation. Hamlet, you will remember, was afflicted by a similar disablement. His professors at Wittenberg university can be seen in this respect as the real villains of the piece.

But it is time to return to the questions with which I started. What does it mean to say that foreign students need to know English? It means, I suggest, that they need to know how to use the resources provided by the language system to realize indexical meanings and this implies the ability to establish relations between the abstract system of symbols and the actual frames of reference or schemata which define their particular areas of enquiry or professional concern. Now where the instructional programmes these students are to follow have primarily a training orientation, then this relationship between system and schema will in large measure be formulated in advance. The language to be used will be formulaic in correspondence with the relatively formulaic nature of the specialist activity the students are to be trained in. And in this case it seems reasonable to talk about being specific in the prescription of language to be learned, although one must always bear in mind that programmes will in practice not usually be located at the extreme training end of the instructional spectrum, so that some allowance will generally have to be made for some educational element which cannot be reduced to formula. With this proviso, however, there are grounds for thinking of English for specific purposes in association with training programmes. It is less easy to justify specificity in respect of *educational* objectives.

For as one moves along the spectrum towards the education end, formulae become increasingly inadequate to the learner's needs, and one finds, accordingly, that one can be less and less specific in prescribing the required language behaviour. What is needed by students of biochemistry, medicine, economics, sociology and so on is the ability to use English to make inferences, to draw conclusions, to relate particular instances to general principles, in short to relate systems to schemata. Such students cannot be served by prescribed formulae; they need the general ability to negotiate meaning, to make sense in flight, *ex tempore* by means of language. Their educational purposes cannot be achieved by a restricted repertoire of system—schema correlates, but only by the use of procedures for inferring indexical meaning in the manner of the natural language user.

How is this procedural ability to be learnt? Only, I suggest, by associating the language to be learned with the kind of activities required of students in pursuit of their specialist objectives, so that the solving of problems in particular subject areas is contingent on the solving of problems in language use, and vice versa.

In learning how to use language, there are no language problems as such, but only problems which need language for their solution. What this means is that the methodology of English teaching designed to service the specialist needs of students must be congruent with the methodology of their specialization: it means, indeed, that it will be difficult to distinguish between them.

But in a good deal of material in the ESP field we find not only a lack of congruence, but a vast disparity between methodologies. Thus students of science who, in their specialist studies, will be engaged in endeavours of an intellectually taxing kind, are required in their English classes to go through mechanical routines of filling blanks in sentences, reading off symbol combinations from substitution tables, repeating structural patterns and so on. These are *training* techniques essentially, and entirely appropriate to training purposes. Thus there is no incongruence in concentrating on drills in the army method. But training techniques cannot of their nature achieve educational aims. You cannot drill people into creativity, or the exercise of critical intelligence. You cannot fix in advance the routes through the mazes of the mind.

ESP has in the past been centrally concerned with the specific *selection* of language to be taught. The argument I have been pursuing in this paper leads to the conclusion that student needs for English can only be met by appropriate methodology. Sometimes this methodology will be specific to suit the specificity of training objectives. Often, however, it will need to correspond to the more general educational requirements of intellectual enquiry and the solving of unpredictable problems. Most students need English for their studies not as a repertoire of formulaic language behaviour but as a creative capacity for achieving meaning by the exercise of thought. To concentrate on the specific is to run the risk of denying the very educational process which the language is intended to serve.

To conclude. We can I think only satisfactorily provide for the English needs of students if we understand that these needs are for language use, for the ability to realize indexical meanings, that language use cannot be defined in dissociation from the *kind* of learning purpose the students are seeking to achieve; that this purpose is itself a matter of pedagogic principle. Language teaching is bound up with issues in general pedagogy.

And in ESP, it is the relationship between E and P, language use and learning purpose, which is crucial (see Widdowson 1983) and this relationship is not self-evidently mediated by S, Specificity, but has to be established, without prejudgement, for every programme. I began with a commonplace. I will end with a paradox: to insist on being specific as a matter of principle is to reveal a misunderstanding of principle and so in this degree to betray one's own lack of education.

Note

Paper presented at a conference of the National Association for Foreign Student Affairs (NAFSA), Seattle, May 1982.

Communicative language teaching

The papers in this Section take up the issues that have been raised in previous papers about a user-oriented model of language, and consider their implication for language teaching and learning in general.

Papers 16 and 17 both discuss the possibility of basing course design on schematic structures (referred to in Paper 16 as routines) which would serve as a framework for procedural activities which it would be the business of methodology to stimulate. In this way, pedagogy creates the conditions for learning by replacing the analyst's model of language with that of the user, as outlined in previous papers, and in particular in those of Section Three, and by focusing, therefore, on capacity rather than on competence.

The idea of capacity is an important one in my scheme of things, and it is discussed in some detail in Paper 18. Whereas competence is taken to be a state of knowledge, stabilized by rules and necessarily an idealized representation of reality, capacity is conceived of as a dynamic set of procedures for exploiting knowledge, for creating meaning which has reference to rules but is not determined by them. Capacity in this sense cannot be accounted for in an analyst-oriented model of language. As Lyons puts it:

> To attempt to build into the linguist's model of the language system all the factors which determine our capacity to interpret utterances would be to nullify the very concept of language system. (Lyons 1977b: 420)

In order to realize meaning in language use, the user has to employ procedures which in effect put the linguist's idealization process into reverse. Furthermore, these procedures can operate to make meanings out of the total resource of the language and not only that part of the resource that has been codified as a rule in the system. Therein lies the potential for creativity and change in language use and this, as is pointed out in Paper 18, is not only realized in literary writing, where it is praised, but also in the deviant utterances of learners, where, generally speaking, it is deplored. This is not to say that learner error is to be equated with literary effect. The former exploits a limited range of linguistic resources and aims at reference, the latter exploits the full range and aims at representation (see Paper 11). Nevertheless, exploitation and the achievement of meaning beyond the confines of competence is evident in both cases. Creativity is common to both.

There is one further point about capacity that it is important to note. Unlike competence it is not language specific, but comprises a set of procedures for the communicative deployment of language in general. The learner of a second language will therefore come to his task already possessed of the capacity he needs to carry it out. If this is so, the teacher's responsibility is to provide language data in such a way that this capacity is engaged and in such a way also that it is constrained to service the acquisition of acceptable competence. The recognition of capacity as the driving force in language use and learning leads logically to a shift away from the idea of teaching as the imposition of patterns of knowledge and behaviour, however benevolently conceived, to an acknowledgement of the learner's claim to responsibility for his own role, even though he will need guidance in the part he has to play.

16 Teaching language as and for communication

While casting about for a suitable title for my talk today I came upon a terminological problem which I think has quite important implications for language teaching pedagogy. The first title that occurred to me was *Teaching Language for Communication* and then I thought I would amend this to *Teaching Language as Communication*. This would give the impression of consistency with, even development from, a book of mine that bears that title and perhaps enable me at the same time to indulge in some discreet publicity. On reflection, though, it struck me that my first title (Teaching Language *for* Communication) in fact captures more accurately what I feel we should be about when we teach language. The other title (Teaching Language *as* Communication) could be (indeed in some places has been) misleading. So let me begin with a brief semantic exercise to consider the different implications these two expressions seem to carry.

If one sets the two expressions into contrastive opposition, 'Teaching language *as* communication' seems to focus attention on the nature of the phenomenon to be taught: it seems to carry the implication, I think, that the teacher's aim should be to present language in such a way as to preserve its communicative character. It seems to suggest that there are aspects of language itself which are communicative and that these should constitute the essential content of courses. 'Teaching language *for* communication', however, seems to shift the emphasis from language as such to the activity of using it to achieve communicative ends, and to focus attention on learning objectives, referring not to what is actually being taught in the classroom but the desired outcome of that teaching activity.

This might appear to be a distinction without any real significance in practice—a typical bit of linguistic pedantry designed to make life more difficult. But I do not think so. The two ways of formulating the language teaching task do seem to point in different pedagogic directions and my purpose today is to explore where they go and see where they lead (or mislead) us.

If you think in terms of the teaching of language *as* (in contrast to *for*) communication you tend to look for ways of characterizing course content with reference to the communicative properties of language, and you will very likely come up with notional and functional categories: time, space, duration, cause, effect, on the one hand; identification, request, description, etc. on the other. These categories derive from the analytic findings of linguists and philosophers of language which are based on an idealization of data which disregards the actual process whereby such notions and functions are realized in acts of communication. This idealization necessarily carries over into the definition of course content so that we are left with a collection of notional and functional categories as analytic isolates associated with their most likely linguistic correlates in particular languages: a Council of Europe inventory. But the question now arises as to how such isolates are to be presented so that they are used in the actual communicative process from which they have been abstracted by idealization. For unless they are used *for* communication in the classroom they remain items to be stored as knowledge not essentially different from sentence patterns but with new labels attached. Consider an example. I have devised for this occasion the first few units of a beginners' syllabus in English along notional-functional lines.

Unit 1
Notional categories   Deixis, present point of time, singular quantity
Functional category   Identification
Unit 2
Notional categories   Deixis, present point of time, singular quantity, space location
Functional category   Locating statement
Unit 3
Notional categories   as above
Functional category   Request for information
Unit 4
Notional categories   As for Unit 2 + plural quantity
Functional category   As for Unit 2
Unit 5
Notional categories   As for Unit 2 but replace space location with attribute

Functional category   Description
Unit 6
Notional categories   Person, present duration of time, direction
Functional category   Commentary

Now what about linguistic realizations of these categories in English? This syllabus outline provides for the following sequence of language items:

Unit 1
This is a pen. This is a book. This is a bag.
That is a pen. That is a book. That is a bag.

Unit 2
The pen is here. The book is here. The bag is here.
The pen is there. The book is there. The bag is there.

Unit 3
Where is the pen? Where is the book? Where is the bag?
The pen is here/there, etc.

Unit 4
These are pens. These are books. These are bags, etc.

Unit 5
The pen is red. The book is blue. The bag is old, etc.

Unit 6
I am walking to the door. I am writing on the blackboard. He is opening the bag.

All very familiar. What's new when all the terminological obfuscation is cleared away? Old wine in new bottles—or perhaps old wine in old bottles with new labels. But this, some will say, is a travesty of the notional/functional approach, a gross distortion. But why? The learners are presented with language in communicative categories and they are being required to use these categories to identify, describe, make statements and commentaries, etc. in the recommended manner. But, you might retort, they are doing these things artificially and not in reaction to normal situations, so the language is not authentic; it is not really being presented as communication at all. These are pens, this is a bag, I am writing on the blackboard! I ask you!

Well now if the presentation of language as communication is not necessarily brought about by focusing attention on the communicative properties of language as identified by analysts, how can it be brought about? One might consider simply exposing learners to raw data—recordings of speech, chunks of written text. This is language in its natural communicative condition. The obvious difficulty here, of course, is that the learners have to recognize it as such. Genuine data though it may be, it would simply appear as incomprehensible gibberish if the learners lack the ability to *authenticate* it as communication. The pedagogic presentation of language, like the analytic description of language, necessarily involves methodological contrivance which isolates essential features from their natural surroundings.

Of course, there are ways of making the contrivance less evident and less of an imposition on the learner, so that he will be prepared to suspend his disbelief in the interests of the game. Or perhaps one could make the contrivance so obvious that its very absurdity is a motivating force, after the manner of Ionesco. It may be that a major deterrent to learning is the fact that learners have to solemnly go through the pretence of being serious when they say such things as 'This is a bag', 'This is my nose', 'My foot is here'. It would perhaps be more effective, with adult learners at any rate, if one acknowledged from the start that language classes were exercises in the theatre of the absurd. Whichever way one plays it, one has to accept the classroom game and work out the rules in such a way as to make the learners want to join in, and provide for the possibility of their actually winning from time to time.

I would argue then that the very principles of pedagogy will tend to work against the presentation of language *as* communication if by that we mean the transference into the classroom of natural uses of the language being learned, without pedagogic modifications of some sort to adjust these uses to a learning purpose. On the other hand, to deal in communicative features analysed out from natural uses will tend to make a communicative syllabus indistinguishable from a structural one. And the attempt to present language as communication may well be unnecessary anyway and so a waste of effort. It is justifiable only if it can be demonstrated that the teaching of language *for* communication depends upon teaching language *as* communication, on the presentation of language in its natural pristine state. And I do not think that it does.

We would agree, I think, that our teaching should be directed towards developing in learners the capacity to achieve their learning objectives and that these objectives have to do with the use of the language for effective communication. Whether or not we teach language *as* communication is an issue that can only be decided by reference to this teaching purpose. There is no merit in doing so as a matter of pointless principle. It may be that an over-enthusiastic belief in communicative presentation and a striving for authenticity in classroom language use could in fact lead a teacher to abandon types of conventional classroom activity which could be put to effective use in teaching *for* communication.

Perhaps I might at this point give one example of what I mean by this: how a too exclusive concern for presenting language *as* communication could lead to the neglect of procedures which contribute to the teaching of language *for* communication. The abilities we bring to bear in the natural use of language are hierarchically ordered in such a way that lower level skills are pushed down into automatic dependency on higher level ones. So it is that the discrimination of sounds in speech is normally carried out below the level of conscious awareness, thus leaving the mind free to handle the negotiation of meaning by reference to larger linguistic units. Obviously if we had to pay attention in language use to all the distinctions described in linguistics at the phonological, syntactic and semantic levels of organization, communication would be an extremely inefficient business. But we cannot do without a knowledge of such levels and the ability to shift down to them, since there will be occasions when the procedures we use to infer meanings from the larger language units will let us down. The lower level skills are a crucial back-up resource. But they have to remain in the background, utilized without conscious awareness, and so they have to become habitual. Since they normally operate at a subconscious level they would not normally have an executive role to play in actual communication and they would not figure very prominently, if at all, in the presentation of language *as* communication, which would be busy with notions and functions. They are crucial *for* communication however, and their function *for* communication depends on their automation, which is where repetitive drills come in. Drills which provide repetitive practice for sound discrimination or for the absorption of sentence patterns into habitual behaviour do not of their very nature deal with authentic language *as* communication. But they could provide an indispensable service in developing language *for* communication. This is not to say that the way they are conventionally used does fulfil that service, but only to say that they could be so used.

What then is involved in the teaching of language for communication? Let me at this point present a rough sketch of how I think communication is conducted, so as to give some idea of what it is that learners have to be able to use the language for. Communication, let us agree, is a function of the discourse process: unless a discourse is enacted no communication takes place, and discourse is not enacted by the simple expedient of expressing individual notions and functions. It is done by the extension of utterance by negotiation. This negotiation is carried out by means of two kinds of device in complementary relationship. These I will refer to as routines and procedures. Extension, negotiation, routines and procedures. The terms proliferate. I apologize. But let me presume on your patience a little to explain what I am getting at.

In natural language use we realize linguistic rules as utterances when we judge that there is good cause for us to do so, when we consider that the situation calls for it. We do not in the ordinary way just mouth sentences to display our knowledge of how to compose them. As children we may do this during one period of our development but we grow out of it and put away such childish things, except when we are constrained to indulge in such display by such people as language teachers. Normally we only produce utterances or receive them from others when the situation requires us to do so. Otherwise we keep our peace or escape out of earshot. And the situation which provides the context for language use also inevitably keys in with it, so that meaning is a function of the linguistic utterance as extended by situational factors. Since the sentence is simply a device for demonstrating the formal properties of language as a system, its meaning is obviously not conditioned by circumstances in this way. The meaning is internally defined and always signalled by formal devices, so it never varies. Not so the utterance: its meaning must always be a function of its extension by situational factors: who produced it for what purpose, against what background of shared knowledge, and so on. The linguistic signals in an utterance always point *outwards* in the direction where meaning is to be found. They are a set of bearings.

Here is a linguistic expression:

The door is open.

What does it mean? Considered as a sentence there is no problem: *the* door, not *a* door, *is*, not *was* or *will be*, or *will have been*, or *has been*, *open* and not *closed*, and a door is a door is a door, as Gertrude Stein might put it. There is only one meaning for this expression as a sentence, and this meaning is established by paradigmatic contrast. But suppose that I uttered the expression with the serious intent of saying something purposeful and did not simply wish to exemplify a structure of English, what then? The door is open. You would want to know which door, and unless you were provided with the information, you would not know what the utterance meant. It would be propositionally deficient. But even if you know which door I was referring to, you would not necessarily know what I was up to in saying that it was open.

The door is open.

So what? I can see that it is. What then would I be doing by coming out with such a remark? Am I inviting you to leave or am I inviting you in? Am I asking you to close the door? Am I issuing a warning? You cannot know, of course, because there is no situation which extends the utterance: there is nothing for the signals to point to. It is incomplete as both proposition and illocution. You do not know what I am saying or doing.

Utterances are extended by negotiation and this is carried out by the use of interactive procedures based on the so-called cooperative principle. This principle embodies the necessary social assumption that when people come together or otherwise make contact with each other in order to communicate, they will cooperate and seek to arrive at an understanding. It is a powerful principle which informs the very nature of social life and it is in fact very difficult to deny. If you deliberately introduce irrelevance into your remarks, it will often be some time before you are discovered: your interlocutor will always give you the benefit of the doubt, assume you are being cooperative and try to make sense of what you say. It is the power of this principle which is used in the creation of poetic effect, as in the following lines by Ezra Pound:

> *In a Station in the Metro*
> The apparition of these faces in the crowd;
> Petals on a wet, black bough.

or again:

> Swiftly the years beyond recall.
> Solemn the stillness of this spring morning.

There are no syntactic signals here to connect the two expressions: you are left to work out the relationship for yourself, on the assumption that if they occur together they must be made sense of in reference to each other. The same principle operates at the humbler level of ordinary conversation and provides for all sorts of nuance, insinuation and *double entendre*, nudge, nudge, wink, wink, say no more, no need to spell it out, or dot the i's or cross the t's. Communication would indeed be an infinitely tedious and inefficient business if we could not count on cooperation to leave things unsaid.

Communication works, then, by the operation of what we can call the cooperative imperative: a necessary requirement for social life. And this imperative leads to a whole set of procedures for making sense. Some are particularly associated with the effective conveyance of propositional meaning, and this is dependent on what has been called the given-new contract. This provides for the expression and organization of information within utterances so that what is new is introduced into a given pattern of existing knowledge, thereby ensuring that propositional meaning is carried like a charge through the text, with each utterance connecting up with the next. Procedures which are used to meet the conditions of this contract include the judicious selection of appropriate pronouns and other proforms and the arrangement of information to conform to expectations. Without such procedures, one would be forced into tedious and confusing prolixity:

> I wrote a letter to my MP last month. I complained about my MP's neglect of local problems in a letter I wrote to my MP last month. I have not received a reply from my MP to a letter I wrote to my MP last month in which I complained about my MP's neglect of local problems. That I have not yet received a reply from my MP to a letter I wrote to my MP last month in which I complained about my MP's neglect of local problems is a serious matter.

And so on. Such uncooperative language use undermines the bases of communication. If my letter—the letter I wrote to my MP last month in which I complained about my MP's neglect etc. etc. and which I have just been telling you about—if that letter were similarly uncooperative, it should not be too surprising that I have received no reply—to the letter I wrote last month to my MP complaining etc. etc. I am not, of course, claiming that if one follows these procedures for propositional development one automatically avoids tedious and confusing prolixity, but only that without such procedures one *cannot* avoid it. There is still plenty of scope for the boring windbag. And with this in mind, I move rapidly on to the next point.

Some procedures then have to do with the conveyance of propositional meaning. Others have to do with the conveyance of illocutionary intent, with what is being done rather than with what is being said. Here we can return to the expression we considered earlier:

The door is open.

Such an utterance could be used to perform a number of different illocutionary acts:

Invitation The door is open. Come on in.
Dismissal The door is open. Clear off and never darken it again.
Request for action The door is open. Close it please.

And so on. The producer of the utterance would rely on the receiver's cooperation in matching interpretation with intention. If both of them can see quite well that the door is open, the receiver would be uncooperatively perverse to react as if the producer were simply providing factual information.

A   The door is open.
B   So I see.

Cooperation involves the receiver relating the utterance to the conditions on a particular illocution which the situation provides for. If the remark is not informative it must be relevant to some illocution other than a factual statement. The receiver scans the situation for the relevant conditions which will provide the utterance with a likely illocutionary value. This is his room. We have just had a fairly violent difference of opinion. He has gone red in the face. He is deeply offended. He wants me to leave.

A   The door is open.
B   All right, all right, I'm leaving.

Of course the receiver may get it wrong and it may turn out that his negotiation with situational factors leads him to a wrong extension.

A   The door is open.
B   All right, all right, I'm leaving.
A   No I don't want you to leave, you fool; close the door. We don't want this to be a public spectacle.

So one needs procedures for clarifying intent and for adjusting interpretation. Such procedures establish situational factors as conditions for various illocutionary acts and, like the propositional procedures mentioned earlier, they function to create a convergence of knowledge for the purpose of conveying information. They provide for individual worlds coming together to achieve social actions: they service the cooperative imperative.

But individual worlds are havens of security. When one cooperates, one encroaches on another person's private territory, and leaves one's own vulnerable to attack. The cooperative imperative impels man towards social contact; but at the same time he feels the need to be protective of the individual domain. This is the counteractive force of the *territorial* imperative. So it is that in their negotiation of meanings, interlocutors are aware of the importance of face. And there are procedures for mitigating and aggravating the force of what one has to say. In the case of a request for action, for example, the most aggravating realization will tend to make use of the imperative, the least aggravating will tend to make use of an interrogative with the declarative intermediate between the two. But apart from the use of these structures, there are other procedures for adjusting the degree of mitigation or aggravation required: for example the use of elaborate modality, or christian names or terms of endearment. So we arrive at a whole range of expressions that can do the same general illocutionary duty:

Close the door.
The door is open.
Can you close the door?
May I ask you to close the door?
Close the door, will you?
I wonder if you would mind closing the door?
Close the door, darling.
Close the door, John.
Close the door, there's a darling, John.
Would you mind closing the door, there's a darling John, my love.
Darling, the door please, would you mind, etc.

Etc. This list is open-ended, the permutations legion, and no useful purpose would be served in attempting to be exhaustive. No useful purpose would be served either in trying to teach all these expressions.

What can be done, however, is to make the learner realize that the foreign language operates by means of the same communicative principles as his own. Means of both propositional and illocutionary kinds have to be negotiated through cooperative interaction, and this negotiation has to be so conducted that the cooperative imperative and the territorial imperative are kept in balance. Procedures for propositional development, illocutionary realization and face preservation are likely to be transferable from mother tongue to foreign language behaviour so long as the way the foreign language is presented in the classroom is congruent with learner experience of natural language and so facilitates the transfer.

What seems to be needed is a presentation which sets problems requiring the contingent use of language for their solution after the manner of other subjects on the school curriculum—problems, therefore, which are situation and not language centred. But the situations do not need to be simulations of real life, any more than what goes on in history, chemistry or mathematics classes is a simulation of real life. The crucial point is that they should provide for the development of abilities for coping with real life subsequently. This is what I mean by language *for* rather than *as* communication.

But the devising of activities which will engage procedures for making sense is a *methodological* matter. How would they be organized into a *syllabus?* How can such activities fit into an orderly learning sequence? You will remember that I said that the negotiation of meaning in discourse is carried out by the use of two complementary devices: procedures and routines. I have discussed procedures and suggested that they relate to methodology. We have now to consider routines, since they, I think, relate to the syllabus.

Procedures can be understood as tactical moves in discourse. Routines are strategic. They represent prototypes of behavioural patterns which we use to understand actuality. These prototypes allow us to project expectation on the occurrences of daily life so that they do not take us by surprise, so that we recognize them as conforming to a predictable pattern. And the language use which services these expected patterns of behaviour conforms, therefore, as Firth pointed out long ago, to a roughly prescribed social ritual. So this is what I intend by routines—predictable patterns of language use. They vary in their predictability of course: some routines, like those followed in church services, allow very little room for tactical manoeuvre, while others, of which academic argument might be an example, allow a great deal. Obviously, the decreasing predictability of a routine will call for an increasing reliance on procedures: this is what I mean when I say that they are complementary.

Examples. Poetry in the eighteenth century was written to routines of very close confinement: there were restrictions on topic, language and metrical measure. Here is Alexander Pope indicating the disadvantage of such predictability in the work of his fellow poets:

While they ring round the same unvaried chimes,
With sure returns of still expected rhymes;
Where'er you find 'the cooling western breeze'
In the next line, it 'whispers through the trees':
If crystal streams 'with pleasing murmurs creep',
The reader's threatened (not in vain) with 'sleep'.
Then, at the last and only couplet fraught
With some unmeaning thing they call a thought,
A needless Alexandrine ends the song.
That, like a wounded snake, drags its slow length along.
(*Essay on Criticism:* 348–357)

We move now from Alexander Pope to seaside postcards. For here too routines come into play. Here too there is a roughly prescribed ritual, a conventional formula which includes a reference to the weather and to the hotel's standards of accommodation and catering; regret at the addressee's absence, and some reference to his/her well-being; mention of next meeting:

Dear Frank and Marjorie,

   Lovely weather here and the sea very warm. The hotel is rather crowded but our room looks out over the promenade and the food is good. Hope you are both keeping well. Wish you were here. See you next Sunday. Arthur and the children send their love.

                                                                            Mildred.

Now I am not suggesting that a second language syllabus should include the writing of heroic couplets and seaside postcards (though one could do worse). But I do think that they indicate a direction for research in syllabus design to follow. Recurrent situations in social life can be studied with a view to establishing the underlying routines they conform to, and one might hope that such a study would yield routines which on the one hand enable us to group apparently different social events together and on the other hand provide some basis for ordering them in a sequence of increasing complexity. In other words, we are looking for a pragmatic analogue of the sentence. What one would like to have is a set of routines as frameworks for procedural activities which enabled us to group together, for example, a whole range of service encounters (buying tickets at the railway station and theatre, reserving rooms or seats at a hotel and a travel agent, etc.) which varied in their selection of optional elements in the routines.

But we do not need to think only of language use outside the classroom. I think that we can, once more, refer our language teaching problems to issues of general education. For it is very much the business of formal education to develop in learners a knowledge of routines of different kinds: routines for the solution of mathematical problems, for example, for the recording of experiments, the description of historical events and their causes, and so on. These routines represent the rhetorics associated with different areas of enquiry. We can learn a great deal about such routines from our colleagues teaching other subjects.

It is time to conclude. We would all agree, I take it, that our business is to develop in learners the capacity for communicative behaviour in the language they are learning. Our aim is to teach language *for* communication. The question at issue is: which pedagogic course of action promises to promote that objective most effectively? Over recent years an assumption has taken root that all that is needed is a redefinition of syllabus content in terms of communicative categories, notions and functions, and that the presentation of language *as* communication will automatically trigger off the use of language *for* communication. But communication is not a simple matter of acquiring a knowledge of language items, however they are labelled. It must involve the use of procedures for negotiating meaning within predictable routines. Somehow or other, we have to develop a methodology which will lead the learner to engage in language use as a dynamic problem-solving activity within the confines of the classroom. The most effective syllabus will be one which provides a framework of routines for such activities. But the main responsibility for the procedural activity of learning within the framework rests where it has always been—with the teachers. And that responsibility remains the same as it has always been: how to set up conditions whereby learners can use what they know already to learn more so that they eventually become independent of your tuition. Ah, I hear you say, under your breath:

Plus ça change, plus c'est la même chose.

But there is never a simple recurrence of the past. Things never are the same. The great benefit of recent discussions on communicative language teaching is that they force us into a reconsideration of what we do and why we do it, to observe our practices from a different point of view. So that, familiar though they are, they in some sense appear to us for the first time, because they appear in a different setting and in a changed perspective.

Note

Paper presented as a plenary address at the Annual SPEAQ Convention, Quebec City, June 1980, and published in the SPEAQ Journal, Vol. 4 No. 2, 1980. Also presented as a paper at the Third National Congress of University English Teachers, Bari, October 1980, and published in Italian in the proceedings *La Lingua Inglese Nell'Universita*. Bari: Adriatica Editrice.

17 Course design and discourse process

Language teachers, taking their lead from linguists, have generally speaking accepted it as a self-evident truth that language is rule-governed behaviour. They have looked to the linguist to reveal what these rules are so that the essential character of language behaviour can be explained. The task of language teaching pedagogy is then seen to be a matter of organizing these rules in the most effective order to produce an appropriate course design, and the devising of activities which will lead the learners to internalize the rules for future use. In other words, the linguist describes *competence* and the teacher then bases course design on this description. On the face of it the operation appears to be unproblematic and it seems a pity to cause trouble by calling it into question. But I think we must; because the whole operation depends so critically on this assumption that language is rule-governed behaviour, that what we do with language is determined by competence, whether this be linguistic or communicative. And I believe this assumption to be mistaken in theory, and in consequence misleading in practice. The description of language knowledge is not the same thing as the explanation of language behaviour.

In Chomsky's original formulation, the term competence refers to the language user's knowledge of rules for the composition of sentences. But we have to note that the language user, in the actuality of communicative behaviour, never in fact uses his knowledge to compose sentences. This is what the language *analyst*, the grammarian, does in demonstrating the operation of rules by citation forms. He displays the system by sample sentences. But the user never does this in the normal circumstances of use. Indeed, when asked to display his knowledge of a language in this way, the language user generally finds it quite difficult to oblige. 'So you speak English', someone might say. 'Say something in English.' The likely result of such a request is some remark of breathtaking banality: 'the sky is blue', 'this is a pen', 'the book is on the table'.

The production of sentences does not come easily to the language user. It is not a natural thing to do.

The user does not exhibit, he exploits knowledge, takes his bearings by it, uses it as a resource, but he does not directly project it into use. To present these rules of grammar as a device for users to generate sentences is misleading because it is only the grammarian who is in the sentence generating business. And to talk about the generation of sentences as if it were synonymous with creativity is even more misleading. For creativity does not in its usual sense mean conformity to rule but on the contrary *non*-conformity, the denial of the determining effect of rules on behaviour.

So what I am saying is that actual language behaviour is not just a reflection of linguistic knowledge, distorted by the particular circumstances of performance. Linguists talk as if utterances were simply tokens of sentence types, tokens of behaviour which can be directly correlated with types of knowledge. But I want to argue that utterances are different in *type* from sentences; they are not the same kind of phenomenon at all. Both sentence and utterance consist of linguistic signs, but the linguistic signs are of a different kind in each case.

The linguistic sign as it is represented in the abstract knowledge system of grammar is a *symbol*. Its meaning, established by convention, is self-contained. And it derives from two sources. First it *denotes* a class of objects, events, and so on in the external world. Consider, for example, the symbol ROSE. It denotes a class of individual flowers of a particular sort. Second, the symbol contracts relationships internally with other symbols as terms in the systems of the language. Hence ROSE is a term which contracts a sense of relationship with terms like GERANIUM, HYDRANGEA, PETUNIA and PANSY, all of which are hyponyms of the superordinate term FLOWER. So within the semantics of English, the word ROSE is a symbol which has a definite sense and denotation and so its meaning is circumscribed and stable, and can be put on lexicographic record. As Gertrude Stein has it: a rose is a rose is a rose.

As with individual words, so with sentences. The meaning of a sentence, what I have referred to elsewhere as its signification, is a function of its *sense* relations with other sentences which manifest terms in the same systems, and of what its elements *denote*, as abstract classes of entities generalized from particular instances in the outside world. The traditional pedagogic device which serves to present and practise the *sense* of sentences is the substitution table.

The device for presenting their *denotation* is the situational demonstration. In both cases, what is being shown is the set of rules that control the combination of linguistic symbols. A pedagogy based on the sentence seeks to implant, as it were, the analytic units of linguistic description, to graft linguistic competence on to the learner's mind. It is an exercise in the direct transference of knowledge. This is why it is so difficult. It tries to bypass behaviour and to create knowledge without experience.

But all this, you might say, is now worn and familiar ground. The arguments against an exclusive concern for linguistic competence are well-known. 'What can I but enumerate old themes?' Surely it was precisely because of this recognition of the inadequacy of equating knowledge of language with knowledge of sentences that the concept *communicative* competence was proposed and notional/functional syllabuses emerged into the light of pedagogic day.

But I am not just saying that *linguistic* competence is inadequate as a definition of objectives in language course design. What I want to do is to assert the inadequacy of competence in general, both linguistic and communicative varieties, as a basis for pedagogy.

Proposals to define course content with reference to communicative rather than formal linguistic categories only tinker with the central problem and do not provide radical repair. The focus of attention is still on competence, on the knowledge of rules. The assumption still is that language behaviour is rule-governed and that once the rules are known, then effective communication will follow as a necessary consequence, since all that is needed is for them to be directly projected into behaviour. It is true that the spotlight shifts to rules of use. But the same mistaken assumption is made as before: that rules *determine* what people do with their language. And they do not. They may guide, but they do not govern.

As a matter of fact, although the proponents of notional/functional course design make the claim that communicative competence is the objective, the rules that define this competence are not generally made explicit. It is supposed that they will be induced from examples. What we normally get in such courses is a collection of correlations between notional and functional labels, and the linguistic expressions most commonly associated with them. The difference between this and the structurally based course is essentially one of degree and not of kind. The structurally based course usually makes similar correlational pairings, indicating, for example, that the interrogative commonly functions as a request for information or action, that certain tenses are associated with different notions of time, and so on. A course based on notions and functions will perhaps make more subtle distinctions, will provide a more refined illustration of meaning potential inherent in linguistic forms, but these forms are still represented as *symbols*, even though tagged more extensively with functional labels. They are still represented as elements in the knowledge system, and it is still supposed that these can be directly projected into use, that the elements of language usage as abstracted out of behaviour, whether tagged with notional/functional labels or not, are essentially the same as elements of language use. But they are not the same. They are crucially different.

The analyst, through his idealization of language data, represents the linguistic sign as a symbol which denotes a class of entities in the outside world and contracts sense relations with other symbols which function as terms in the same semantic and syntactic systems of the language. But when the linguistic sign is actually put to use in naturally occurring communication, it ceases to function as a symbol. It functions now not as a symbol but as an *index*. It does not carry its own self-contained meaning but indicates where meaning is to be found, points the user in the right direction, as it were. The linguistic element in language use becomes a clue that calls for interpretation. The ability to engage in communicative activity crucially depends on knowing how to realize the particular indexical value of signs as they appear in the context of actual use. It is not enough to know what general signification they have as symbols.

Consider a simple example:

She gave the rose to the waiter.

Considered as a sentence, as a combination of linguistic symbols, this expression is easy to understand. You know what the words GIVE and ROSE and WAITER denote; you know that SHE denotes a female individual (to the extent that male chauvinism still accepts this possibility); that the term contracts a contrastive sense relationship with HE and IT in the pronoun system in English. You know that GIVE contracts the sense relationship of converseness with the term TAKE, that ROSE is a hyponym of FLOWER. This knowledge of the sense and denotation of symbols enables you to recognize that the sentence:

She gave the rose to the waiter

has a different meaning from:

He gave the rose to the waiter
She *gives* a rose to the waiter

and the same meaning as

The waiter took the rose from her
The rose was given by her to the waiter

and so on. And that this meaning will always be invariant: the sentence has one meaning and one meaning only by virtue of the established conventional signification of the symbols that comprise it.

Considered as an *utterance*, however, this expression takes on a very different character. If I were to utter it with the serious intention of engaging you in communication, then you would be entitled to some further elucidation as to my meaning.

She gave the rose to the waiter.

Who's she? Which waiter? Which rose are you referring to? What do you mean in saying this? What propositions are you intending to express? In other words, you now treat the linguistic elements not as self-contained symbols but as indices which indicate meaning beyond themselves, which need to be extended by reference to knowledge other than that of language. And this is essentially what we mean when we say that a particular expression refers to something: we mean that it refers *us* to something, it provides a direction for us to follow, to discover what particular instance is intended. The sense and denotation of a sentence signal themselves. But sentences do not refer to anything. Only utterances refer. And the reference in an utterance has always to be discovered elsewhere.

But the linguistic sign in the utterance does not only act as an index to *propositional* value. It also indicates *illocutionary* value. Even if you know who she is and which rose and which waiter I am referring to, you may still not be at all clear about my point in providing you with this information. You may know what I mean *in* saying something but still not know what I mean *by* saying something. So when I say:

She gave the rose to the waiter

your reaction might well be: so she gave the rose to the waiter, so what? What is the point of your making this observation? What are you up to? What are you implying?

Taken as a sentence, the expression *She gave the rose to the waiter* excites little interest. A typical textbook offering. She gave the rose to the waiter; the man gave the book to the boy; the postman gave the letter to the man. But as an utterance, it is full of exciting possibilities. What is the hidden significance of this rose, redolent of romantic association? Who is this woman? The daughter of a rich aristocrat in a small Spanish town arranging secret assignations with her lover Manuel the waiter? The utterance releases us into creativity, into a range of possible interpretations, sends us out in quest of meaning. The sentence confines us to the limited meaning codified in language itself.

So the linguistic signs in utterances are *indicative* of but not *expressive* of propositional and illocutionary meaning and the ability to interpret them depends on the language user's ability to follow these indications and to use them as evidence. The interpretative procedures which are engaged in the discourse process, in both spoken and written language use, serve to realize the indexical value of linguistic signs in the contexts of actually occurring instances of communication. These procedures mediate between the abstract systems of knowledge, which constitute competence and the actuality of *behaviour*. They are procedures for converting symbols into indices.

So I think a distinction must be made between what we know of language, our competence, and how we activate this knowledge in particular instances of actual language behaviour, what I shall call our *capacity* for realizing the indexical value of language elements in the communicative process. The linguist is in the business of making models of competence, and capacity is beyond his scope.

The linguist can afford to concentrate on competence. He is not accountable to practical effectiveness. But the language teacher cannot so conveniently ignore capacity because it lies at the heart of language use and therefore, as I shall argue presently, at the heart of the language learning process itself.

But how can we characterize this competence and this capacity, and the relationship between them? Competence, as Chomsky originally used the term, meant a knowledge of the symbolic meaning of linguistic forms and their combinations in sentences. Subsequently the term was extended to mean a knowledge of the communicative properties of these forms, of the notions and functions they are used to express: communicative competence. This extension is, however, misleading since it implies that communicative competence is of the same essential character as linguistic competence; that is to say that the correlations between form and function can be reduced to rule in much the same way as the symbolic relationship between items in the language system. But these correlations between form–notion and form–function are not a matter of rule government. They are, rather, schemes of prediction and expectation, records of probable patterns of co-occurrence of form with notions and functions which derive from past experience of language use. They are not rules, but guiding schemata of sorts, habitual frames of reference and communicative routines which we have generalized from previous occasions of language use and which we exploit as useful approximations to reality. They represent a second level of language organization: a level which linguists have been inclined to ignore, a level of what we might call preparedness for use.

Our experience of language provides us with data which we internalize both as linguistic rule at the systemic level and as contextual association at the schematic level. In other words, we convert experience into both *symbols*, the categories of linguistic competence, and commonly occurring schematic *indices*, the categories of communicative competence. Linguists often talk as if symbolic conversion, the acquisition of system, were the *only* language learning process, as if all that happened to the immensely complex experience of language in childhood was that it was ground up into the linguistic categories of the language system and became entirely separate from the contexts in which it occurred. Language use is in this view simply fodder to feed the language acquisition device. I would argue, however, that the language we learn retains traces of its contextual origins and that it is associated with the recurrent patterns of social interaction in which it is used. It is this association that creates the schemata I have been referring to: patterns of language tagged as it were with contextual labels. Put another way, schemata represent the organization of language at the pragmatic level of communicative readiness, whereas linguistic rules represent the context-free organization of language at the symbolic, the syntactic and semantic levels of the formal system.

An example would no doubt be welcome. Imagine it is midday in London. I am hungry. I go to a lunch counter to get something to eat. My previous acquaintance with lunch counters elsewhere has provided me with relevant schemata for this situation: I know that the propositional schema will define a particular frame of reference which links egg, let us say, with sandwich rather than with chicken and farmyard or with embryo and fertilization, and that links coffee with cream rather than cash crop economy. So I engage the frame of reference associated with lunch counters and not that which is associated with agriculture, economics, or animal husbandry. I know too that the illocutionary schema, or rhetorical routine, will involve a sequence of communicative acts, a particular exchange pattern along the following lines: optional greeting, request for particular item of food, payment, reciprocal thanks. Armed with this schematic knowledge, I can conduct my lunch counter business very briskly. Knowing what to expect, and what is expected of me, I am not involved in the careful decoding of every utterance into a corresponding set of sentential symbols.

A Morning.
B Morning.
A Could I have two cheese sandwiches.
B Two cheese.
A How much?
B Eighty p.
A Thanks.
B Thanks.

What I do in these circumstances, then, is to engage the schematic level of my language knowledge and take my communicative bearings from there. This enables me to take short cuts. Thus, the lunch counter exchange might be much more brusque:

A Two cheese.
B Eighty p.

The interlocutors here do not ponderously reconstitute sentences from this degenerate data in order to interpret the utterances. They would understand them as indexical of meaning at the schematic level.

But we must note that schemata only provide approximate guidelines to actuality: there is no guarantee that a particular instance of use will conform to the prototype image in our heads. To return to the lunch counter. It is possible that my propositional schema, my frame of reference for lunch counters does not match up with that of the person serving me. In such circumstances, I shall find myself involved in meaning negotiation of a kind all too familiar with foreigners.

A Two cheese sandwiches please.
B Chutney?
A Pardon?

The person serving at the counter realizes that schematic guidance has broken down but he believes that it is the illocutionary aspect that has gone wrong and that I do not understand that the simple utterance of the word 'Chutney' is intended as a question, a request for information. So he tries to repair the fault by making the illocutionary force more explicit.

B Chutney. Do you want any chutney? Would you like to have some chutney on your cheese sandwich?

There is a schematic breakdown here, which has serious effects on my sense of security, particularly if there are people behind me waiting to be served. If chutney is not in my lunch counter frame of reference, there will be a pause while I make the necessary adjustment. A minor hitch in the proceedings. But I may not even know what the term *denotes*, what its *symbolic* meaning is and in this case, negotiation is necessary.

A What is chutney?
B This stuff here. This is chutney [*denotation*]. Kind of pickle [*sense*].
A No thank you.
B OK. Two cheese sandwiches without chutney. Take away?
A I beg your pardon?

Here we go again. If I do not have in my lunch counter routine the alternative of eating food on the premises as opposed to taking it off the premises to eat, then I am in trouble. I try to work out the indexical value of the expression by looking up, as it were, its symbolic meaning first, its semantics. *Take away*. It could mean an enquiry as to whether I wish to take my sandwich away from the counter myself rather than have it taken by, say, a waiter. If I acted on this interpretation, I would no doubt be corrected. The experience leads me to modify my schematic knowledge and prepares me for similar encounters in the future.

It has often been supposed that a knowledge of symbolic meanings is both necessary and sufficient as a precondition for understanding utterances in discourse, both spoken and written. But clearly this is not the case. Consider, as further illustration, the problem posed by riddles and other dark sayings:

Alive without breath
As cold as death
Never thirsty ever drinking
All in mail never clinking.

What is being referred to? You may know what the expressions denote, but you cannot interpret them as indexical clues because you do not have the frame of reference. Once you have it, then the meaning falls neatly into place. *Fish.* All becomes clear: the scales, as it were, fall from your eyes.

Furthermore, once the right schematic frame is engaged, it provides contexts whereby the meaning of unknown expressions can be inferred. Symbolic meanings are acquired as a function of the interpretative process.

What I am trying to suggest is that actual communication involves the use of interpretative procedures to associate particular instances of behaviour with familiar schemata and to modify them where necessary by using a knowledge of syntax and semantics as a resource. These procedures, then, exploit and extend knowledge of language at the level of communicative schema, communicative competence, and at the level of system rules, linguistic competence. It is ability to engage or activate this knowledge for actual behavioural outcomes by means of these interpretative procedures that I refer to as communicative *capacity*. It is this which mediates between knowledge and behaviour and which is exercised in the discourse process.

Now what, you might ask, has all this to do with course design? I take it that the purpose of any language course is to develop in learners the ability to engage in communicative behaviour and this, I have argued, must mean that there has to be a concern for capacity, for the procedural activation of competence. To coin a slogan: no course without discourse. But language courses have generally concentrated on competence and left capacity out of account. The structurally ordered course concentrates attention on linguistic competence as such but does not effectively indicate how this competence can be drawn upon as a communicative resource. It is true that words and sentence patterns will often be associated with situations, but these situations are designed simply to reveal the symbolic signification of linguistic forms. The direction of fit, as it were, is situation to language.

In courses which have a notional/functional orientation, the focus of attention is on the schematic level and the direction of fit is reversed. That is to say, the starting point is a particular notional frame of reference or, more usually, a particular functional routine: asking the way, asking and granting permission, apologizing and so on. The language is then brought in to service the presentation of these schemata. In both cases the whole business of language behaviour is presented as a straightforward matter of projecting knowledge. One gets the image of the language user as somebody going around with bits of language in his head waiting for the appropriate occasion to insert them into the right situational slots.

But as our lunch counter exchanges make clear, actual language use is not like this at all. It is rather a series of problems that have to be solved on the spot by reference to a knowledge of linguistic systems and communicative schemata. This knowledge does not provide ready-made solutions which are simply selected from storage and fitted in. But language courses have generally been based on the assumption that it does. Whether they are structurally or functionally oriented, what they have tended to do is to present and practise solutions. What they need to do, I suggest, is to create problems which require interpretative procedures to discover solutions by drawing on the knowledge available as a resource. In other words, they need to encourage the exercise of the capacity for negotiating meaning and working out the indexical value of language elements in context.

There is a further point to be made which supports the emphasis on procedural problem-solving activity in course design. I have suggested that capacity mediates between competence and actual behavioural outcomes, that it is the ability to exploit existing knowledge. But it is also the ability to create new knowledge. Capacity, in other words, is not only a fundamental principle in processing discourse in reference to what is known, it is also, necessarily, a fundamental principle in learning, the acquisition of new knowledge. Consider again the lunch counter episode. The unexpected occurrence of the expressions *chutney* and *take away* obliges me to engage procedures for making appropriate meaning out of them. Once I have negotiated their meaning in the discourse, I am able to extend my vocabulary by internalizing the denotation of the term CHUTNEY which I did not previously have in my semantics, and also include it in my frame of reference, my pragmatic schema for lunch counters. This schema is also extended by my learning of the value of the expression *take away* in this particular context of situation. It is not simply that my discourse engagement here produces new knowledge: the very process of meaning negotiation is itself a learning process. The acquisition and use of language are in this sense alternative terms for the same basic phenomenon.

If this is so, then it follows that course designers need to pay particular attention to the kind of activity that they require learners to undertake. But the kind of procedural activity which develops capacity has not been greatly in evidence in language courses. Activities have been seen as a *means* for facilitating the storage of forms, tagged or not with notional and functional labels, but not as *ends* in themselves and representative of the very process of language use. They are commonly devices for the repetition and practice of ready-made solutions. Where they present problems they are essentially problems within language and not, as in normal communication, problems *outside* language which call for the contingent and discriminating use of language knowledge to solve. In these circumstances a gap opens up between the language to be learned and language used in learning. In ESP, for example, a great deal of attention has been devoted to the specification of the language to be learned. This language has sometimes been specified at the system level in terms of the linguistic properties of particular registers of English. Sometimes it has been specified at the schematic level as well, with linguistic expressions tagged with notional and functional labels. There has been less attention paid to the methodological matter of what kind of problem-solving procedural activity is appropriate for the realization of this content as actual communicative behaviour. Often ESP course content has been associated with activities which are simply transferred from standard, language teaching practice and which are extremely remote from the kind of procedural work that has to be done in interpreting the actual discourse of particular specialities. Asking engineers or research chemists to fill in the blanks, change active to passive, or learn sets of form/function correlates in simulated dialogues is not likely to engage them in the procedural activity so necessary for authentic use and, equivalently, for learning.

Authentic. The term is much in vogue in ESP at present. But authenticity is not achieved by simply working from genuine texts. It has to be a function of an engagement with discourse whereby students exercise their capacity for making indexical meaning out of signs in utterances. And they will not be engaged unless they are involved in achieving solutions to problems they feel are worth solving—problems which are conceptually related to their specialist activities even if they are not drawn from the specific topics of their speciality. Authenticity is not a matter of selection but of methodology.

I hope I shall not myself be misinterpreted. I am not saying that we should ignore linguistic forms and their symbolic signification, that we should not associate these forms with their common indexical features in particular frames of reference and routines. Linguistic rules and communicative schemata are necessary features of language use and language learning. And they provide us, particularly in ESP, with an operational starting point in course design. But they are not sufficient. We need also to take the procedural dimension into account. We must also have a mind to the development of communicative capacity. Only then can we ensure that the experience of language use during the course of instruction continues to extend language learning through use after the course is over.

We are after all principally concerned with setting up conditions for learning, for preparing our students to cope with contingencies that cannot be specified in advance. So when a situation comes up that has no ready-made solution in knowledge, they will know how to use their experience to learn more. And this is true whether we are talking about a treatise on relativity, a textbook on heat engines or electrical wiring, or buying a cheese sandwich at a lunch counter. With or without chutney.

Note

Paper given as a plenary address at MEXTESOL, National Convention, Guadalajara, October 1981.

18 Competence and capacity in language learning

It is generally assumed as self-evident that language learning is a purposeful goal-oriented activity, its objective being the internalization of a system of rules which define correct linguistic comportment, that is to say the acquisition of competence. The learner is thus represented as directing his efforts, either under his own volition or with pedagogic persuasion, towards a submission to authority. But can we really account for the process of language learning by characterizing it in this way as an urge towards conformity? Do learners only learn the rules, the linguistic code of conduct, and nothing more? Can they indeed function as language users at all if this is all that they learn? Codes of conduct, linguistic and otherwise, are necessary social controls on behaviour but they rarely determine what people do in any absolute sense. Indeed in the very process of learning them we discover ways of evading them or turning them to our own individual advantage. And so it is with the rules of language. In the process of acquiring them as a social convenience we learn how to exploit them and how to escape from their confinement in order to express individual experience. In learning competence we also learn how to exercise our capacity for making meaning in language.

The orderly conduct of human affairs requires individuals to conform to social convention. There are patterns of acceptable behaviour, exigencies of etiquette, which control the wilder impulses of eccentricity and keep us to our orbit. We are socialized into acceptance of the established order in the very act of acquiring our first language.

> The heavens themselves, the planets and this centre
> Observe degree, priority and place,
> Insisture, course, proportion, season, form,
> Office, and custom, in all line of order.
> (Shakespeare: *Troilus & Cressida*)

Of course there will always be some people who will openly flout authority and assert the primacy of self by denying the social contract to conform: drop-outs and other disaffected elements. But then they risk losing the benefits that the system provides for those who subscribe to it, and the consequences of challenging the established order can be serious. There are, thus, very strong pressures on people to accept the constraints of social convention and they will in general seek some scope for individual initiative within it rather than try to break it down at the barriers.

Take but degree away, untune that string
And hark what discord follows.
(Ibid.)

Let me give you some examples of discord in language, examples of language, that is to say, that untunes the sentence strings and disrupts the order of established grammatical rule.

He saw not the beautiful lady.
You love not me.
He has a fill of humility in nature.
Terrifying are the attent birds on the lawn.

How are such discordant instances of language to be characterized? They are in certain respects expressions in English since they are combinations of English words and not, for example, French, Spanish, or German words. But the combinations are not in accord with standard syntactic and semantic rule. They are deviant, discordant; they offend against established order. They are, indeed, not English, even though they are *in* English. They draw on the resources of the language without commitment to the rules which normally constrain their use. In this respect, we may say that they reveal not competence but capacity.

When such expressions are produced by language learners they are characterized as errors, evidence of inadequate competence or, more positively, as evidence of an interim interlanguage system of the learner's own devising. In both cases, the expressions are seen as makeshift efforts patched up from a partial knowledge of the target language, and indicative of a transitional stage in the learning (or acquisition) of the standard system. And in both cases, glosses would be provided in standard form to reveal what the learner should have said, would have said if he/she had been fully competent in the language.

He saw not the beautiful lady.

This is cited as an error in the compendium of learner errors compiled by Burt and Kiparsky and called *The Gooficon*. We are told that

> Students need to learn the rule for negative placement: *Do* appears in negatives when there is no auxiliary, and *not* follows it. (Burt & Kiparsky 1972: 27–8)

Application of this rule yields the correct sentence:

> He did not see the beautiful lady.

This seems entirely reasonable, and the same correction procedure would presumably apply to the expression:

> You love not me.

But here we come up against a difficulty. For the source of this expression is not the faltering effort of a student essay but the selected poems of Thomas Hardy:

> You love not me
> And love alone can lend you loyalty;
> I know and knew it. But, unto the store
> Of human deeds divine in all but name,
> Was it not worth a little hour or more
> To add yet this: once you, a woman, came
> To sooth a time-torn man; even though it be
> You love not me?

We do not suppose that Hardy needs instruction in the rule for negative placement. We assume he knows the rule but chooses to disregard it because it does not provide him with the precise expression he needs to match his meaning, even though the correct form *you don't love me*, would fit just as well into the rhyme scheme.

Again, consider the discordant expression:

> Terrifying are the attent birds on the lawn.

If this were uttered by a learner what would our likely reaction be? 'Well I can see what you mean but actually that isn't English. What you ought to say is:

> The birds on the lawn are terrifying.

And they are attent*ive* not attent.

> The attentive birds on the lawn are terrifying.

That is right. Good.'

And so we coax our learners towards correction, towards the standard codification of meaning that represents competence in a language. But the very same deviation occurs in these lines from a poem by Ted Hughes:

> Terrifying are the attent sleek thrushes on the lawn,
> More coiled steel than living—a poised
> Dark deadly eye, those delicate legs
> Triggered to stirrings beyond sense ...

We do not think of adjusting the structures to make them accord with correctness. We know that to regularize the language into conformity here would be to diminish its meaning, that to reform the expression would be to deform the poem. So in this case we apply different criteria in our evaluation and engage standards not of correctness but of communicative effectiveness. We recognize that deviant expressions may be evidence not of deficiency but of a more than common ability to realize the resources of the language for making meaning.

Now what about the fourth example I mentioned:

He has a fill of humility in nature.

You will by now, I hope, be uncertain how to react to this deviant expression. Is it an error to be corrected or an invention to be admired? This time its source reveals it as an error (Burt & Kiparsky 1974) and I have no literary example to offer. But it is not difficult to imagine that it could without incongruence appear in a poem. Or perhaps in a Shakespeare play:

> This was the noblest Roman of them all:
> All the conspirators save only he,
> Did that they did in envy of great Caesar;
> He only, in a general honest thought,
> And common good to all, made one of them.
> *He had a fill of humility in nature.*
> His life was gentle; and the elements
> So mix'd in him that Nature might stand up
> And say to all the world *this was a man.*
> (Shakespeare: *Julius Caesar*)

So it would appear that discord, the violation of conventional norms of correct linguistic conduct, can be attributed to two different and apparently opposite causes. On the one hand it is the result of *deficiency* in a language, in which case we call it error, and on the other hand it is the result of a heightened *proficiency* in a language, in which case we call it art. But the deviations themselves may look alike. We cannot judge by appearances. In one of his letters somewhere, Charles Dickens complains:

> I generally find that when I write a line which I believe to be a fresh thought expressed in an original way, that the passage is marked 'query' in the proof when it comes back from the printers.

The committing of an error and the creation of an artistic effect can result in the same kind of linguistic object. But although the products are similar, we generally make the assumption that the processes are different: we do not talk about creating an error or committing a line of poetry (except to memory). What I want to suggest is that in fact the processes are essentially the same, and that both represent the creative force of what I have called *language capacity*. I mean by this the ability to exploit the resources for making meaning which are available in language whether these have been codified or not.

The knowledge one has of the codified language constitutes linguistic competence. But although this is what we learn as a function of socialization into the conventions and customs of our particular speech community, it represents only that part of the total meaning potential of our language which has been given social sanction. It may constrain our capacity into appropriate channels but it does not suppress it by complete confinement. We can, and do, find ways of expressing individual concepts and perceptions by innovative turns of phrase. There is scope for invention. Poets are not endowed with any special capacity for creativity which is denied to ordinary mortals; if they were, their work would defy interpretation. They simply have a greater talent for exploiting this capacity to artistic effect.

The human capacity for making meaning out of linguistic resources is not, then, confined within competence. Nor is it simply converted into competence in the language acquisition process. One is sometimes given the impression that the sole purpose of innate language capacity is to activate the acquisition of competence in a particular language and that its vital force is thereby exhausted; in discharging this function, we might say, it decharges itself. We are led to believe that the creative force is channelled into a code and finds expression only in the production of sentences according to rule. But the fact that we are able to produce and interpret utterances which do violence to such rules makes it clear that creative capacity has an independent existence.

This capacity is of course available to us as learners of another language, and so-called errors are evidence of its survival. They are the results of the learner exploiting whatever resources are available to him to achieve his meanings. This exploitation is comparable with what Levi-Strauss calls *bricolage*: the activity of altering an established order of elements to make a new pattern of significance. As Levi-Strauss puts it (in translation), the bricoleur

> ... interrogates all the heterogeneous objects of which his treasury is composed to discover what each of them could 'signify' and so contribute to a set which has yet to materialise but which will ultimately differ from the instrumental set only in the internal disposition of its parts. (Levi-Strauss 1966: 18)

> This logic works rather like a kaleidoscope, an instrument which also contains bits and pieces by means of which structural patterns are realised. These patterns actualise possibilities ... these patterns project models of intelligibility. (Levi-Strauss 1966: 36)

This bricolage, this kaleidoscopic actualization of possibilities is, as Levi-Strauss implies, a primal activity of the human mind. The learner as a kind of inventive handyman (or handyperson I suppose I should say), a bricoleur of makeshift utterances, simply follows his natural bent as a language user. If there is a ready-made, reach-me-down pattern available for a particular purpose, all well and good; if not, then one will have to be put together for the occasion with whatever material comes most readily to hand. This is what the poet does; this is what the learner does; and this is what we all do. We are all, in varying degrees, do-it-yourself bricoleurs, fashioning our own devices by rummaging in the established system for spare parts.

But it will be objected that the learner is surely in a quite different situation. We cannot, and should not, confuse his idiosyncrasies with those of the literary writer. He, poor fellow, cannot help producing oddities because he only has scant materials to work with, whereas the literary writer has complete mastery at his disposal and is deviant by choice. To confuse the two, it might be argued, is to equate the cripple with the contortionist. My argument is that although they may not have the same amount of material to work with, both are in full possession of their creative faculties. The essential difference is that the learner is generally speaking discouraged from using them, and when he does so he is likely to be put in his place and penalized for ineptitude. In this way the learner's creative instincts are suppressed and his individual identity correspondingly diminished.

All this, you might say, has a splendid humanistic ring to it, but surely the language learner's efforts are essentially transitional and tentative, simply a means for finding the right direction to follow. As such, they are the testing out of hypotheses about the target language and are directed at the eventual acquisition of the standard system. In this sense they represent temporary interim approximations, interlanguage staging posts on the road to native speaker competence. Learner language is simply a kind of discovery procedure, a device for internalizing a system, and nothing more.

This seems to be the accepted way of conceiving of learner effort, whether stigmatized as error or not. But it does not on the face of it seem very plausible that the learner moves towards some predetermined goal like this. It presupposes that he has a target before him at which he takes deliberate aim with every expression he utters or is drawn willy-nilly towards competence by some atavistic homing instinct. I find it hard to accept that learner behaviour is controlled by either purpose or predestination in this way. It seems to me much more plausible to suppose that he behaves in the natural manner of the language user, that his deviant utterances are patched together from whatever knowledge he can press into service, including knowledge of his own language, in order to get his meaning across. If he follows his normal practice as a language user in this way, he will naturally only fashion his utterances into correct form to the extent that experience indicates that he needs to do so, either to make his meaning plain or to conform to the accepted norm of conventional behaviour. I am suggesting, then, that the oddities of learner language are the creations of his capacity for making sense as the communicative occasion requires. They are the results of bricolage, makeshift combinations devised from whatever bits and pieces are available, and cobbled together to cope with immediate contingencies. They only get fashioned into stable codified form under social pressure from outside.

This pressure in the formal teaching/learning situation is applied by the teacher, who seeks to show the learner the error of his ways and to guide him along the straight and narrow path of correctness. The good shepherd. But there are grave difficulties inherent in this task and, more importantly, grave dangers.

The difficulties first. Learners, like the ordinary people they are, adjust their language to an acceptable norm for two reasons: either in order to be more effectively *communicative* or in order to indicate a sense of identity with a particular group of language users. Both the communicating and the identifying or indicative functions of language call for conformity. But if the teacher appeals to the principle of correctness in spite of the fact that what the learner says is perfectly intelligible, then she is in effect invoking the identifying function. That is to say, if the teacher makes a remark of the kind: 'Well I understand what you mean, but actually we do not say it like that: the correct way is X', what she is saying is that correctness in this case is not necessary for the satisfactory operation of the communicative function, but is only required for the learner to be eligible to join the exclusive club of standard speakers of English. But the likelihood is that learners do not want to join such a club, do not wish to be identified with such a group, since they might feel, justifiably enough, that their primary social allegiances lie elsewhere and that they wish to learn another language without being encumbered with the identity of its users. It is difficult to correct learner error which has little or no communicative consequence because to do so is to ask learners to subscribe to an etiquette which may seem alien to them, quaint, even ridiculous; to conform to standards of behaviour that represent a code of conduct for particular social groups with which they have no social connection and no real affinity.

It is pronunciation, of course, which most obviously proclaims group membership, and it is not therefore surprising that accents cling to their owners with such tenacity. For they are the emblems of identity; badges, blazons, rosettes, college scarves, rugby club favours, and the old school tie. Major Thompson and Hercule Poirot are figures of fun, stereotypes of ethnic images, but they are significant of a serious point: people do not lightly expose their precarious sense of security to risk by exchanging one social identity for another.

So to correct learner language without communicative warrant in order to bring it into line with what an alien society regards as proper comportment is to impose standards of behaviour which in all probability the learner cannot identify with and in which he has no social investment. The codes of conduct of other communities have no psychological jurisdiction over our behaviour. This is why foreigners, for example, are capable of uttering taboo words of the most awful obscenity in serene unawareness of their effect.

But the imposition of correctness may be mistaken for another and more important reason. And here I come to the danger of

pedagogic ministrations and return to the question of the relationship between competence and capacity. The aim of language
teaching has generally been understood as the gradual consolidation of competence in the learner's mind. Correction is crucial to
this operation since competence in a language means conformity to
rule. Any expression that does not conform is by definition ill-
formed and a sign of incompetence. But to force the learners into
compliance in this way is to suppress the very creative capacity by
which competence is naturally achieved. It is not surprising,
therefore, that attempts at error elimination by exhortation and
drill are so seldom effective. The natural instincts of the bricoleur
continually assert themselves and the learner engages his capacity
for making meaning out of language despite the best efforts of the
teacher to deter him.

The logic of the line of argument I am pursuing here leads us to
the conclusion that it is counter-productive to focus attention on
competence in our teaching as we are at present prone to do;
whether this be of a linguistic or communicative variety. We would,
I think, be better employed setting up conditions in the classroom
which will engage the natural language capacity of the learners,
allowing competence to grow out of such activity as a consequence
of communicative requirement. Competence in this view is not
something that is directly taught but something that learners
fashion for themselves by recognizing the need for conventional
controls over their creative efforts in the interest of better communication. In this way, competence comes as a corollary to
effective communicative use. And correctness is what the learner
moves towards, not what he begins with; something he achieves
and not something that is thrust upon him.

Now, if the language learning process is conceived of in this way
as the gradual achievement of competence by the exercise of
capacity, then the teacher's role has to be re-defined. It can no
longer be a matter of handing out parts from a language kit with
instructions on how to proceed stage by stage to put them together
to make the approved model. Instead the teaching task is to involve
the learners in activities which will lend purpose to their bricolage,
and to guide them towards ways of assembling the parts which
gradually approximate to standard structures as a function of their
increased effectiveness for communication.

This is all very well, you may say, but what if the learners never
arrive at the standard structures and so remain incompetent,
content with the makeshift bricolage of their own contrivance. I do

not think it is very probable that learners will persist in the use of linguistic forms which manifestly do not work in preference to those that do. Like the rest of us, they are likely to take the line of least resistance, and incline to orthodoxy because it is convenient.

But although communicative effectiveness may exert conforming influence it does not guarantee correctness because, as I have argued earlier, correctness is not only a matter of effectiveness but also a matter of etiquette. This cosmetic aspect of correctness is difficult to acquire, precisely because of its lack of communicative relevance. Learners who are impressionable will acquire it and those who are not won't. But it seems to me that learners are more likely to be influenced into cosmetic correctness by its being represented as a contingent aspect of purposeful activity than if it is imposed upon them by pedagogic fiat.

But even if learners fall short of competence, this is not, I think, an important failure. For they will have been engaged in learning through the exercise of their capacity for making meaning from the resources available in a new language. This, I would argue, is the essential creative process of language learning as language use. The extent to which it produces native speaker competence is of secondary and contingent concern.

Note

Paper presented as a plenary address, TESOL Convention, Honolulu, May 1982, and published in Clarke and Handscombe, 1983.

Bibliography

Alderson, C. and A. Urquhart (eds.) 1984. *Reading in a Foreign Language*. London: Longman.

Allen, J.P.B. and P. van Buren. 1971. *Chomsky: Selected Readings*. London: Oxford University Press.

Argyle, M. 1967. *The Psychology of Interpersonal Behaviour*. Harmondsworth: Penguin.

Banton, M. 1965. *Roles: An Introduction to the Study of Social Relations*. London: Tavistock Publications.

Bartlett, F. 1932. *Remembering*. Cambridge: Cambridge University Press.

Bates, E. 1976. *Language and Context*. New York: Academic Press.

Bateson, F.W. 1961. *English Studies Today* ii. Bern.

Bauman, R. and J. Sherzer (eds.). 1974. *Explorations in the Ethnography of Speaking*. Cambridge: Cambridge University Press.

Bazell, C.E., J.C. Catford, M.A.K. Halliday and R.H. Robins (eds.). 1966. *In Memory of J.R. Firth*. London: Longman.

Beaugrande, R. de. 1980. *Text, Discourse, and Process*. London: Longman.

Beaugrande, R. de and W. Dressler. 1981. *Introduction to Text Linguistics*. London: Longman.

Berlin, Isaiah. 1957. *The Hedgehog and the Fox*. New York: Mentor Books.

Berne, E. 1968. *Games People Play*. Harmondsworth: Penguin.

Bernstein, B.B. 1971. *Class, Codes and Control*, Vol. 1. London: Routledge and Kegan Paul.

Bever, T. 1970. 'The cognitive basis for linguistic structures' in Hayes 1970.

Bobrow, D.G. and A. Collins. 1975. *Representation and Understanding. Studies in Cognitive Science*. New York: Academic Press.

Bolinger, D.L. 1952. 'Linear modification'. *PMLA* 67: 1117–44.

Bolinger, D.L. 1975. *Aspects of Language* (2nd edition). New York: Harcourt Brace Jovanovich.

Bransford, J. D. and **M. K. Johnson**. 1972. 'Contextual prerequisites for understanding: some investigations of comprehension and recall'. *Journal of Verbal Learning and Verbal Behaviour* 11: 717–26.

Brazil, D., **M. Coulthard**, and **C. Johns**. 1980. *Discourse Intonation and Language Teaching*. London: Longman.

Brown, P. and **S. Levinson**. 1978. 'Universals in language usage: politeness phenomena' in Goody 1978.

Brown, R. 1976. *A First Language*. Harmondsworth: Penguin.

Brown, R. and **A. Gilman**. 1960. 'The pronouns of power and solidarity' in Sebeok 1960.

Brumfit, C. J. 1979a. 'Accuracy and fluency as polarities in foreign language teaching materials and methodology'. *Bulletin CILA* 29: 89.

Brumfit, C. J. 1979b. '"Communicative" language teaching: an educational perspective' in Brumfit and Johnson 1979c.

Brumfit, C. J. and **K. Johnson** (eds.). 1979c. *The Communicative Approach to Language Teaching*. Oxford: Oxford University Press.

Burt, M. and **C. Kiparsky**. 1972. *The Gooficon*. Rowley, Mass: Newbury House.

Butler, C. and **A. Fowler** (eds.). 1971. *Topics in Criticism*. London: Longman.

Canale, M. and **M. Swain**. 1980. 'Theoretical bases of communicative approaches to second language teaching and testing'. *Applied Linguistics* I/1: 1–47.

Chomsky, N. 1957. *Syntactic Structures*. The Hague: Mouton.

Chomsky, N. 1965. *Aspects of the Theory of Syntax*. Cambridge, Mass.: M.I.T. Press.

Cicourel, A. 1973. *Cognitive Sociology*. Harmondsworth: Penguin.

Clark, H. and **E. Clark**. 1977. *Psychology and Language: An Introduction to Psycholinguistics*. New York: Harcourt Brace Jovanovich.

Clark, H. H. and **S. E. Haviland**. 1977. 'Comprehension and the given-new contract' in Freedle 1977.

Clarke, M. A. and **J. Handscombe** (eds.). 1983. *On TESOL 82*. Washington, D.C.: TESOL.

Cole, P. and **J. L. Morgan** (eds.). 1975. *Syntax and Semantics Vol. 3: Speech Acts*. New York: Academic Press.

Cooper, R. L. 1982. Review of Peñalosa, F. *Introduction to the Sociology of Language*. *Applied Linguistics* III/3: 276–80.

Corder, S. P. 1973. *Introducing Applied Linguistics*. Harmondsworth: Penguin.

Corder, S. P. 1979. 'Language distance and the magnitude of the language learning task'. *Studies in Second Language Acquisition* 2/1.

Corder, S. P. and J. P. B. Allen. 1974. *The Edinburgh Course in Applied Linguistics. Vol. 3: Techniques in Applied Linguistics*. Oxford: Oxford University Press.

Crystal, D. and D. Davy. 1969. *Investigating English Style*. London: Longman.

Culler, J. 1975. *Structuralist Poetics*. London: Routledge and Kegan Paul.

van Dijk, T. A. 1977. *Text and Context: Explorations in the Semantics and Pragmatics of Discourse*. London: Longman.

Empson, W. 1961. *Seven Types of Ambiguity*. Harmondsworth: Penguin.

Ervin-Tripp, S. 1972. 'On sociolinguistic rules: alternation and co-occurrence' in Gumperz and Hymes 1972.

von Faber, H. 1980. *Leserverstehen im Fremdsprachen Unterricht*. München: Goethe Institut.

Fillenbaum, S. 1974. 'Pragmatic normalization: further results for some conjunctive and disjunctive sentences'. *The Journal of Experimental Psychology* 102: 574–8.

Firth, J. R. 1957. *Papers in Linguistics 1934–51*. London: Oxford University Press.

Fisher, J. C., M. A. Clarke, and J. Schachter (eds.). 1981. *On TESOL 80: Building Bridges*. Washington, D.C.: TESOL.

Floyd, A. 1976. *Cognitive Styles: Personality and Learning (Block 5)*. Milton Keynes: The Open University Press.

Fodor, J. A. and J. J. Katz (eds.). 1964. *The Structure of Language*. New York: Prentice-Hall.

Forster, E. M. 1927. *Aspects of the Novel*. London: Edward Arnold.

Freedle, R. O. (ed.). 1977. *Discourse Production and Comprehension*. Norwood, NJ: Ablex Publishing.

Freedle, R. O. and J. B. Carroll (eds.). 1972. *Language Comprehension and the Acquisition of Knowledge*. Washington, D.C.: V. H. Winston and Sons.

Freedman, A., I. Pringle, and J. Yalden (eds.). 1983. *Learning to Write: First Language/Second Language*. London: Longman.

Galbraith, J. K. 1977. *The Age of Uncertainty*. London: BBC and André Deutsch.

Garfinkel, H. 1972. 'Studies of the routine grounds of everyday activities' in Sudnow 1972.

Garfinkel, H. and H. Sacks. 1970. 'On formal structures of practical actions' in McKinney and Tiryakian 1970.

Giles, H. and P. M. Smith. 1979. 'Accommodation theory: optimal levels of convergence' in Giles and St Clair 1979.

Giles, H. and R. St Clair (eds.). 1979. *Language and Social Psychology*. Oxford: Basil Blackwell.

Godard, D. 1977. 'Same setting, different norms: phone call beginnings in France and the United States'. *Language in Society* 6/2: 209–19.

Goffman, E. 1976. 'Replies and responses'. *Language in Society* 5/3: 257–313.

Gombrich, E. H. 1960. *Art and Illusion*. London: Phaidon.

Goodwin, C. 1979. 'The interactive construction of a sentence in natural conversation' in Psathas 1979.

Goody, E. M. 1978. *Questions and Politeness: Strategies in Social Interaction*. Cambridge: Cambridge University Press.

Greene, J. 1972. *Psycholinguistics: Chomsky and Psychology*. Harmondsworth: Penguin.

Gregory, R. L. 1966. *Eye and Brain*. London: Weidenfeld and Nicolson.

Grice, H. P. 1975. 'Logic and conversation' in Cole and Morgan 1975.

Gumperz, J. J. and D. Hymes (eds.). 1972. *Directions in Sociolinguistics: The Ethnography of Communication*. New York: Holt, Rinehart and Winston.

Halliday, M. A. K. 1961. 'Categories of the theory of grammar'. *Word* 17/3: 241–92.

Halliday, M. A. K. 1964. 'Syntax and the consumer' in C. I. J. M. Stuart (ed.). *Report of the 15th Annual Round Table Meeting on Linguistics and Language Study*. Washington, D.C.: Georgetown Monographs 17: 11–24.

Halliday, M. A. K. 1966. 'Lexis as a linguistic level' in Bazell *et al.* 1966.

Halliday, M. A. K. 1968. Notes on 'Transitivity and theme in English: Part 3'. *Journal of Linguistics* 4/2: 179–216.

Halliday, M. A. K. 1969. 'The relevant models of language'. *Educational Review* (University of Birmingham) 22/1: 26–37. (Reprinted in Halliday 1973.)

Halliday, M. A. K. 1970. 'Language structure and language function' in Lyons 1970.

Halliday, M. A. K. 1973. *Explorations in the Functions of Language*. London: Edward Arnold.

Halliday, M. A. K. 1975. *Learning How to Mean*. London: Edward Arnold.

Halliday, M. A. K. and R. Hasan. 1976. *Cohesion in English*. London: Longman.

Halliday, M. A. K., A. McIntosh, and P. D. Strevens. 1964. *The Linguistic Sciences and Language Teaching*. London: Longman.

Harré, R. 1972. *The Philosophy of Science*. London: Oxford University Press.

Hatch, E. M. 1976. 'Discourse analysis and second language acquisition' in Hatch (ed.), 1976. *Second Language Acquisition*. Rowley, Mass.: Newbury House.

Hawkes, T. 1977. *Structuralism and Semiotics*. London: Methuen.

Hayes, J. (ed.). 1970. *Cognition and the Development of Language*. New York: John Wiley.

Heritage, J. C. and D. R. Watson. 1979. 'Formulations as conversational objects' in Psathas 1979.

Hinde, R. A. (ed.). 1972. *Non-Verbal Communication*. London and New York: Cambridge University Press.

Hines, M. and W. Rutherford (eds.). 1982. *On TESOL 81*. Washington, D.C.: TESOL.

Hockett, C. F. 1968. *The State of the Art*. The Hague: Mouton.

Holec, H. 1980. 'You did say "oral interactive discourse"?'. *Applied Linguistics* I/3: 189–200.

Hough, G. 1969. *Style and Stylistics*. London: Routledge and Kegan Paul.

Hudson, L. 1966. *Contrary Imaginations*. London: Methuen (Penguin 1967).

Hudson, L. 1972. *The Cult of the Fact*. London: Jonathan Cape.

Jacobs, R. A. and P. S. Rosenbaum (eds.). 1970. *Readings in English Transformational Grammar*. Waltham, Mass.: Blaisdell.

Jakobson, R. 1960. 'Concluding statement: linguistics and poetics' in Seboek 1960.

Jakobson, R. and M. Halle. 1956. *Fundamentals of Language*. The Hague: Mouton.

Joos, M. 1962. *The Five Clocks*. The Hague: Mouton.

Just, M. A. and P. A. Carpenter (eds.). 1977. *Cognitive Processes in Comprehension*. Hillsdale, NJ: Lawrence Erlbaum.

Kaplan, R. B. (ed.). 1980. *On the Scope of Applied Linguistics.* Rowley, Mass.: Newbury House.

Katz, J. J. 'Semi-sentences' in Fodor and Katz 1964.

Kellerman, E. 1979. 'Transfer and non-transfer: where are we now?'. *Studies in Second Language Acquisition* 2/1.

Kelvin, P. 1971. *The Bases of Social Behaviour.* London: Holt, Rinehart and Winston.

Kuhlwein, W. (ed.). 1983. *Texte in Sprachwissenschaft, Sprachunterricht, Sprachtherapie.* Tübingen: Gunter Narr Verlag.

Labov, W. 1970. 'The study of language in its social context'. *Studium Generale* Vol. 23 (reprinted in Labov 1972).

Labov, W. 1972. *Sociolinguistic Patterns.* Philadelphia: University of Pennsylvania Press.

Labov, W. and **D. Fanshel.** 1977. *Therapeutic Discourse: Psychotherapy as Conversation.* New York: Academic Press.

Lackstrom, J. E., L. Selinker, and **L. Trimble.** 1970. 'Grammar and technical English: English as a second language' in R. C. Lugton (ed.). *Current Issues.* Philadelphia: Centre for Curriculum Development.

Lackstrom, J. E., L. Selinker, and **L. Trimble.** 1972. 'Technical rhetorical principles and grammatical choice'. *TESOL Quarterly* 7: 127–32.

Leech, G. N. 1974. *Semantics.* Harmondsworth: Penguin.

Leech, G. N. 1977. Review of Sadock 1974 and Cole and Morgan 1975. *Journal of Linguistics* 13/1: 133–45.

Leech, G. N. and **J. Svartvik.** 1975. *A Communicative Grammar of English.* London: Longman.

Levelt, W. J. M. 1975. 'Skill theory and language teaching'. *Studies in Second Language Acquisition* 1/1.

Levi-Strauss, C. 1966. *The Savage Mind.* London: Weidenfeld and Nicolson.

Lyons, J. 1966. 'Firth's theory of meaning' in Bazell *et al.* 1966.

Lyons, J. (ed.) 1970. *New Horizons in Linguistics.* Harmondsworth: Penguin.

Lyons, J. 1972. 'Human language' in Hinde 1972.

Lyons, J. 1977a. *Chomsky* (2nd edition). London: Fontana/ Collins.

Lyons, J. 1977b. *Semantics I, II.* Cambridge: Cambridge University Press.

Mackay, W. F. 1965. *Language Teaching Analysis*. London: Longman.

Matthews, P. H. 1972. Review of Paul Gavin (ed.): *Method and Theory in Linguistics* (1970). *Lingua* 29: 67–77.

McIntosh, A. 1961. 'Patterns and ranges'. *Language* 37(iii): 325–337. Reprinted in McIntosh and Halliday 1966.

McIntosh, A. and M. A. K. Halliday. 1966. *Patterns of Language. Papers in General, Descriptive, and Applied Linguistics*. London: Longman.

McKinney, J. C. and E. A. Tiryakian (eds.). 1970. *Theoretical Sociology*. New York: Appleton-Century-Croft.

McRae, A. 1977. Comprehension: the psycholinguistic view' in *The Teaching of Comprehension*. London: The British Council, 1977.

Miller, G. A., E. Galanter, and K. Pribram. 1960. *Plans and the Structure of Behaviour*. New York: Holt, Rinehart and Winston.

Munby, J. 1978. *Communicative Syllabus Design*. Cambridge: Cambridge University Press.

Neisser, U. 1976. *Cognition and Reality. Principles and Implications of Cognitive Psychology*. San Francisco: W. H. Freeman.

Ochs Keenan, E. 1976. 'On the universality of conversational implicatures'. *Language in Society* 5/1: 67–80.

Oldfield, C. and J. C. Marshall (eds.). 1968. *Language*. Harmondsworth: Penguin.

Olson, D. R. 1972. 'Language use for communicating, instructing and thinking' in Freedle and Carroll 1972.

Olson, D. R. and N. Filby. 1972. 'On the comprehension of active and passive sentences'. *Cognitive Psychology* 3: 361–81.

Palmer, F. R. (ed.). 1968. *Selected Papers of J. R. Firth 1952–59*. London: Longman.

Parkinson, G. H. R. (ed.). 1968. *The Theory of Meaning* (Oxford Readings in Philosophy). London: Oxford University Press.

Parret, H. (ed.). 1974. *Discussing Language with Noam Chomsky*. The Hague: Mouton.

Pask, G. and B. C. E. Scott. 1972. 'Learning strategies and individual competence'. *International Journal of Man–Machine Studies* 4: 217–53.

Peirce, C. G. *Collected Papers, 1931–58* (ed. C. Hartshorne and P. Weiss). Cambridge, Mass.: Harvard University Press.

Philp, P. 1962. *Antique Furniture for the Smaller Home*. London: Arco.

Piaget, J. 1952. *The Origins of Intelligence in Children*. London: Routledge and Kegan Paul.

Popper, K. 1976. *Unended Quest*. London: Fontana/Collins.

Psathas, G. (ed.). 1979. *Everyday Language. Studies in Ethnomethodology*. New York: Irvington.

Reibel, D. A. 1969. 'Language learning analysis'. *IRAL* VII: 283–94.

Richards, J. C. (ed.) 1978. *Understanding Second and Foreign Language Learning*. Rowley, Mass.: Newbury House.

Ross, J. R. 1970. 'On declarative sentences' in Jacobs and Rosenbaum 1970.

Rottman, Milton A. 1962. *The Laws of Physics*. Harmondsworth: Penguin.

Roulet, E. 1980. 'Interaction markers in dialogue'. *Applied Linguistics* I/3: 224–33.

Sachs, H. 'On the analyzability of stories by children' in Gumperz and Hymes 1972.

Sadock, J. M. 1974. *Toward a Linguistic Theory of Speech Acts*. New York: Academic Press.

Sampson, G. 1975. *The Form of Language*. London: Weidenfeld and Nicolson.

Sanford, A. J. and **S. C. Garrod.** 1981. *Understanding Written Language: Explorations in Comprehension Beyond the Sentence*. New York: John Wiley and Sons.

de Saussure, F. 1966. *Course in General Linguistics* (trans. W. Baskin). New York: McGraw Hill.

Schegloff, E. A. 1972a. 'Notes on conversational practice: formulating place' in Sudnow 1972.

Schegloff, E. A. 1972b. 'Sequencing in conversational openings' in Gumperz and Hymes 1972.

Schegloff, E. A. 'Identification and recognition in telephone conversation openings' in Psathas 1979.

Scholes, R. 1974. *Structuralism in Literature*. New Haven and London: Yale University Press.

Schumann, J. H. 1978. 'Social and psychological factors in second language acquisition' in Richards 1978.

Searle, J. R. 1969. *Speech Acts*. Cambridge: Cambridge University Press.

Searle, J. R. 1975. 'Indirect speech acts' in Cole and Morgan 1975.

Sebeok, T. A. 1960. *Style in Language*. Cambridge, Mass.: MIT Press.

Selinker, L., E. Tarone, and V. Hanzeli. (eds.). 1981. *English for Academic and Technical Purposes. Studies in Honour of Louis Trimble*. Rowley, Mass.: Newbury House.

Shank, R. C. 1975. 'The structure of episodes in memory' in Bobrow and Collins 1975.

Sinclair, J. McH., and R. M. Coulthard. 1975. *Towards an Analysis of Discourse*. London: Oxford University Press.

Slobin, D. I. 1966. 'Grammatical transformations and sentence comprehension in childhood and adulthood'. *Journal of Verbal Learning and Verbal Behaviour* 5: 219–27.

Slobin, D. I. 1975. 'The more it changes ... on understanding language by watching it move through time'. *Papers and Reports on Child Language Development* 10: 1–30.

Stevick, E. W. 1976. *Memory, Meaning and Method*. Rowley, Mass.: Newbury House.

Stevick, E. W. 1980. *Teaching Languages: A Way and Ways*. Rowley, Mass.: Newbury House.

Strawson, P. F. 1950. 'On referring'. *Mind* Vol. 59 (reprinted in Parkinson 1968).

Sudnow, D. (ed.). 1972. *Studies in Social Interaction*. New York: Free Press.

Swales, J. 1974. 'The function of one type of particle in a chemistry textbook'. Reprinted in Selinker, Tarone and Hanzeli, 1981.

Thomas, O. and E. R. Kintgen. 1974. *Transformational Grammar and the Teacher of English* (2nd edition). New York: Holt, Rinehart and Winston.

Thorne, J. P. 1965. 'Stylistics and generative grammars'. *Journal of Linguistics* 1/1.

Turner, R. (ed.). 1974. *Ethnomethodology*. Harmondsworth: Penguin.

Wason, P. C. 1965. 'The contexts of plausible denial'. *Journal of Verbal Learning and Verbal Behaviour* 4: 7–11 (reprinted in Oldfield and Marshall 1968).

Widdowson, H. G. 1968. 'The teaching of English through science' in J. Dakin, B. Tiffen, and H. G. Widdowson (eds.). *Language in Education* (Oxford University Press, 1968).

Widdowson, H. G. 1974. 'Stylistics' in Corder and Allen 1974.

Widdowson, H. G. 1975. *Stylistics and the Teaching of Literature.* London: Longman.

Widdowson, H. G. 1977. 'Description du language scientifique'. *Le Français dans le Monde* 129: 15–21.

Widdowson, H. G. 1978a. 'The partiality and relevance of linguistic descriptions'. *Proceedings of the Sixth Neuchâtel Colloquium.* Indiana Linguistics Club. (Reprinted in Widdowson 1979b.)

Widdowson, H. G. 1978b. *Teaching Language as Communication.* Oxford: Oxford University Press.

Widdowson, H. G. 1979. *Explorations in Applied Linguistics.* Oxford: Oxford University Press.

Widdowson, H. G. 1983. *Learning Purpose and Language Use.* Oxford: Oxford University Press.

Wilkins, D. 1976. *Notional Syllabuses.* London: Oxford University Press.

Winograd, T. 1977. 'A framework for understanding discourse' in Just and Carpenter 1977.